Slavery in Sma

Slavery in Small Things

Slavery and Modern Cultural Habits

James Walvin

WILEY Blackwell

This edition first published 2017
© 2017 John Wiley & Sons, Inc.

Registered Office
John Wiley & Sons, Ltd, The Atrium, Southern Gate, Chichester, West Sussex, PO19 8SQ, UK

Editorial Offices
350 Main Street, Malden, MA 02148-5020, USA
9600 Garsington Road, Oxford, OX4 2DQ, UK
The Atrium, Southern Gate, Chichester, West Sussex, PO19 8SQ, UK

For details of our global editorial offices, for customer services, and for information about how to apply for permission to reuse the copyright material in this book please see our website at www.wiley.com/wiley-blackwell.

The right of James Walvin to be identified as the author of this work has been asserted in accordance with the UK Copyright, Designs and Patents Act 1988.

Library of Congress Cataloging-in-Publication Data applied for.

9781119166207 (hardback)
9781119166221 (paperback)

A catalogue record for this book is available from the British Library.

Cover image: Arne Thaysen/Gettyimages

Set in 11.5/15.5pt MinionPro by Aptara Inc., New Delhi, India

Printed in Singapore by C.O.S. Printers Pte Ltd

1   2017

Contents

Acknowledgments

The idea for this book germinated at two places in the USA. When I was researching the history of one particular painting (J.M.W. Turner's *The Slave Ship*) I encountered the astonishing riches housed in Boston's Museum of Fine Arts. At much the same time, I was working in the collections of the Colonial Williamsburg Foundation, Williamsburg, Virginia. The books, manuscripts, furnishings, tableware, and portraits housed in the Rockefeller Library and various locations around Williamsburg (and in storage) provide a lavish version of life in colonial America. The longer I worked in Williamsburg, however, on what became annual visits, the clearer it became that there was a 'back-story' – a context – to many of the artifacts on display, but one which often goes unnoticed. So many of the material objects derived directly or indirectly from the efforts of African slaves, or provided an entrée into the story of the lives of enslaved Africans in the Americas. Yet who thinks of slaves when looking at a beautiful 18th-century sugar bowl, or a piece of mahogany furniture?

This simple question applies not only to North America but is equally relevant (and perhaps even more so) in Britain itself. Galleries, museum, private collections, stately homes, and palaces – all these and more boast of and display items which belong not merely to the story of wealth, style, and fashionable taste, but to the astonishing history of African slavery in the Atlantic world. The link – between voguish taste and brutal slavery – generally goes unnoticed. This simple point set me off in search of the background. What is the connection between African slavery in the Americas and the development of key features of Western taste and style from the 17th century onward? This book tries to offer an answer.

Like all my earlier books, what follows has been made possible by the help, co-operation – and friendship – of people on both sides of the Atlantic. At the Colonial Williamsburg Foundation James Horn proved a stout friend and supporter over many years. He and his colleagues, notably Inge Flester and more recently Ted Maris Wolfe, but above all the staff in the Rockefeller Library, have always made my visits fruitful and enjoyable.

I made an initial effort to explain my ideas at a Conference on 'Visualizing Slavery and British Culture in the 18th century' at Yale University in November 2014. There, David Blight and his colleagues at the Gilder Lehrman Center provided their traditional warm welcome, and an invigorating forum for what I said. Richard Rabinowitz again showed that his friendship does not obstruct his critical and imaginative approach to the study of history. Over many years, my work in the USA has been made possible – and worthwhile – by the kindness of a number of friends: Tolly and Ann Taylor, and Marlene and Bill Davis in Williamsburg, Bill and Elizabeth Bernhardt in New York City, and Fred Croton and Selma Holo in Los Angeles. Caryl Phillips, always willing to listen and to lend invaluable support, seems untroubled by my tendency to talk as much about football as history. Through thick and thin, all these friends have listened more patiently than I have a right to expect. Above all others, and as on so many other occasions, Jenny Walvin has lived at close quarters with my current interests, and makes everything possible.

In Hull, John Oldfield and David Richardson, and Richard Huzzey in Liverpool have proved great supporters. Most important of all, Peter Coveney at Wiley accepted the initial proposal for this book, and was hugely influential in seeing it through, though he had moved on before it appeared. The anonymous reviewers he commissioned to read the draft manuscript provided invaluable help in making what follows an infinitely better book than the one they read initially. This book was also improved by the efforts of Fiona Screen, an exemplary copy editor.

For years, Katie Campbell and Michael Davenport have provided a welcoming home-from-home in London. This time, Michael did not live to see the book materialize. I would have given a copy to him, but now, alas, I can only dedicate it fondly to his memory, echoing his favorite phrase, as we topped up his whisky glass, *'Un tout, tout petit peu.'*

James Walvin
March 2016

Introduction
Slavery in Western Life

Our understanding of slavery has been totally transformed in
the past fifty years. Between 1960 and 1964 I studied history
as a British undergraduate. Or rather I studied British political
history. I still have all my undergraduate notes and essays, and
looking through them, and thinking about what I was taught
(and on the whole taught well), I am now struck by how curiously insular – how 'British' (English even) – were the historical
issues on offer. What has become my major historical preoccu-
pation – slavery – was not even mentioned. In lectures, tuto-
rials, seminars, and essays, I can recall no mention whatsoever
about slavery – not one. The book of documents used for a Special Subject on the American Revolution mentions slavery on
a mere 19 of the 368 pages, and even then largely in passing.[1]
It was of course a very long time ago, and historical interests,
trends – fads even – have changed substantially: some have simply come and mercifully gone. In large measure the curricu-
lum we studied was a reflection of how our teachers perceived
and presented the subject, and what they thought suitable for
undergraduate study. At the time slavery was only one of many
topics which effectively did not exist in British undergraduate
studies but which, today, are in great demand. The absence of

Slavery in Small Things: Slavery and Modern Cultural Habits, First Edition. James Walvin.
© 2017 John Wiley & Sons, Inc. Published 2017 by John Wiley & Sons, Inc.

slavery, in common with other areas of history, was partly a reflection of prevailing knowledge (or lack of it) and the consequent paucity of appropriate literature. There were no obvious books or studies of British slavery that would have provided students with the necessary materials. Equally, the teaching staff were interested in other historical problems for their own research careers. Social history, for example had only begun to make its first transformative impact in Britain. It was hardly surprising, then, that slavery did not even register as a noise off-stage.

Today, fifty years later, if any history department were *not* offering courses on slavery this would be viewed as seriously remiss, and undergraduates and graduate students turn to the history of slavery because of its inherent interest and because of the intellectually exciting prospects available. Slavery is now accepted as a defining historical element in the shaping of the Western world in the post-Columbus period, its importance amply confirmed by a massive (and growing) accumulation of research evidence from all corners of historical enquiry. Even science (in the form of DNA) now lends itself to the study of slavery.

The story of the study and teaching of slavery in the USA in the same period has taken a very different trajectory. Moreover, what happened there was to have major consequences for the study of slavery in Britain (and the Caribbean). In the USA, slavery has an immediate presence and a powerful historical resonance, and naturally enough there has been a long, imaginative, and often fiercely contested historiography of slavery. For decades, arguments about slavery spawned distinct and sharply divided schools of historians. The slave South had its scholarly defenders, and their influence spread far beyond academe. They gave intellectual sustenance to the world of segregated US life and politics, and even helped to shape a romanticized view of the South that permeated popular culture. But all that began to sag, and eventually collapse, in the late 20th century, under the sheer weight of scholarship into the social history of slavery. By the turn of the century, it had become indisputable that slavery in the USA was not simply an interesting, *regional* issue – not solely a matter for the South, with consequences for the North. On the contrary, slavery was exposed as a central institution in the development of the modern USA.[2] Indeed, the modern American state came into being in 1787 *arguing about* slavery. Inevitably, debates continue among historians, but the days have gone when slavery could be regarded as a peripheral, largely Southern issue. What has happened, in the space of an academic lifetime, is that the study of slavery has shifted from the margins to occupy a pivotal position in US historical concerns (with all the political and cultural consequences that follow).

While Americans have for decades wrestled with the question of slavery throughout their history, the British, on the other hand, suffered a prolonged bout of forgetfulness about their own entanglement with slavery, and only recently seem to have emerged from this historical amnesia. At first sight, this forgetfulness about slavery (which lasted effectively until the 1960s) seems very odd indeed, though what underpinned it now seems clear enough. Most significant perhaps, and unlike the North American version, British slavery was not a *domestic* matter. Whereas in 1860 the USA was home to four million people of African descent – all of them slaves or freed slaves – Britain's slave population had evolved thousands of miles away from Britain itself. There had been, it is true, a small black presence in Britain for centuries, and slavery itself had existed, however small-scale and marginal, despite various legal challenges, right up to full emancipation in 1833.

Yet the British, despite having no substantial slave population at home, had been responsible for scattering millions of enslaved Africans across their American colonies, from Demerara in South America, throughout the Caribbean, and into North America. As the leading slave trader in the North Atlantic, the British had also shipped and sold armies of Africans to other European colonies, notably those controlled by Spain. It is hard to exaggerate Britain's involvement in the Atlantic slave system. Nor should we underestimate the enormous benefits which accrued to Britain as a result – a point first effectively asserted in the 1930s and 1940s by C.L.R. James and Eric Williams. Still, the centers of gravity of British slaving activity, the regions where they engaged *directly* – face-to-face – with African slaves, were located thousands of miles away from Britain itself. When the British thought and talked about slavery, the images that came to mind were of slave trading on the African coast, slave ships in mid-ocean packed with Africans, or gangs of field slaves working on plantations in the Americas. Slavery took place and thrived a long way away.

The sense that this involvement with slavery was physically very distant from Britain is itself a curious issue. After all, thousands of ships sailed from dozens of British ports on slave trading ventures, and a myriad British industries and businesses thrived on their dealings with slave ships (and with the slave-grown produce brought back by those vessels from the colonies). Major cities (most notably London, Bristol, Liverpool, and Glasgow) thrived on their commerce with slavery. Furthermore, over a period of more than three centuries, many thousands of Britons had *direct* experience of the Atlantic slave system: they manned the ships, they organized the purchase of slaves on Africa's Atlantic coast, and they marshalled gangs of field slaves throughout the American colonies. Less visible, but no less important, Britons master-minded the entire system from their business premises: the dock-side counting houses, the metropolitan (and increasingly provincial) centers of finance, commerce, and manufacture. By, say, 1750, it was clear enough that slavery had become part of the warp and weft of British commercial and social life. And yet....

By and large, slavery remained out of sight, thriving in distant locations which were, quite literally, over the horizon and invisible to the British eye. This physical distance between the homeland and its slave colonies had profound effects on the way the British experienced slavery. It greatly influenced what they knew – or did not know – about slavery. This geographic remove created a cultural detachment from slavery which could never have been the case in the USA itself. Put crudely, geography had a distorting effect on Britain's understanding of slavery, and therefore on the way the British subsequently constructed their historical memories about slavery. To borrow a phrase from one of Australia's most eminent historians writing about his homeland, there was a "tyranny of distance" involved in the complex relationship between Britain and slavery.[3] A vast watery expanse separated the British Isles from their slave colonies, and created a sense of detachment that was more pervasive than simple geography. There was, until very recently, a gulf of understanding and appreciation which has served to divorce the British from the world of Atlantic slavery.

This geographic divide was compounded by the unfolding of historical events, especially by the story of British abolition. In large measure, the way the British *ended* their involvement with slavery also helped to distance them from their slaving past. Having been the undisputed masters of North Atlantic slave trading in the late 18th century, the British became the self-appointed global abolitionists in the 19th century. The campaigns to end the slave trade (1807) and then to emancipate colonial slaves (1833) were carried along by remarkable domestic popular backing. Thereafter, not only did the British lead the attack on slavery worldwide (via international treaties, often imposed on weaker partners, and by the power of the Royal Navy), but they continued to congratulate themselves on their collective virtue in being the world's pioneering and dominant abolitionist nation. It was as if the world's leading poacher had, within a mere fifty years, become the world's self-appointed game-keeper. Henceforth, the British came to think of themselves as the nation which had brought slavery to its knees. In the continuing campaigns against slavery, throughout the 19th and into the 20th century,[4] the British were proud to proclaim themselves as an abolitionist people, their representatives, statesmen, and military keen to bring the benefits of freedom to people still oppressed by slavery.

The power and persistence of Britain's abolitionist activities in the 19th century generated a smokescreen behind which the British could hide their slaving past. Indeed, it was often difficult even to *see* the history of British slavery behind the decoy of abolition. This ideology of abolition – the sense that the British were a people characterized by a deep-seated abolition sentiment – had a remarkable impact on the writing of British history. Historians looked not to a slaving past, but to the British achievement in bringing slavery to an end. In the process, readers were presented with a historical saga that could make the British feel proud of themselves. There were strident critics, of course, most notably Eric Williams in his book *Capitalism and Slavery* (first published in 1944), but for decades such criticism failed to deflect the triumphalist tone of British historiography.[5] What, then, are we to remember about British history? The nation's pre-eminence as an abolitionist power, or its earlier involvement with slavery itself?

Since roughly 1960 there has been a fundamental revision in the way slavery is seen. It is a complex story at both scholarly and popular levels, involving major changes in academic history, but more fundamentally, it also stems from some extraordinary transformations in the demographics of British life. What had previously been a relatively racially homogenous society was changed by large-scale immigration and the emergence of a British black population which was keen to know about its own history. Britain was also greatly influenced by events in the USA, especially by the American campaigns for full racial equality. All this paralleled independence for former colonies in Africa and the Caribbean. There, the development of new systems of higher education also created demands for a new kind of history: one which addressed local needs and interests rather than the concerns of the old imperial powers. African history, Caribbean history, African-American history, British black history: all of them critically intersected in places to create a cultural ferment which focused on the history of slavery. It was clear enough, for instance, that US slavery had important ties to Britain itself. Equally, British scholarly interest in slavery began to flourish under the influence of some innovative scholarship about slavery in the USA, and about the Atlantic slave trade. This ought not to have been surprising. After all, North American slavery had its roots both in the Atlantic (mainly British) slave ships, and in a British colonial past. Most Africans shipped to North America had been transported in British ships, while the main commodities cultivated by North American slave labor (tobacco initially and cotton later) were vital features of Britain's booming economy in the 18th and 19th centuries.

Throughout the 1960s and 1970s, in what was a confusion of cultural change and historical debate, it became increasingly clear that slavery was of great importance not only for the Americas but for a fuller understanding of Europe itself. It had, for example, been European colonial powers which had conceived and nurtured African slavery throughout the Americas (all with

dire consequences for Africa itself). In addition, the more we
learned about the detailed mechanics of slavery, the more integrated and far-reaching the world of Atlantic slavery proved to
be. Thus the basis was laid for the idea that slavery was perhaps *the* major building block of an 'Atlantic' history, though
even this broad concept had its limitations. Despite the enormous geographic and temporal range of the concept of Atlantic
history, research revealed that the full story of slavery could not
easily be accommodated within it. For all its enormity, slavery
in the Atlantic formed only one *region* of a slaving system that
spilled over, well beyond the boundaries (and definitions) of the
Atlantic. Students of slavery came to appreciate that slavery had
significant worldwide dimensions.

Slavery's *global* significance emerged most clearly via
research into the enforced movement of Africans from their
homelands, and not merely westward into the Americas. The
overland migrations of enslaved Africans northward across the
Sahara, the slave trades from East Africa to Arabia or India,
each formed discrete and major histories of slavery. (And this
is not to include other forms of slavery in other parts of the
world.) Above all, however, it was the shipping of millions
of Africans to the plantations of the Americas that exposed
both the enormity and the historical importance of slavery.
It was both a massive enforced migration of peoples, and a
system of extreme human and social complexity. European,
American, and Brazilian ships carried a multitude of goods,
from all corners of the globe, to exchange for African slaves
on the Atlantic coast. Their African victims then endured a
pestilential experience like no other, before finding themselves
landed in the Americas. They were then forced onward to even
more distant destinations. Finally, and often far from their first
landfall, Africans were set to a lifetime's labor, overwhelmingly
producing export crops for the markets of the Western world.

Not long ago, all this had been thought of, and written about, as a simple story: 'the triangular trade' of popular imagination. Today it is recognized as an astonishingly complex global process. Its most obvious end result was the Africanization of swathes of the Americas. David Eltis has noted that so huge were the numbers of Africans landed in the Americas that, until 1840, the Americas were an outpost, not of Europe, but of Africa. Equally, the labor of enslaved Africans served to transform the habits of the wider world. Tobacco quickly became an addiction in Europe, the Americas, Africa, and Asia. Sugar made tea and coffee palatable to millions. By the time of the American Civil War, slave-grown cotton clothed the world in cheap textiles. All this, and much more besides, is now so familiar, so commonplace, that it hardly needs repeating. Yet to have made such claims in, say, 1960, would have been to invite historical derision. No longer.

Today, historians and writers face a very different challenge. We now have so much information about slavery that it is difficult to know how to take stock of so vast and sprawling a topic. It sometimes seems easier to provide a detailed case study, a microcosm of the story (the history of a single person, a place, a ship even) than to try to make sense of a topic that involves so many people, during such a prolonged period, and which spans such geographic expanse. To put the matter crudely, slavery in the Atlantic world bound together the continents, economies, and the peoples of Europe, Africa, and the Americas – with onward links to the trade routes and cultures of Asia. How can we hope to write a broad outline of that entire story?

My aim here is to tell that story by taking a very different approach, certainly different from any other book I have written about slavery. Slavery in the Americas was designed to produce commodities for the consumption and pleasure of the Western world, and many of the habits conceived and nurtured by slavery survive, in modern form, down to the present day. Similarly, a number of major artifacts (some of them so commonplace that they are unexceptional – banal even) have their origins and dissemination in the world of slavery. This book seeks to tell the story of slavery by discussing a number of those *things*. In recent years material culture has become of great interest to historians, in the process spawning some best-selling books (mainly when linked to exhibitions of those material artifacts).[6] I am trying to follow a similar path: exploring a broader story via a range of small items, in this case, objects and customs which emerged from the world of slavery. I have chosen a number of small pegs on which to hang the very big story of slavery itself. What follows is an attempt to tell the story of slavery by looking at the history of slavery in small things.

Notes

1. S.E. Morison, *Sources and Documents Illustrating the American Revolution, 1764–1788 and the Formation of the Federal Constitution*, Oxford, 1962 edn.
2. For the discussion about the central role of slavery in the shaping of US history see Edward E. Baptist, *The Half Has Never Been Told: Slavery in the Making of American Capitalism*, New York, 2014; Walter Johnson, *River of Dark Dreams: Slavery and Empire in the Cotton Kingdom*, Cambridge MA, 2013; Sven Beckert, *Empire of Cotton: A New History of Global Capitalism*, New York, 2014. But see also David Eltis and Stanley L. Engerman, 'The importance of the slave trade to industrializing Britain,' *The Journal of Economic History*, vol. 60, No. 1, March 2000.
3. Michael Blainey, *The Tyranny of Distance*, Melbourne, 1966 edn.
4. James Walvin, *Crossings: Africa, the Americas and the Atlantic Slave Trade*, London, 2013, Chapter 10.
5. For a wider discussion of the relevant historiography see Gad Heuman, 'Slavery and abolition,' Chapter 20, and B.W. Higman, 'The British West Indies,' Chapter 7, in Robin Winks, ed., *The Oxford History of the British Empire*, vol. V, Historiography, Oxford, 1999.
6. Neil McGregor, *A History of the World In 100 Objects*, London, 2012 edn., and *Germany: Memories of a Nation*, London, 2014. See also Laurel Thatcher Ulrich, Ivan Gaskell, Sara J. Schechner, Sarah Anne Carter, *Tangible Things: Making History Through Objects*, New York, 2015.

1

A Sugar Bowl
Sugar and Slavery

In November 2014 a sugar bowl sold at Christie's in London for £3,500. True, it wasn't an ordinary sugar bowl. This one was a piece of Sèvres, a Vincennes blue lapis (*Pot à sucre 'Herbert' et couvercle, 2me grandeur*) – an exquisite piece of 18th-century craftsmanship from the porcelain workers and artists at the French factory in Sèvres. The company had been founded in 1738, moving to Sèvres, close to Madame de Pompadour's palace (today the Elysée Palace), in 1756, and becoming a royal factory three years later. Its porcelain ware quickly established itself as the most desirable of luxury items for wealthy elites across Western Europe. Prosperous Britons traveled to Paris simply to acquire their own Sèvres. In 1756–1757 Horace Walpole, for example, (though not so prosperous) spent £400 on Sèvres porcelain during a trip to Paris. A decade later the actor-manager David Garrick returned from Paris with his own Sèvres tea set. The sugar bowl from that collection eventually found its way into the Victoria and Albert Museum in London. There, it jostles for space with numerous other 18th-century sugar bowls; in porcelain, earthen ware, silver and pewter, all of them testimony not merely to fashionable table ware, but to the astonishing Western addiction to sugar.

Slavery in Small Things: Slavery and Modern Cultural Habits, First Edition. James Walvin.
© 2017 John Wiley & Sons, Inc. Published 2017 by John Wiley & Sons, Inc.

Sèvres porcelain was (and is) so beautiful, so exquisite in design and decorative finish, that it created its own voracious demand among wealthy people anxious to display their taste and opulence. Yet behind the Sèvres factory (and similar companies – notably Dresden, Meissen, Worcester, and Wedgwood) there lies a more complex history. At first glance the story of European porcelain in the 18th century seems but one aspect of the remarkable expansion of material and luxurious consumption during that century. But it was also directly related to the much less obvious story of global trade, empire – and slavery.

Sèvres sugar bowls were normally manufactured as integral items of larger sets of table ware – tea and coffee sets – all aimed at the appetite for tea and coffee. Tea (from China) and coffee (from the Horn of Africa, from Arabia and later from newly acquired European tropical colonies, from Java to Jamaica) had, by the 1700s, established themselves as fashionable drinks of the wealthy. Soon they also became the ubiquitous drinks of ordinary people. But tea and coffee (like chocolate – the other emerging drink) had a naturally bitter taste, and were enjoyed in their native regions in their bitter form. Western consumers, however, came to expect their drinks to be sweetened by the addition of cane sugar. This was no accident: the transformation from bitter to sweet drinks took place when sugar from Europe's slave colonies began to flow back to Europe in remarkable volumes. The tea and coffee sets, disgorged in ever growing numbers from the factories and workshops of Western Europe and North America, provided all the accessories familiar today: tea and coffee pots, cups and saucers – and beautiful and delicate sugar bowls. It is, at the very least, an astonishing curiosity that this single fashionable item – porcelain sugar bowls from Sèvres and other manufacturers – were filled with a commodity cultivated in the most brutal and degrading of circumstances: sugar from the slave colonies of the Americas. Here was one of the paradoxes of slavery: callous oppression bringing forth Western fashion and luxury.

* * *

At the time Louis XV designated Sèvres a royal factory, France's major Caribbean colony had become the world's largest exporter of sugar. By 1770, St. Domingue (later Haiti) produced 60,000 tons a year (compared to Jamaica's 36,000 tons.[1]) All this was made possible by massive importations of Africans. By the time slavery in that colony, and the economy which it sustained, were destroyed by the great slave upheaval after 1791, no fewer than 790,000 Africans had been imported into St. Domingue. Of course, by then the West's addiction to sweetness in all things was well established. But who, even at the time, made the link? Who realized that the refinement of the Sèvres tea and coffee services, and their sugar bowls, was connected to the brutalization of armies of Africans in the Americas? It is a curious story which needs further explanation. But so too do many other historical artifacts: everyday items of 18th-century life, common today in museums and galleries, and all related to slavery.

* * *

The history of the world's taste for sweetness in food and drink is intimately linked to the story of African slavery.[2] Before the development of plantation societies in the Americas, cane sugar had been rare and costly. Though honey had been the traditional sweetener in the West, small quantities of sugar had reached Europe from early plantations in the Mediterranean. Sugar cane cultivation had spread slowly from New Guinea, across Asia, each stage characterized by improvements in cultivation and sugar technology. This geographic spread of cultivation and consumption gathered pace under the wing of Arab expansion and trade. When Europeans moved outside the traditional center of their trading world, in the Mediterranean, and into the Atlantic, settling islands and making maritime contact with the Atlantic coast of Africa, sugar traveled with them. Long before Europeans crossed the Atlantic, they were cultivating sugar cane in Madeira, the Azores, Cape Verde, and on Sao Tome in the Gulf of Guinea.

Sao Tome, only 320km from the African coast, was a well-watered location, and ideally placed for replenishing ships' supplies as they explored and traded up and down the African coast. It proved an ideal location for sugar cultivation. Moreover, close by, on the coast of Africa, there were plentiful supplies of slaves to toil in the labor-intensive work of the sugar plantations. Clearing land, planting cane, harvesting the sugar cane, all demanded regular and plentiful supplies of labor, and Africa offered labor in abundance. Plantations in the Mediterranean had traditionally used a combination of free and unfree labor, but on Sao Tome in the 15th century, the pattern began to change. As that island's landscape came to be dotted with plantation settlements, its laboring population became predominantly African – and enslaved.

The capital needed for these pioneering settlements was available from Italian and Spanish merchants, keen to find new outlets for their money. To round off this increasingly complex commercial nexus, the finished product – raw sugar – required further refinement in distant refineries. Starting in Antwerp, but soon spreading to a growing number of major European port cities, sugar refineries were constructed to provide the finishing touches. Cane sugar was then dispatched for sale to the increasing number of European shops and outlets, via traveling salesmen and peddlers. Sugar thus passed to consumers across the length and breadth of Europe, and all this was in place *before*

European explorers and settlers put down roots in the tropical Americas. What had emerged was a remarkable commercial and laboring network which drew together the continents of Africa and Europe. It was a system lubricated by the sweat of a burgeoning population of enslaved Africans.

Sao Tome's planters were easily persuaded of the benefits of slave labor because African slaves regularly passed through the island on a slave route between Kongo, Old Calabar, and the Gold Coast. In the early 16th century, Sao Tome boomed, with a population of 100,000, dominated by Portuguese planters, and its landscape dotted by as many as 200 sugar mills. But the island went into rapid decline when Portugal began to settle the apparently unlimited bounty that was Brazil and by 1700 the Sao Tome sugar industry had all but vanished. Compared to what was to follow in the Americas, the numbers of Africans involved looks insignificant (except for the individuals concerned). Perhaps 2,000 Africans were landed as slaves each year in Sao Tome. Yet those figures tell only part of the story.

What had happened on the Atlantic coast of Africa, in the Atlantic islands, and in Sao Tome had established an economic and social pattern, and a highly profitable one at that, which became a blueprint for pioneers and settlers on the far side of the Atlantic. Even before Columbus crossed the Atlantic, Europeans became accustomed to acquiring Africans to work as slaves on plantations. Europeans also recognized that the plantation provided a social and economic tool for bringing untapped but luxuriant lands into profitable cultivation. Behind it lay European consumers with their apparently insatiable appetite for sugar. Sugar from Madeira, the Canaries, and then Sao Tome whetted the European appetite for sweetness.

Like many other exotic products, sugar had gained an initial foothold in Western societies as a medicine. Long a part of Arab pharmacology and medicine, it was prescribed for a host of ailments and cures. Along with other exotic crops from the East, sugar arrived via trade routes from societies influenced by Arabic science and medicine (themselves well ahead of their European counterparts). Sugar had long been advocated as an important medicine in a handful of Arabic scientific writings. Those medical texts, translated from Arabic into Latin, encouraged the use of sugar in Western medicine. Crusaders, for example, returning from the Eastern Mediterranean brought with them not only cane sugar itself, but knowledge of the way sugar was used for medical purposes. Greek and Byzantine physicians and writers thus incorporated sugar as an ingredient in contemporary pharmacology and medicine, and their influence spread throughout Europe in the late Middle Ages. Though some scientists and philosophers disputed its benefits, sugar rode the controversies to maintain a niche in Western medicine through to the apogee of slave-grown sugars and beyond.

When in the 16th and 17th centuries cane sugar began to arrive in Europe in ever greater (and cheaper) volumes, it became a familiar aspect of contemporary medical practice and learning. It was to be counted among the standard items found in European apothecary shops. Like other medicines, however, it had its opponents: doctors and writers who challenged its alleged medical virtues and who argued that sugar was actually harmful. Yet sugar was to triumph not as a medical ingredient but as a sweetener. The medical harm of *mass* and massive sugar consumption belongs to a more modern era, by which time sugar had long since lost its medical pretensions.[3]

The European settlement in the tropical Americas, especially in Brazil and the Caribbean, transformed everything. Brazil led the way, with early sugar plantations in Bahia and Pernambuco copying the patterns of Portuguese planters in Sao Tome. As Brazilian sugar production grew, so too did the importation of African slaves. By the mid-17th century, the Dutch were carrying tens of thousands of Africans across the South Atlantic. (By the time the Dutch abolished their slave trade, they had shipped more than half a million Africans to the Americas.[4]) As early as 1630, more than one quarter of a million Africans had been loaded onto slave ships bound for Brazil, setting a pattern in the South Atlantic that was to dwarf all other regions of Atlantic slave trading. By the time the trade to Brazil ended, Brazilian and Portuguese slave traders had carried more than six million Africans across the South Atlantic.[5] No less astonishing is the fact that 2.8 million Africans were loaded onto slave ships from a single African port: Luanda in Angola. Brazil was, then, the first and the last: the first to establish a slave-based sugar economy in the Americas, and the last to abolish it – in 1888.

Slavery was an adaptable institution which could be turned to a huge range of activities. The vastness of Brazil allowed slavery, in time, to be adapted to a wide range of economic enterprises (mining, forestry, cattle, coffee, and tobacco). But sugar led the way: the original crop which proved that the rich lands of Brazil could produce a lucrative export crop. And it was sugar which persuaded planters to turn to Africa for slave labor to make everything else possible. Brazilian sugar plantations thus established the pattern for colonial settlement and development which encouraged other settlers, in other parts of the Americas, to do the same.

The British followed in the early 17th century, settling smaller islands in the Eastern Caribbean (notably St. Kitts and Barbados), then Jamaica in 1655. Colonists there tried a range of crops, and experimented with a number of labor systems before they, like the Portuguese before them, realized that sugar cultivated by enslaved Africans on plantations offered the best chance of commercial success. As ever more Africans were shipped into the islands, increasing volumes of sugar flowed back to Britain's major ports, and thence onward throughout

Britain and Western Europe. The figures involved are staggering. Eventually, almost one million Africans were landed in
Jamaica (though many were promptly shipped elsewhere; some
485,000 went to the tiny island of Barbados). The French, starting slightly later, did much the same. Their Caribbean islands
of Guadeloupe and Martinique absorbed 290,000 Africans, and
St. Domingue 750,000. On all these islands, and throughout the
Americas, Africans and their enslaved descendants undertook
every job imaginable – from sailor to cowboy, from seamstress
to nurse, miner to craftsman. But *the* dominant form of slave
work, throughout the tropical Americas, was sugar. Indeed, an
estimated 75% of all Africans crossing the Atlantic were destined, initially at least, to work in sugar.

Slave-grown sugar was produced in enormous volumes,
packed into large barrels (hogsheads) and shipped to European ports, where newly established sugar refineries converted
the crude sugar into the different forms of marketable sugars
which were then dispatched, as sugar cones, to commercial outlets across Europe. At first the price of sugar remained high,
partly because the initial costs of cultivation, production, and
shipping (over enormous distances) were high. Sugar plantations were, from first to last, dependent on the outside world,
and could only function thanks to regular importations of people and goods: labor from Africa, and goods from Europe and
North America. The finished products – sugar and rum – were
then shipped thousands of miles by sea (with all the attendant
dangers) to Europe and North America. In 1600 the only American exporter of sugar was Brazil, but from mid-century, a string
of Caribbean islands were producing their own sweet product
(after experimenting with a number of other crops – notably
tobacco). With Spain preoccupied in Central America, it was
the island colonies of Britain and France that began to export
substantial volumes of sugar. In 1650 Barbados was exporting

7,000 tons. Fifty years later, British Caribbean colonies dispatched 25,000 tons – more even than was exported from Brazil (22,000 tons). By 1700, ten colonies in the Americas exported 60,000 tons of sugar (half of it from the Caribbean).[6] Yet even this astonishing figure was surpassed, within a lifetime, as new colonies, and newly settled regions, turned to sugar cultivation – and slave labor. In 1750, 150,000 tons of sugar left the slave colonies. On the eve of the American War of Independence it stood at 200,000 tons (90% of it coming from the Caribbean). This huge expansion in sugar production was not due to new systems of cultivation, or of production. It was a result of the rapid expansion into new sugar lands. And that meant a need for ever more African slaves.

The fate of the Africans involved – their torments on the Atlantic slave ships, their wretched health and difficulties as they adjusted (or failed to adjust) to the new environment and work in the first years (the years of greatest mortality and sickness among newly imported Africans) – forms the grotesque backcloth to this entire story. The starkest yet most revealing evidence is the crude data. Although some 11+ million Africans stepped ashore from the slave ships, more than one million had not survived the Atlantic crossing. For the survivors, the years that followed were years of suffering – that 'time on the cross' most vividly etched on popular imagination (in part because the slaves' anguish became the core of fierce abolitionist agitation in print, and in politics from the late 18th century). Graphic images of slave distress became an obscene caricature in an expansive illustrative culture designed to foster hostility to slavery in all its forms. Yet the misery of the slaves stood in stark contrast to the fruits of their labor, most strikingly in the wealth and luxury of the most successful planters and slave traders. Of course, not all planters were successful, and many lived more humble lives than is often imagined. Even the prosperous could be brought down, without warning, by natural disaster, a twist of economic circumstance, or warfare. Still, the richest and most powerful, owning an assortment of estates and possessing hundreds, often thousands, of slaves, lived in considerable material splendor. Wealthy beyond the dreams of avarice they were able, in the most spectacular cases, to return 'home' to Europe and live in a style which befitted their wealth and status (though it often belied their humble origins). These were the 'sugar barons' and 'plantocracy', able to hold their own in the socially competitive world of home-grown aristocrats and Indian nabobs. Often the object of derision and scorn by those to whose company they aspired, the émigré planters surrounded themselves with the lavish trappings of 18th-century wealth and splendor, often in custom-built stately homes and grand rural retreats which stood in landscaped gardens and grounds, and which they filled with treasures and paintings. They were paragons of taste and wealth. But it came courtesy of African sweat on the sugar lands.[7]

Britain's major slave ports – London, Bristol, Liverpool, and Glasgow – were dotted with grand homes belonging to returned planters, but especially to merchants, traders, and shippers involved in the slave business.[8] Yet it was the West Indians who caught the eye, living up, as they did, to the popular phrase, 'As wealthy as a West Indian.' The most prosperous planters established a reputation for conspicuous wealth and consumption. The family of Edwin Lascelles, who had once been modest farmers in North Yorkshire, acquired fabulous riches in the Caribbean, as traders, contractors to the Royal Navy, merchants, money-lenders, and finally planters, mainly in Barbados but also on other islands. Edwin Lascelles crowned the family fortunes by building Harewood House between Leeds and Harrogate. The family's status was confirmed when Edwin was made Baron Harewood.[9] A similar pattern of striking opulence can be seen wherever sugar grandees put down local roots: the

Codringtons of Barbados, for example, developed an estate at Dodington in Gloucester. But the grandest – and most famous by far – were the Beckfords.[10] A family of Jamaican planters, they returned 'home' to move in high political circles and display their fabulous wealth in their lavish home at Fonthill Splendens. The Beckfords were friends to Prime Ministers, and were collectors on a grand scale, as well as hosts of legendary dinner parties. They also spawned eccentricities and eye-catching excess at home and abroad. By the time slavery was ended, the Beckford fortunes had also disappeared: swallowed by mad, spendthrift recklessness.

Others were more cautious, buttressing their British positions by political power in parliament – their access to plentiful cash guaranteed the purchase of parliamentary seats and hence political sway. By 1765, no fewer than forty MPs were 'West Indians,' and were able to secure and promote the interests of the slave-based sugar lobby against all-comers. Until, that is, they were outmaneuvered and out-gunned, quite suddenly, by the abolitionists in the last twenty years of the 18th century. Prior to that, the West India lobby ensured that the interests of those producing slave-grown commodities (and those providing the vital supplies of African slaves) remained a prime concern in the corridors of power in London.

It was relatively easy for the West India lobby to persuade London's political elites of the importance of the slave system. They had only to point to the crowded British quaysides, packed with vessels heading for, or returning from, West Africa and the slave colonies. In the background was a supporting chorus of financial interests, of money-lending and insurance, which underpinned everything, and a huge array of industries and manufacture which sustained Britain massive maritime fleet, and which filled outbound vessels with goods and equipment for sale and barter on the African coast and in the plantation colonies of the Americas. Here, by the mid-18th century, was a commercial cornucopia, the benefits of which seemed unchallengeable. *Everyone* seemed to benefit, from the rough deck hands manning the slave ships, through the workers constructing and sustaining the ships and their cargoes, right up to the greatest sugar planters returning with their extremes of wealth. Yet behind it all, out of sight and largely out of mind, lay the armies of Africans, 5,000 miles distant, literally over the horizon, toiling to make it all possible.

*   *   *

Though slaves in the Americas produced a range of commodities for export, sugar dominated, at first. It employed the largest numbers of Africans, who lived and worked in the largest slave concentrations. Sugar was the cause and occasion of some of the harshest of working conditions on slave plantations. And it was sugar, directly and indirectly, that dominated the shipping patterns to and from the Caribbean and Brazil. But *why* had sugar become so dominant? What was so special – distinctive – about sugar?

The taste for cane sugar began as a luxury among the rich. Initially it often took the form of fashionable and elaborate creations, molded and shaped into impressive decorative forms for the tables of rulers and the wealthy. Extravagant carvings and ornate displays shaped from sugar graced the homes and social worlds of elites. These ostentatious sugary exhibitions of wealth and power were also signs that the hosts and organizers had the wherewithal to acquire exotic sugar and transform it into fanciful objects for entertainment and taste.[11]

From the very first, there was a stark, glaring contrast between the lives of African slaves on the sugar plantations and the extravagance of early sugar consumption which was at its most elaborate – outrageous even – among Europe's monarchs and rulers. In 1549 a feast given by Mary of Hungary in honor of Philip II included sculptures of deer, boar, birds, fish, and fruit – all fashioned from sugar. More elaborate still, in 1566 when Maria de Aviz married the Duke of Parma, the city of Antwerp gave her a gift of 3,000 sugar sculptures, which included whales, ships, and even a model of her new husband, fashioned from sugar. Courtly excesses across Europe made use of sugar to entertain, feed, and amuse the court and its guests. Queen Elizabeth – famed for her sweet (and rotten) tooth – was entertained to a 'sugar banquet' in 1591.[12]

Naturally enough, men whose wealth could match that of their rulers (wealth acquired from Europe's burgeoning trade and commerce) sought to emulate and even surpass their social betters. We can even catch a glimpse of the process in the pages of the new cooking and domestic handbooks which began to appear in the 16th and 17th centuries. (Between 1651 and 1789, at least 230 were published in France alone.) The world of 18th-century popular and accessible print utterly transformed the Western world, from politics to cooking. As sugar entered the culinary and social world of less vaunted people, the earlier sugary sculptures were rivalled by something quite different: an array of simple, sweet desserts which were much less extravagant than earlier versions. European cooks and households adapted sugar to their cooking, in the process learning to discriminate between different kinds of sugars. Sugar thus entered the mainstream European diet and found a place in a range of desserts gracing the tables of prosperous people. The list of sugary dishes which became popular in the 17th century is remarkable, not least because they remain so familiar to modern readers – and diners. "Hot puddings, cold puddings, steam puddings, baked puddings, pies, tarts, creams, moulds, charlottes and bettys, trifles and fools, syllabus and tansys, junkets and ices, milk puddings, suet puddings...."[13] Most famously perhaps, sugar formed the basis of ice cream, which became hugely popular on both sides of the Atlantic by the late 18th century. However, the spread of sugar consumption was driven forward not by foods and desserts, but by drinks. Sugar became popular, rapidly and unpredictably, in the course of the 17th century in particular, via its close association with the new fad for exotic drinks – themselves imported from far-flung regions. The British took to tea from China.

By 1600, the Dutch had established trading links to Asia, and had developed a complex network of trading and military routes linking Europe to South Africa, India, Indonesia, and on to China. Exotic commodities of unknown places began to arrive back in Europe via Amsterdam, and the Dutch trade inevitably attracted other European maritime powers. Most of them established trading companies to Asia (East India Companies), all keen to share the astonishing riches and valuable commodities of Asia – among them tea. Tea from China (where it was consumed as a bitter drink without any additives) was introduced to Europe by Portugal, which had pioneered trading links to China. British tea drinking was first adopted in the court of Charles II after the arrival of his Portuguese queen, Catherine. Within a generation, courtesy of the recently developed sugar islands in the Caribbean, the British were sipping their tea sweetened with sugar.

The British developed their own trade to Asia, greatly assisted by new types of ship, managed and directed by the East India Company. But the key to the burgeoning British success in Asia was the tea trade to and from China. It involved, however, a long, perilous voyage, at risk from pirates, hostile European powers, and the natural dangers of oceanic travel. The British developed an effective monopoly in tea, providing a lucrative commodity that amply compensated for the risks. Though Europeans knew little about how the tea was cultivated in China, or even how it reached the dockside of Canton (thence onto the European-bound ships), they purchased it in growing volumes.

The British market for tea was small in the mid-17th century. Samuel Pepys confessed to his first drink of tea in 1660, but seven years later his wife was making a pot of tea at home, because the apothecary had recommended it as a cure for a cold. (Like all the other new-fangled spices and drinks from exotic lands, tea was initially promoted for its medicinal qualities, and could be purchased from apothecaries.) Tea drinking on a mass scale seems to have taken off in the 1690s, and rapidly became a feature in London shops and in the social routines of polite metropolitan and fashionable society in the provinces.

By the 1720s the price of different types of tea had dropped substantially, greatly accelerating the consumption of tea among people previously excluded by cost. The Scottish theologian and lawyer Duncan Forbes noted at mid-century that the price of tea had fallen so low "that the meanest laboring Man could compass the Purchase of it...."[14] Thereafter, tea became a major industry, imported in increasing volumes, both by the monopolistic East India Company and by gangs of smugglers. The early problems of securing tea from China were overcome after 1713 when the East India Company struck a deal to ship tea direct from Canton. Four years later British ships began to trade directly to and from that distant port. These home-bound ships, packed with silks, porcelains – and tea – made possible the development of the fashionable taste for *chinoiserie*. And as more tea arrived, the price dropped and tea drinking spread. Yet because of a thriving smuggling industry (mainly via the West Country), and largely in response to the excessive duties on tea, there were periods when the East India Company imports accounted for only a quarter of the nation's consumption.[15] A substantial part of the 13.5 million pounds of tea shipped to Europe was re-exported – smuggled – into Britain. Indeed, throughout much of the 18th century, a great deal of the demand for tea was satisfied by smugglers. Even respectable people who traveled to Europe resorted to returning with tea hidden about their person.

The British simply could not get enough of it, and by the mid-18th century, more than one pound of tea was being landed for every head of the population. By the time the government slashed the duties on tea, in 1784 (from 120% to 12.5%), the British were each consuming two pounds of tea every year.[16] In 1820 something like 30 million pounds of tea were consumed in Britain, accounting for 5% of the British gross domestic product.[17]

In the course of the 18th century, tea drinking, with its complex social rituals, became a familiar aspect of British life. Tea-drinking rituals, in fashionable homes, in poor dwellings, and in a variety of public places, became a characteristic feature of British social life by the mid-18th century, the habit, like sugar, moving down the social scale from the prosperous to the poor. In Bath, for example, fashionable society revolved around the town's various assemblies, adjourning when the mood took them to the Assembly Rooms' smaller tea rooms for refreshments. More formal balls in the same building began at 6pm: about 9pm… "the gentlemen treat their partners with tea…."[18] At much the same time, people keen to escape the noise and smell of Central London would decamp to the summer tea gardens of Bagnigge Wells and White Conduit House, in Islington and Primrose Hill.

> Ah I loves life and all the joy it yields,
> Says Madam Fussock from Spittle Fields,
> Bon ton's the space twixt Saturday and Mundy,
> And riding in a one-horse chair 'Sunday:
> 'Tis drinking tea on Summer's afternoons
> At Bagnigge Wells with China and gilt spoons.[19]

These, and many others, were favorite weekend haunts of family groups, who wished to get away from the city for a short while to enjoy the refreshments on offer. The *Universal Chronicle*'s Zachary Treacle (created by Dr. Johnson), dragged out by his wife to one such tea shop on Sunday, begrudged the cost of "tea, and hot rolls, and syllabubs for the boy."[20] It was no accident that in the 1790s, the campaign against the slave trade targeted the fashionable use of slave-grown sugar. That campaign, in its turn, attracted the mischievous attention of caricaturists – mocking both the fashion of sweet tea and the abolitionist campaign.[21] By then, tea drinking was virtually a universal habit among working people and their social superiors.

The tea chests loaded onto the *East Indiamen* contained much more than tea. Tea leaves were ideal packing material for the delicate 'China' which was exported in astonishing volumes. The rise of Western tea drinking confirmed the pre-eminence of the Chinese porcelain industry. At a time when Europeans had not mastered the skills of manufacturing porcelain, the Chinese produced exquisite items which quickly became fashionable and were sought after in Europe and North America, and feverishly copied once Europeans learned the techniques of porcelain manufacture. But initially the Chinese alone could provide what their European customers wanted: both the finest of craftsmanship from the 3,000 kilns of the great factories of Ching-te-Chen near Nanking, and then, increasingly, huge volumes of less elaborate but serviceable tableware: tea and coffee sets for the homes of ordinary people in all corners of Europe and colonial North America.

For years, European manufacturers tried in vain to copy the Chinese prototypes but did not make a breakthrough until after 1712 (and then only via leaks provided by insiders). Thereafter, the French, Germans, Flemings, and English began their own mass production of refined porcelains and ceramics. By then, Chinese tableware and tea services had become commonplace. Curiously, porcelain had initially been shipped to Europe as ballast to the main cargoes of Chinese tea and silks. Six tons of porcelain were loaded for every ton of tea, and Chinese porcelain quickly acquired a market of its own. As more arrived, as taste and demand spread, there was a consequent drop in the price asked for Chinese porcelains. In 1723, 5,000 imported teapots cost one penny and a half each. The numbers involved were amazing. At its peak, some 5 million items were imported *each year*. In 1718, for example, a 29-ton lot contained 250,000 pieces. A 40-ton lot, imported six years later, contained 332,000 items. By 1791, when the East India Company stopped shipping porcelain imports, an estimated 215 million items had been imported. Objects which had once been rare and exotic had, in a cheaper, simpler format, become mundane and unexceptional features of domestic life across a wide social spectrum of Western society.[22] Yet even the finer items of Chinese porcelain sometimes had a way of finding their way down the social scale, as employers handed on chipped, damaged, and broken tableware to their servants and helpers. The end result, in what became a familiar pattern, was that previously exotic and costly objects were now commonplace.

Not everyone approved of the rising popularity of tea drinking. To some it seemed bizarre that the poor and even the wretchedly humble came to regard tea as a necessity. Here was an exotic produce, imported from the far corners of the world, now vital to the lives of the poor. One diarist recorded "with some Degree of Indignation" that "a ragged and greasy Creature" came into a shop, with her filthy children "asking for a Pennyworth of Tea and Half pennyworth of Sugar...."[23] This was the critical mix – tea and sugar – which came together to form a brew of two exotic products, the one from China, the other from the tropical Americas where it was cultivated by African slaves. For all the fashionable etiquette of tea drinking in London and the spa towns, the practice became a simple domestic habit. It was easy and cheap to make and was consumed overwhelmingly in the home. In fashionable houses it was served via the most lavish of tea services, but in the humblest of garrets and cellars, tea was drunk from chipped and broken cups and mugs, acquired in the way the poor acquired all their meager personal effects. Over the course of the 18th century, families came to own more and more *things* – clothing, furnishings, and kitchenware. On both sides of the Atlantic families left an increasing number of material objects from one generation to another. And among the most striking features of those possessions were the tea and coffee accessories which had been effectively unknown until the mid-17th century.[24] Even among the 'lower class' in France in the 18th century, historians have found a striking increase in the ownership of accessories for tea.[25]

The Chinese manufacturers of tea and coffee sets, alert to what was required in Europe, *adapted* their products to the market. The Chinese did not brew their tea in the type of teapots favored by Europeans and Americans, for example, nor did they sip tea from cups with handles, but from small rimless, bowl-like cups, as they still do. But both were now provided in shapes which conformed to Western taste. More striking still, though the Chinese did *not* add sugar to their tea, Chinese manufacturers were more than happy to provide sugar bowls for the purpose. The success of imported 'China' (the name itself an abbreviation of 'China-ware') can be seen by the fact that the name was absorbed into the vernacular by the late 17th century as a generic term for crockery of all kinds.[26] Enterprising Europeans were also prompted to imitate these China wares. There was, however, more to this than merely copying the finest and most costly of elaborate fashions, once Europeans had learned how to create and work with porcelain. It was clear enough that there was a growing market for *locally* made tableware. Josiah Wedgwood led the way in Britain, aiming initially at the fashionable tastes of the wealthy. His new London showroom offered a variety of attractive items for the kitchen and dining room. But Wedgwood also set out to *popularize* his wares, manufacturing goods at prices within the reach of the middling orders. A clever mix of new manufacturing systems and – above all – marketing techniques enabled Wedgwood's products to find their way into all corners of British domestic and social life. He also aimed at an international market, and soon his pottery could be found scattered around Europe. His salesmen's efforts were helped by fashionable society's adoption of Wedgwood products as gifts for like-minded friends. Much of his trade was, however, exported to the tables of Britons wherever they lived and worked, from North America to India and beyond. Travelers regularly noted the presence of Wedgwood pottery wherever they traveled abroad: in France, the Low Countries, and Russia, in Spain, in North America, and in the slave colonies of the Caribbean. At his death in 1795 Josiah Wedgwood left a fortune of half a million pounds.

Wedgwood's commercial success provides an important clue to a much broader process of social change. He aimed initially at the prosperous, at the very people first influenced by the habit of tea drinking. In the process he helped to create a mass market with high prices. Once his goods had secured their niche in fashionable society, others – less fashionable and less wealthy – followed. He spotted and capitalized on one simple principle: fashion tended to start at the top and work downward. Thus it was with tea drinking and with the domestic acquisitions of tea sets.

The British had become infamous tea drinkers by 1800, and tea drinking was firmly rooted as a feature of public, social, and domestic life. Something like 30 million pounds of tea were consumed in Britain by then. As we have seen, for the British, tea and sugar went together, and the graph for the import and consumption of the one more or less mirrored the graph for the other. Supporters of the sugar lobby – planters and slave traders – knew that their firmest support was to be found not only among those who favored slavery and the slave trade, but also among those who promoted the importation of tea. Like tea drinkers, the West Indian sugar planters *needed* tea from China.

Europeans, by contrast, tended to prefer coffee, though the development of coffee drinking took a similar pattern to that of tea. It, too, took hold initially in elite circles, before becoming a popular habit via the proliferation of coffee shops and cafes throughout urban Europe. A common drink in Arabia and Turkey for centuries (British coffee shops often went under the sign of 'The Turk's Head'), coffee created a distinctive niche in Western city life. Served in bowls or cups, with sugar added to remove its naturally bitter taste, coffee drinking became the focus for male social and economic life across Europe. In Paris, cafes multiplied, the cost of coffee fell, and coffee drinking established itself as part of public and private social life. The French heaped so much sugar into their coffee that, according to an English visitor, the spoon could stand up in the cup. It was consumed in royal palaces and sold on the streets of Paris by vendors working from a wooden bench in the street. Parisian coffee shops came in an enormous variety by the late 18th century, from the most fashionable and costly to the lowest of dives offering warmth and shelter for the poor – alongside a cup of hot sugary coffee. Men on their way to work early in the morning could buy a cup of cheap coffee – made from coffee dregs mixed with warm milk – from female street pedlars.[27]

London had its own coffee culture. In the City of London alone there were 82 coffee shops by 1662, perhaps 550 in Greater

London by 1740. Over the period 1650 to 1850, 2,000 coffee shops existed in London. The coffee house had become "a chief focus of social life."[28] Here was the key to its universal importance. Men gathered over coffee to conduct business, to organize finances, to provide insurance, to supervise and scrutinize shipping and manufacture. In time the coffee shop became a gathering point for political and sectional interests. They were home to thespians and the world of theater, trade associations, political groups, and conspirators. They attracted high life and the lowest of low life. They became the natural habitat of London's great artists and caricaturists of the 18th century, and some were famed for their gatherings of writers and wits. Others were infamous as brothels and bagnios. This extraordinary variety of coffee shops provided a meeting place where coffee (and tobacco) was consumed, and where sugar was added to the black bitter drink, as taste required. In the coffee shop, as in the servants' quarters and in kitchens across Europe, the dictum 'sweeten to taste' was the golden rule. It was also an unmistakable sign of the pervasiveness of slave-grown sugar.

Coffee itself had, like tea and chocolate, come from an exotic location, and as with other exotica, it arrived on a wave of medical and social controversy. Like sugar, tea, and tobacco, coffee had its medical backers (and it too, initially, could be bought in the apothecary shop). Some worried that coffee attracted groups of men who wished to take part in nefarious discussions: in societies beset by political and religious strife, another venue for political and perhaps seditious debate was a worrying trend. But the drift to coffee proved impossible to stop, not least because of the simple social pleasures it afforded, especially when assisted by tobacco. The coffee shop thus became an essential feature of Western urban social life. Men gathered round their bowls of coffee, sweetening them with slave-grown sugar, their pipes filled with the new-fangled weed of tobacco (from the slave fields of the Chesapeake), for the prospects of good company and the inevitable arguments about any topic under the sun. Unlike the tavern and ale house, where arguments could disintegrate into drunken dispute, the coffee shop debates remained rational and controlled (despite the stimulus of coffee itself). Not surprisingly, some called them 'penny universities.'

The medicinal qualities claimed for coffee were soon set aside in favor of its simple personal and social pleasures. Like tea and sugar, coffee could be had in ever greater (and cheaper) volumes, thanks to coffee cultivation in Europe's tropical possessions. Europeans settling into their new tropical colonies were always on the hunt for commercial tropical produce, transplanting crops from one corner of the world to another. Coffee was henceforth cultivated in new colonial locations; at higher altitudes in the Dutch settlements in Java, in the Blue Mountains of Jamaica, and in the hilly and mountainous spine of St. Domingue (Haiti) – and much of it was cultivated by African slaves. At first the bulk of coffee in Britain was imported from the Levant and the Mediterranean (much of it had originated in the Yemen) but by 1720 coffee from the Red Sea port of Mocha was being imported by the East India Company, with substantial volumes of British imports of coffee re-exported to European customers (overwhelmingly to Holland). The data is again confused by the story of smuggling, that contraband industry which sought to evade state duties on imported coffee. *The* peculiar feature of this story, however, is the parallel trajectories of tea and coffee. Just when the British were re-exporting much of their coffee to their coffee-drinking European neighbors, British coffee drinking was being overtaken – and at a remarkable pace – by tea. Stated simply, in the course of the 18th century, tea replaced coffee as the national drink in Britain. Today, and despite a thriving coffee culture, we simply assume that the British are primarily a tea-drinking people. Yet the British consumed ten times as much coffee as tea in 1700.

By the 1720s, all that had changed. In that decade the value of imported tea (most of it for domestic consumption) was much higher than that of coffee. But as the cost of tea fell, the popularity of tea drinking was confirmed and expanded.[29] At much the same time, and as coffee took root in Europe's various tropical colonies (the Dutch in Java and Surinam, the French in the Indian Ocean and the Caribbean), Europeans were no longer reliant on coffee from the Red Sea. In the British case, tea held its commercial advantage by being cheaper. Hot sweet tea was the undisputed king by the late 18th century: it was now the drink of British working people. Those so poor in the 1790s that they could not afford to buy tea would simulate it by pouring hot water over a burnt crust.[30] Contemporaries regularly scratched their heads at the apparent contradiction; the very poor had come to think of hot sweet tea as a vital ingredient of everyday life. In 1757 Jonas Hanway was irritated that "your servants' servants, down to the very beggars, will not be satisfied unless they consume the produce of the remote country of China."[31] In Europe, it was different. In Germany, coffee was "the drink of all, to the very porters and postilions." So too in France, where coffee was enjoyed by the highest and the poorest of French society by the late 18th century.[32] But in Britain, coffee had lost out to tea.

Three hot drinks (tea, coffee, and, to a lesser extent, chocolate) which were widespread and popular by the late 18th century were made palatable to Western tastes by the addition of sugar. So, too, was a range of Western food. The very phrase 'sweeten to taste' could now be found where it remains to this day: in cookbooks, domestic manuals, and recipes. Cooking – like beverages – had absorbed sugar, part of the broader process which saw diet and taste transformed by Western involvement with foodstuffs from throughout the world. The data, again, provides a statistical outline for what had happened. Sugar, which had cost about one shilling per pound in 1660, cost half that twenty years later. In 1700, the English consumed 7lbs of sugar a year – each – the equivalent of two tablespoons a day. Sugar was used not only in drink and food but was also incorporated into a growing number of manufacturing processes (brewing and distilling, for example), in preservatives and medicines. Sugar was a feature of British cooking by the late 17th century and became even more widespread as the 18th century advanced, especially via the spread of 'French cuisine', with its widespread use of sugar for its great variety of desserts and puddings.[33] By then, sugar was indispensable and integral to Western taste.

The whole process was dependent on African slaves in the Americas. Yet who even thought of the slaves in St. Domingue as they lavished sugar into their Parisian coffee? Who even considered the African slave when they spooned sugar into their coffee in Philadelphia, or into tea in British homes? Indeed, what could be more British than a sweet cup of tea? Did anyone think about the role played by gangs of Africans toiling in the Caribbean when they lovingly handled their Sèvres sugar bowls?

Notes

1. B.W. Higman, *A Concise History of the Caribbean*, Cambridge, 2011, p. 104.
2. For the classic study of sugar, see Sidney Mintz, *Sweetness and Power: The Place of Sugar in Modern History*, New York, 1986.
3. Jessica Mudry, 'Sugar and health.' In Darra Goldstein, ed., *The Oxford Companion to Sugar and Sweets*, Oxford, 2015, pp. 670–673.
4. Jelmer Vos, David Eltis, and David Richardson, 'The Dutch in the Atlantic World.' In *Extending the Frontiers: Essays on the New Trans-Atlantic Slave Trade Database*, New Haven, 2008, Chapter 8.
5. David Eltis and David Richardson, *Atlas of the Transatlantic Slave Trade*, New Haven, 2010, Table 2, p. 23.
6. B.W. Higman, *A Concise History of the Caribbean*, p. 104.

7. Matthew Parker, *The Sugar Barons: Family, Corruption, Empire and War*, London, 2012.

8. See Madge Dresser, *Slavery Obscured: The Social History of the Slave Trade in an English Provincial Town*, London, 2001, Chapter 3.

9. S.E. Smith, *Slavery, Family and Gentry Capitalism in the British Atlantic: The World of the Lascelles, 1648–1834*, Cambridge, 2006.

10. Matthew Parker, *The Sugar Barons*, p. 300.

11. Ivan Day, 'Sugar sculptures.' In Darra Goldstein, ed., *Sugar and Sweets*, pp. 689–693.

12. Elizabeth Abbott, *Sugar: A Bittersweet History*, London, 2009, Chapter 2.

13. Elizabeth Abbott, *Sugar*, pp. 48–50.

14. Sidney Mintz, *Sweetness and Power*, p. 114.

15. James Walvin, *Fruits of Empire: Exotic Produce and British Taste, 1660–1800*, London, 1997, p. 17.

16. James Walvin, *Fruits of Empire*, pp. 17–19.

17. James Walvin, *Fruits of Empire*, p. 30.

18. Quoted in Paula Byrne, *The Real Jane Austen*, London, 2013, p. 167.

19. M.D. George, *Hogarth to Cruikshank: Social Change in Graphic Satire*, London, 1968, p. 77.

20. M.D. George, *Hogarth to Cruikshank*, p. 77.

21. See James Gillray, 'The Anti-Saccharites' (1792), in M.D. George, *Hogarth to Cruikshank*, p. 69.

22. John Brewer and Roy Porter, eds., *Consumption and the World of Goods*, London, 1993, Part II, Chapters 5–8.

23. Quoted in Dorothy George, *English People in the Eighteenth Century*, London, 1956, p. 172.

24. Jan de Vries, 'Between purchasing power and the world of goods.' In John Brewer and Roy Porter, eds., *Consumption and the World of Goods*, Chapter 5.

25. Cissie Fairchilds, 'Populuxe goods.' In John Brewer and Roy Porter, eds., *Consumption and the World of Goods*, p. 230.

26. 'The rage for China.' In Markman Ellis, Richard Coulton, Matthew Mauger, *Empire of Tea: The Asian Leaf that Conquered the World*, London, 2015, pp. 150–157.

27. Fernand Braudel, *Capitalism and Material Life, 1400–1800*, London, 1967, pp. 186–188.

28. Vic Gattrell, *The First Bohemians*, London, 2014 edn., pp. 178; 433, n. 32.

29. Brian Cowan, *The Social Life of Coffee: The Emergence of the British Coffee-house*, London, 2005, p. 75.

30. E.P. Thompson, *The Making of the English Working Class*, London, 1968 edn., p. 351.

31. Quoted in A. Hope, *The Londoner's Larder*, London, 1990, pp. 88–89.

32. Fernand Braudel, *Capitalism and Material Life*, pp. 184–188.

33. Nuala Zahedieh, *The Capital and the Colonies: London and the Atlantic Economy, 1660–1700*, Cambridge, 2010, pp. 221–223.

2

Cowrie Shells
Slavery and Global Trade

The cowrie shell, famous the world over for its simple beauty, has for centuries been used as an item of personal decoration, as jewelry, and as an accessory in hairstyles and clothing. Today, there are fashion companies specializing in cowries, offering a range of stylish items, all incorporating cowrie shells as part of their commercial wares. Metal and leather bracelets, necklaces, pendants, hair accessories, earrings, baskets and bowls, musical instruments, rings – even denim jeans – all come bedecked with cowrie shells. You can even buy large bags of cut and polished cowrie shells for personal adaptation.[1] Cowrie shells and their related fashions are aimed primarily at the African-American market, with companies often promoting their products to people of African descent through an appeal to an African past. For some, the cowrie has even become a symbol of African identity and an imagined African history. Wearing or sporting a cowrie shell is not only a fashion statement but also an affirmation of personal identity. Sometimes this simple shell is promoted by some far-fetched claims: a shell rooted in an Africa shrouded in myth and legend, with links to the world of spirits, beliefs – and with tantalizing hints of prosperity and personal health.

Slavery in Small Things: Slavery and Modern Cultural Habits, First Edition. James Walvin.
© 2017 John Wiley & Sons, Inc. Published 2017 by John Wiley & Sons, Inc.

Such commercial claims for the cowrie shell generally fail to take note of the shell's intimate connection to the history of the Atlantic slave trade. The small shell (*Cypraea moneta*) was "by a large margin the most important money import to West Africa in the era of the slave trade...."[2] The volume of shells involved in the slave trade was astounding, and the figures are hard to grasp at first sight. Historians calculate that *ten billion* cowrie shells (1,143 metric tonnes) were landed on the West African slaving coast in the years 1700–1790, largely along the coast between Accra and what is now Nigeria. Even more remarkable, perhaps, is the fact that most of those shells came from the Maldive Islands in the middle of the Indian Ocean, and had found their way to West Africa via India and Europe. There they were bartered for African slaves. The vast geography of this commercial transaction is staggering: shells shipped from the Maldives to India, to Europe, thence to the African coast to be bartered for slaves, with the slaves then shipped to the Americas. The story of the cowrie shell reveals that the Atlantic slave trade did not exist as a discrete, isolated system but was a commercial enterprise sustained by people scattered over an enormous geographical area. It embraced commodities and people from India and the Indian Ocean, from the interior of Africa (itself largely unknown to the coastally rooted Europeans), from the insecurely settled frontiers of the Americas, and of course from the old established societies and economies of Europe. The cowrie shell, then, provides an avenue through which to explore the complex economic and geographic enormity that was the Atlantic slaving system. This simple, beautiful object is also a cautionary reminder of the need to locate the Atlantic slave system in a much broader context than is normally the case.

*   *   *

There are 250 species of cowrie shell, but only two really matter here: *Cypraea moneta* and *Cypraea annulus*. Long before the cowrie shell made its commercial impact on West Africa it had been a basic form of currency – "the most widely used primitive currency in world history" – and an item of personal adornment, in widely separated parts of the world unknown to Europeans. Various sorts proved fashionable and useful in all corners of the globe: in Hawaii and among native peoples in the Americas, for example. Its great attraction as a currency was that it was impossible to counterfeit.[3] For millennia, the shell had been taken eastward across the Indian Ocean to Asia, where it penetrated societies far from its homeland. As such it provides evidence of the extensive oceanic and overland trade routes which linked those small dots in the Indian Ocean to distant civilizations. Recent archaeological digs in China, for example, have revealed large hordes of cowrie shells in the burial chambers of monarchs and leaders. Chinese rulers were frequently buried alongside symbols of their power and prestige, and these often took the form of cowrie shells. For example, the wife of a Chinese ruler in the Shan dynasty (12th century BCE) was buried along with a large collection of bronze pieces, jade – and 6,800 cowrie shells. From there they had traveled into northern India, and even further afield into South East Asia. Archaeology, again, has unearthed cowries in widely scattered communities, from Burma to Vietnam and Central Asia, carried there along the trading systems of the Silk Road and via the maritime trading links of Asia.[4] Cowries had also traveled westward, to Arabia and Africa. By the time Europeans began their tentative exploration of the East African coastland and the Indian Ocean – making contact with trading systems which had existed for centuries – they were curious to find the widespread presence of cowrie shells. Long before Europeans established trading bases on the West African coast, cowries had penetrated deep into a number of African societies. They were to be found, for instance, in upper and middle Niger, and in the great Mali and Songhay empires.

Above all, however, Europeans were struck by the cowrie's impact in India and Asia. Reports came back to Europe from early voyagers (the first ambassadors to China, and the first European visitors to India and China) of cowrie shells in Bengal and in the ports of South East Asia and Burma. Early visitors to the Maldives described how locals harvested the shells.

> As to their cowries: the people there collect them and pile them into heaps like mountains; they catch them in nets and let the flesh rot: they transport them for sale.[5]

A fourteenth-century visitor to the Maldive Islands told how cowries were sold in baskets of 12,000:

> They sell them in exchange for rice to the people of Bengal, who also use them as money, as well as to the Yemenites, who use them instead of sand [as ballast] in their ships. These shells are used also by the negroes in their lands.[6]

A Frenchman, shipwrecked in the Maldives in 1602, wrote that 30–40 shiploads of cowries were being exported from there to Bengal each year. When the Portuguese encountered the Indian Ocean cowrie trade, they naturally began to make use of it for their own purposes. In 1515 the King of Portugal licensed a Portuguese merchant to import cowries as ballast from India to Sao Tome. With the expansion of Portuguese trade and exploration, cowries inevitably ended up in Portugal itself and by the early 16th century Portuguese ships were regularly using cowries as ballast on their trading legs between Asia and the Atlantic. Thus did cowries find their way, on early Portuguese ships, to the newly opened slave trading locations on the West African coast, sometimes as ballast, but increasingly as a means of exchange. In West Africa, as in Bengal and Asia many centuries earlier, the humble cowrie shell proved an ideal means of exchange. Europeans came to realize that the cowrie shell was a perfect form of currency.

Though it is true that cowrie shells were available in other parts of the world, notably on the East African coast, those, especially the smaller shells, from the Maldives, were the most prized of all. By the early 18th century, regular supplies of cowrie shells were arriving in Europe, through Rotterdam and London, thence to France, but all were destined for the African slave coast. As the Europeans expanded their trading presence on that coast, and as the American appetite for slaves grew, the cowrie shells of the Maldives established themselves as a major form of currency in the complex slave trading and commercial systems of West Africa.

At first, the British, French, and Portuguese bought their cowrie shells at auctions held by the United East India Company (the VOC) at Amsterdam, Middleburg, and Rotterdam. Even at first glance, this seems a very unusual trade. Sea shells shipped enormous distances, from the Indian Ocean, round the Cape, to Europe, where they were sold on, in auctions, to other European traders who wanted them for their own commerce in African slaves on the Atlantic coast. It was a trade which stretched 16,000 miles, "equivalent to more than half the earth's circumference."[7]

Cowrie shells began to follow the new routes and locations of Dutch commercial and maritime power, arriving in Holland, packed in bundles, or barrels. The standard basket of cowries arriving in Rotterdam contained 12,000 shells. At much the same time, they arrived in Britain, and both the Dutch and the British quickly appreciated the economic value of the shells as a means of exchange in their burgeoning trade on Africa's Atlantic coast. Britain's new and increasingly important bases in India also encouraged the shipping of cowrie shells.[8] Others followed suit and soon most of the major European slave trading nations on the African coast adopted cowrie shells as part of the complex payment for African slaves. The resulting volume of cowries exported from the Indian Ocean (normally via India) to Europe and thence to Africa was simply amazing. The Dutch, the British, and the French all wanted cowries to assist their trade, and accumulated them in huge quantities. By the 1720s, an estimated one million pounds in weight of cowries were being shipped *every year*: something in the order of 400 million shells per year.[9]

The sheer *volume* of shells involved is sometimes hard to believe. In the period 1699–1790, the Dutch exported an annual average of 81 tons of shells to West Africa (in 1749 it reached 304 tons). When we recall that each ton contained three-quarters of a million shells, the actual *number* of cowrie shells involved is truly bewildering. (And this was simply the Dutch trade.) The British trade was equally enormous. In the equivalent period, British exports averaged 57 tons a year. Between them, the British and the Dutch shipped an annual 138 tons of cowrie shells in the 18th century, with something like 40 million shells landed each year in West Africa. (And this does *not* include the French trade.)

The Portuguese had introduced cowries into Sao Tome, thence to Benin and Whydah, in the 16th century. The shells moved inland, along existing trade routes, and took firm root in a variety of African societies: into regions effectively unknown to European traders on the coast. The shells remained embedded there for centuries. Time and again, visitors, traders, and colonial administrators in the heartlands of Africa commentated on the use of cowries in distant interior societies, long after the slave trade had been abolished.[10]

Throughout, cowrie shells were also used as items of personal decoration. In certain places it was even thought they brought health benefits or had spiritual qualities. Above all, however, the shell had a *value*. Wherever it was used, the cowrie shell was a vital currency, not merely a local means of exchange, but an *international* currency which could be traded and exchanged in vastly different societies across huge distances of the world's surface. By, say, the mid-18th century, it had become like a traveler's check – or a modern US dollar bill: an item which was recognized and accepted for its universal ability to buy goods and services, as a Dutchman noted in 1747.

> What we call money being arbitrary, and its nature and value depending on a tacit convention betwixt men, these [cowrie] shells, in several parts of Asia and Africa, are accounted current money, with a value assigned to them. This is established by a reciprocal consent, and those who are pleased to show a contempt of them don't reflect that shells are as fit for a common standard of pecuniary value as either gold or silver.[11]

Cowrie shells were not, of course, the only commodity which Europeans used to acquire African slaves. Indeed, there were some African coastal regions where cowries were *never* used in the slave trading system. Even so, this small, delicate item, from the middle of the Indian Ocean, exposed a central feature of Europe's involvement in the African slave trade. Here was a massive international trade of much greater commercial and geographic complexity than the simple 'triangular trade' of popular imagination. It involved societies and economies far beyond the regions traditionally associated with the Atlantic trade. We only need peer inside the holds of European ships heading to West Africa to grasp this simple but far-reaching point.

European (later American and Brazilian) ships converged on the African coast packed with goods for the awaiting African merchants and traders. Though the initial trading forays were for the obvious and well-known commodities (notably the gold which had long been one of Africa's prime attractions), the growing demand for slaves created an immense market for imported goods. It formed a coastal market which stretched from Senegambia in the north to Angola in the far south, and eventually round the Cape to Mozambique and Madagascar. What evolved, at all the coastal locations, were sophisticated commercial transactions. These were not raids, where Africans were simply grabbed and taken away (though such violent raids were often the *initial* source of distant, inland slaves), but forms of commercial bargaining. Those with Africans to sell had firm ideas about what they wanted in return. John Barbot, describing trade on the African coast in the late 17th century, wrote:

> ...the Blacks of the Gold Coast have traded with the Europeans ever since the beginning of the fourteenth century, are very skilled in the nature and proper qualities of all the European wares and merchandize vended there...In short, they examine every thing with as much prudence and ability as any European trader can do.[12]

As the trade evolved, the range of goods disgorged from the Atlantic ships became more varied, but their *quality* was always important to African traders. If slave traders could not deliver the expected goods, they often returned home with unsold cargo. One Bristol slave captain sailed home with 7 tons of iron bars and 728 pounds of beads unsold in his ship's hold.[13] Africans were choosy about what they wanted, and were insistent upon the *quality* of imported goods. Ships' captains could not fob them off with inferior goods. Europeans went to great lengths to find precisely what Africans wanted. As European trading and colonial interests crept into all corners of the world, they were able to find goods from distant sites to trade in Africa. Commodities and products from far-flung European outposts in India, Asia, and the Americas became the common currency of European trade and dominion, alongside items from the economies of Europe. The pioneers in all this were the Portuguese and then the Dutch.

Dutch traders, like those who followed, shipped an enormous variety of goods into West Africa. Textiles from Asia, Indian cotton textiles (which had been dyed in Holland) from the Low Countries, England, and Spain, woollen goods from France, cotton from Cape Verde, calico from Gujarat, cloth from Bengal and Seurat, striped cottons from Sindh, bedspreads from China, woven goods from North Africa, shawls from southern India. All these were in addition to beads, shells, and precious stones from India, and more mundane items – hats and cloaks, codfish from the Newfoundland fisheries, wines and food from France.[14] At first, the British played a minor role, but their own expanding commercial and geopolitical strength in the 17th century saw them overtake the pioneering Dutch and Portuguese. Propelled by the growing power of London, with its important financial and political elites, the British became the dominant force in the North Atlantic. And, like their predecessors in the Atlantic trade, they ferried enormous volumes of goods to West Africa in return for slaves. Ships left their home quaysides, from an expanding number of British ports, loaded with goods demanded by African middlemen. By the early 18th century, something like two-thirds of those goods, dominated by textiles and woollens, were British. Second in importance was metal ware: raw iron bars (much of it, at first, trans-shipped from Sweden) for Africans to refashion to their own local use, weapons and guns, nails and shot, plus a range of luxury items, notably wines and brandy. But textiles dominated. Upward of 50% of all goods shipped to Africa were textiles. In 1688, for example, the Royal African Company shipped £13,713 of woollens and £ 11,105 of East India textiles to Africa. When, after 1740, Liverpool emerged as the new dominant British slave port, it rose to prominence in large part because of the nearby textile regions of Yorkshire and Lancashire.[15]

The British trade to Africa had initially been the monopoly of the Company of Royal Adventurers Trading into Africa (1660–1672), later known as the Royal African Company (f. 1672 – its monopoly ended in 1692). But over *one half* of the Company's exports were goods of foreign origin, re-packaged and trans-shipped through London. Pre-eminent among those goods were Indian textiles. (This pattern continued in the next century, long after the Company's monopoly had ended. Between 1699 and 1800, 27% of the value of *all* goods shipped to Africa were East Indian textiles.[16]) The Company also re-exported iron and copper ware from Sweden and Germany. In 1685, for example, of 36 Company ships sent to Africa, only six sailed without iron exports. Other re-exported items carried in the ships of the Royal African Company included amber and textiles from Germany. At first, many of these goods were bought via agents working in Amsterdam (the Dutch had well-established trading links to Africa, Asia, the Baltic, and Eastern Europe). In the space of twenty-four years, the Company re-exported to Africa no less than half a million sheets of textile (into which Africans wrapped themselves at night). More than 3,000 gallons of French brandy were shipped to Africa each year.[17]

African tastes and demands were *cultivated* by the remarkable commercial cornucopia disgorged by the European ships. With the development of direct slave routes, to and from the

Americas, from Brazil, from the Caribbean, and from North America, goods from those burgeoning American economies also found their way to West Africa. Merchants from Pernambuco exported tobacco (grown by slaves, of course) on the ships sailing east to the African coast. African traders in the Bight of Benin developed a fondness for tobacco coated in molasses from slave merchants in Bahia. Ships from Barbados exchanged local rum for new African slaves.[18] What lurks behind these small snippets of evidence is a very complex trade in African slaves. Ships were sailing from Europe to Africa, thence home via the Americas. Others sailed east and west across the southern Atlantic; still more sailed direct from North America and the Caribbean to Africa. And each of those vessels carried varied cargoes which the merchants hoped would catch the eye, and pander to the taste of African traders who had been primed by earlier voyages, or by commercial contacts and tip-offs. Each ship carried something *local*; from Britain or France, from Barbados or Brazil. Many also carried items which had already been trans-shipped from an even more distant corner of European trade and dominion.

The mixed nature of this trade is visible in the cargoes of individual ships, or when we track the exports from particular ports. The case of Liverpool is a good example. In 1709 that port dispatched only one ship to Africa. One hundred years later, 134 Liverpool ships were trading for African slaves. Though the Liverpool cargoes to Africa formed only a small proportion of the city's export trade, the *value* of those cargoes was high, largely because the cargoes destined for Africa were primarily comprised of manufactured items: textiles, guns, and knives, metal ware, brass cooking pots, bottles, clay pipes. Many of these goods had been manufactured by craftsmen in Liverpool itself; others had been shipped into the city by coastal vessels or along inland canals from industries and craftsmen elsewhere. Cargoes to Africa were the most costly of all export trades and comprised 65% of the total cost of a voyage – a far higher figure than for other forms of export trade. When we add to this evidence the size of Liverpool's shipbuilding industry, with all its associated trades and industries, the economic and social centrality of slave trading to Liverpool becomes even clearer. Perhaps 40% of the city's income derived from the slave trade.[19]

Liverpool's was the biggest and most striking example of Britain's export trade to Africa in the mid- and late 18th century. Yet the story can be replicated in a host of other ports, many of them small, some of them rarely associated with the slave trade, but all of them anxious to profit from the export of local, regional, or trans-shipped goods, on local ships, to African merchants on the African coast. Many of the goods in demand on the African coast were readily available at different British regional ports (though the ports' geographic locations were equally important in gaining successful access to the Atlantic trade). Experience showed that African traders expected British ships to deliver mixed cargoes:

> Keep your cargo well assorted, for shou'd the Traders
> there learn you are short of any article commonly carried
> there, it may detriment your purchase.[20]

As we have seen, Africans were choosy customers; choosy about the commodities, their quality, color – and sizes. And, of course, African demand changed from place to place and across time. Iron bars, hugely popular in Gambia in the 17th century, gave way to textiles a century later. All this meant that European slave traders needed to be alert to different (and changing) African tastes and demands. For that, they needed good personal contacts and intelligence on the African coast. Merchant houses of London, Bristol, and Liverpool developed a finely tuned sense of the changing commercial demands on the African coast, just as they did for other forms of maritime trade, to Europe or the Americas, for example.[21]

With Indian textiles, as with the cowrie shells which accompanied the textiles in the ships' holds, we find confirmation of the global complexity of the slave trade. Large volumes of a wide range of Indian textiles, shipped to Britain, were trans-shipped in Britain, then dispatched to the Atlantic coast to find a suitable market place among local African slave traders. Many then went to consumers in the unknown reaches of inland African markets.

As we have seen, many of these items were bought and shipped through Amsterdam. But the rise of British commercial (and military) power, the lowering of costs, and the demands of new mercantile policies saw London emerge as the major *entrepôt* for goods passing from their place of origin (India, Italy, the Baltic, or France) *en route* to West Africa.[22] The rise of British manufacture in the 18th century, and the dictates of governmental commercial policy, saw a substantial change in the trade, with Africa-bound ships filling their holds with *British*-made goods, though this did not eliminate the re-exports of goods in great demand in Africa: beads from Italy, iron from Sweden, textiles from India.[23] From the 1740s, however, a growing volume of textiles exported to the African coast were produced by Lancashire manufacturers: one of the reasons which underpinned the rise of Liverpool to pre-eminence in the 18th-century slave trade. Lancashire cotton goods were ideal for light clothing in tropical climates. Yorkshire woollens also became popular (ideal for wraps and shawls) and became an established item in slave ship cargoes. Thus the economies of the north-west of England began to funnel their products, along the new canal systems, to the burgeoning port of Liverpool – and thence to African markets.

With the cargo securely stowed and the ship ready, the captain headed for Africa, often via the Atlantic islands where fresh supplies were picked up. Often, too, they also acquired more goods destined for the African markets. A ship's captain left his home port clutching precise instructions about his destination and route: he was often instructed to deal with *specific* people on the coast known to the ship's owners: the agents, traders, and contacts, and those likely to yield the most profitable trade.[24] Not only did slave captains need to be master mariners, familiar with the risks and dangers of sailing in tropical waters, but they were also expected to be canny traders. Then, as African slaves began to accumulate below deck, they also became jailors, often of the most brutal kind.

The major British slave ports (London, Bristol, and Liverpool) dominate our knowledge and understanding about the British slave trade. But even smaller ports confirm what we know from the dominant ones. In fact, 32 British ports dispatched vessels to Africa.[25] Everyone seemed keen to become involved. In an early voyage, the *Daniel and Henry* had sailed from Exeter for West Africa and Jamaica in 1700. She was financed by two merchants from Exeter, and one from Dorchester. She, too, was freighted with a mixed cargo of goods. Local manufacturers provided items of serge, while more exotic goods included alcohol, Indian textiles, and beads from further afield. There were also firearms, gunpowder, alcohol, glass and brass ware, pewter, basins, and tallow – much of it apparently of foreign origin.[26] Like Exeter, Lancaster might, today, seem an unlikely candidate for slave ships, yet 122 voyages originated in that town to trade on the African coast. When the *Hope II* departed Lancaster in 1792 it carried a remarkable range of goods. Brass and wire from Cheshire, knives from local craftsmen and from Liverpool, cotton goods from Manchester, more delicate textiles from India, earthenware (from Preston), flagons, glass, canvas (from a sail-maker in Kirkham), guns and cutlasses (made in Liverpool), local foodstuffs (beans and barley to feed the Africans *en route* to the Americas), chests from a Lancaster cooper. It seems likely that other local ships were loaded with a similar range of commodities, alongside goods bought from Sheffield, Birmingham – and the Baltic.[27]

When we examine the nature of the cargoes loaded onto outbound slave ships, we can begin to appreciate the remarkably varied and even global nature of the Atlantic trade. Goods were gathered from throughout the British Isles: foodstuffs from Scotland and Ireland, manufactured goods from industries and craftsmen in distant hinterland towns and communities, from South Wales to North Yorkshire, from the West Country, and from the ports themselves. British manufactured goods jostled for space with items imported to Britain from across Europe, from Scandinavia in the north, to Italy in the south, and they rested in the hold alongside wares from the very edges of European settlement and trade, in India and the Indian Ocean. Other ships arriving off West Africa from the Americas carried goods from other distant economies: tobacco and rum (cultivated by African slaves in the Americas) to tickle the fancy of African merchants on the coast – and all in return for still more African slaves.

The rise of British power, from the late 17th century onward, ensured that an ever greater share of the merchandise heading to Africa was made in Britain. That, after all, was the central principle of the nation's mercantilist policies. But of all the goods involved – of all the items shipped to West Africa to be bartered for slaves – none had the durability and appeal of the simple cowrie shell. Cowries were still being used in regions once blighted by the slave trade well into the 20th century. Even the creation of new, postcolonial currencies in West Africa did not totally erase the shadow of the cowrie shell. Modern Ghana chose an image of the shell as a symbol on its independent currency.[28] In the process, something very odd happened. The cowrie shell morphed into a symbol of African independence, style, and beauty, used to enhance and adorn clothing, hairstyles and personal items. This had been true, of course, for centuries, notably in India, where hair, dress, and jewelry had traditionally been enhanced by the addition of cowrie shells. But in the late 20th century, and especially in the USA and in black communities of the African diaspora, the cowrie shell came to denote more than simple beauty and attraction: it proclaimed an attachment to Africa and an African heritage.

Of all the tens of millions of items shipped into the slave markets of West Africa from all corners of the globe, which had the most lasting, most durable and most physical legacy? It must, surely, be the humble cowrie shell from the Maldive Islands. Textiles perished with age, metal goods rusted, rotted, and decayed, drink and tobacco were consumed. But the cowrie lived on, down to the present day, both in material reality and in the imagination. But who even recognizes its links to the slave trade when looking at a Ghanaian coin, or when wearing or admiring a modern necklace of cowrie shells today?

Notes

1. 'The meaning and history of the cowrie shell' (retrieved from www.africa imports.com/cowrieshell, 30/12/2015). See also www.pinterest.com, and search 'cowrie shell.'
2. Jan Hogendorn and Marion Johnson, 'A new money supply series for West Africa in the era of the slave trade: the import of cowrie shells from Europe,' *Slavery and Abolition*, vol. 3, No. 2, Sept 1982.
3. Mary Ellen Snodgrass, *Coins and Currency: An Historical Encyclopaedia*, London, 2003, p. 122.
4. Bin Yang, 'The rise and fall of cowrie shells,' *Journal of World History*, vol. 22, No.1, March 2011.
5. Quoted in in Bin Yang, 'The rise and fall of cowrie shells,' p. 16.
6. Marion Johnson, 'The cowrie currencies of West Africa, Part I,' *Journal of African History*, vol. 11, No. 1, 1970, p. 19.

7. Jan Hogendorn and Marion Johnson, 'A new money supply series', p. 156.

8. Marion Johnson, 'The cowrie currencies', pp. 20–21.

9. Marion Johnson, 'The cowrie currencies', p. 21.

10. Marion Johnson, 'The cowrie currencies', pp. 32–37.

11. Quoted in Marion Johnson, 'The cowrie currencies', p. 17.

12. John Barbot, *A Description of the Coasts of North and South Guinea…in Six Books*, London, 1744 edn., vol. 5, pp. 273–274.

13. Madge Dresser, *Slavery Obscured: The Social History of the Slave Trade in an English Provincial Town*, London, 2001, p. 35.

14. James Walvin, *Crossings: Africa, the Americas and the Atlantic Slave Trade*, London, 2013, p. 77.

15. Nuala Zahedieh, *The Capital and the Colonies: London and the Atlantic Economy, 1660–1700*, Cambridge, 2010, pp. 248, and Table 6.2, p. 249.

16. Kenneth Morgan, *Bristol and the Atlantic Trade in the Eighteenth Century*, Cambridge, 1993, pp. 133–134.

17. K.G. Davies, *The Royal African Company*, New York, 1970, pp. 171–173.

18. David Eltis and David Richardson, *Atlas of the Transatlantic Slave Trade*, New Haven, 2010, Maps 38–41, pp. 66–70.

19. James Walvin, *Crossings*, p. 79.

20. Quoted in Kenneth Morgan, *Slavery and the British Empire*, Oxford, 2007, p. 67.

21. Kenneth Morgan, *Slavery and the British Empire*, pp. 67–68.

22. K.G. Davies, *The Royal African Company*, pp. 174–175.

23. K.G. Davies, *Royal African Company*, pp. 175–179.

24. Kenneth Morgan, *Slavery and the British Empire*, pp. 68–69.

25. David Eltis, Lecture delivered at the University of Pittsburgh, April 17th, 2015.

26. For a complete cargo of this vessel, see Nigel Tattersfield, *The Forgotten Trade: Comprising the Log of the Daniel and Henry of 1700 and an Account of the Slave Trade from the Minor Ports of England*, London, 1995, pp. 41–45.

27. Melinda Elder, *The Slave Trade and the Economic Development of 18th-Century Lancaster*, Halifax, 1992, pp. 47–48; 211–212.

28. 'Money in Africa: Understanding the past and present of a Continent.' British Museum website, www.britishmuseum.org/research/research_projects/all_current_projects/money_in_africa.aspx, retrieved 29/11/2015.

3

Tobacco
The Slave Origins of a Global Epidemic

As you drive down Route 5, along the north shore of the James River in Virginia, between Williamsburg and Richmond, you pass a string of fine plantation houses. Today many of them are tourist sites, offering the visitor wonderful views across the land that slopes down to the river, which runs into the Chesapeake Bay and thence to the Atlantic. The houses are fine brick constructions, set in handsome ornate gardens, their interiors filled with stylish furnishings. One of them, Shirley plantation, was founded in 1613 (with claims to being the oldest family business in North America), though the mansion itself was begun a century later. Today, visitors are invited to admire its architectural beauties and unique fixtures. Close by, Berkeley plantation boasts a mansion founded in 1726 along with a 'magnificent collection of 18th-century antiques and artefacts.' Neighboring Westover plantation is an equally splendid mid-18th century mansion, and perhaps the finest building of its kind in North America. It, too, has beautiful formal gardens rolling down to the James River.

That river itself is the key. It was the lifeline, to European markets and to Africa. All three plantations – and many similar ones – produced tobacco, and, after a different start,

Slavery in Small Things: Slavery and Modern Cultural Habits, First Edition. James Walvin.
© 2017 John Wiley & Sons, Inc. Published 2017 by John Wiley & Sons, Inc.

increasingly relied upon African slave labor to bring their land into profitable cultivation. These remarkably beautiful places are also an indication of the great changes which transformed the colony of Virginia. The pioneering small-scale husbandry which used a mix of free, indentured, and slave labor to produce a host of crops, made way for large tobacco plantations which relied overwhelmingly on slave labor. Oddly, today you have to look very closely for evidence of slaves and slavery on the major James River plantations. Yet the main crop that enabled their founders to construct such stylish monuments to their success and wealth was cultivated by African slaves. Successful planters waxed fat and rich on tobacco, but they were nothing without their imported African labor force.[1]

African slaves first arrived in Virginia in the 1610s, though indentured labor from Britain was more common in the early days of settlement, and the colony did not become a slave colony until the end of that century. Most of Virginia's African pioneers came, in the first instance, from other colonies, and it was only the consolidation of tobacco cultivation into larger holdings that confirmed the drift to slave labor in the colony. Though an ever greater proportion of slaves in the Chesapeake region lived on tobacco plantations, these tended to be relatively small plantations, housing upward of twenty people.[2] Sugar plantations in Jamaica and Brazil, at the same time, counted their slaves in gangs of hundreds. Even so, the numbers of slaves toiling in Virginia were huge. In 1700 there were some 13,000, increasing to 105,000 fifty years later. The total stood at more than one third of a million by 1800.[3] Not all worked in tobacco of course, but that crop was the prime reason and cause of the Africanization of Virginia's laboring population. The consequences of their labor went far beyond the colony itself, for it set in train the development of a cultural habit – the consumption of tobacco – that became a global habit – and today a man-made global epidemic.

This simple weed, cultivated and consumed since time out of mind by indigenous peoples in the Americas, very quickly transformed not merely swathes of the Americas but soon established itself as an essential feature of social life across the Western world – and far beyond. By the end of the 18th century, tobacco had become a global commodity, and was shipped from the Americas to Europe and to Africa. It was consumed in pipes, rolled into cigar-shapes, and then lit, it was chewed and was ingested as snuff. It was valued in society, high and low, on both sides of the Atlantic, and became an essential item in the cargoes of ships in all corners of the Atlantic and beyond. Sailors and soldiers everywhere came to think of tobacco as vital, and it was used as a mean of bargaining and trading the world over. In time it even became a form of currency (in prisons and post-war societies wrecked by warfare). But its fame and its stature as a global commodity were established by Africans working on tobacco plantations in the Americas.

* * *

Early explorers had noticed Indian peoples smoking tobacco in rolled leaves, and they copied the habit, but it was not until the late 16th century that tobacco made a major impact in Europe itself. Its popularity, however, spread at astonishing speed. In 1603 an estimated 25,000 pounds of tobacco were imported into Britain from Spanish America. As the British settled their own colonies, they began to cultivate tobacco alongside other crops. In Bermuda, St. Kitts, Barbados, Maryland, and then Virginia, settlers turned to tobacco cultivation, often using seeds from Spanish America. Pioneering tobacco farmers in Virginia soon realized that tobacco was an ideal export commodity. (Other European colonists also appreciated the link between colonization and tobacco in their Americas colonies.) It became clear that European consumers wanted tobacco – in huge and growing volumes. As early as 1628 (only fifteen years after the first Virginia tobacco arrived), England imported 370,000 pounds. It has been calculated that, fifty years later, enough tobacco was shipped into England to allow a quarter of the population to have one pipe a day. In the last thirty years of the 17th century, the years when tobacco produced by small planters in the Chesapeake took off, demand increased by leaps and bounds. By 1700, the British imported 38 million pounds of tobacco from their own colonies, and on the back of that tobacco consumption the Virginia economy boomed.[4] Similar patterns unfolded in Europe, notably in the Netherlands, though France was later coming to the habit.

Tobacco cultivation became a powerful commercial incentive in the European settlement of key areas of the Americas. Those colonies were, after all, designed as commercial investments, with companies settling lands beyond the seas with an eye to the development of trade and commerce. Tobacco seemed to hold out the best, most alluring initial prospects. Thus it was that European settlement and tobacco cultivation went hand in hand, and as it did so, colonial settlers became not only exporters of tobacco but they led by example: they consumed it, smoking and chewing it, much as their European customers did. The profits on early tobacco exports spurred the massive expansion in its cultivation. Europeans also started tobacco cultivation in Europe itself, but the outcome was never as good – or as profitable – as American tobacco. Caribbean tobacco also declined, though it never faded away, giving way from the mid-17th century, before the rise of the sugar economy. Above all it was the cultivation of tobacco that taught settlers critical lessons about how to organize plantation labor and resources, and how to ship their product across the Atlantic.

As impressive as the 17th-century tobacco numbers are, they pale when we consider what happened in the 18th century. All Europe's tobacco colonies produced huge volumes, but the Chesapeake surpassed them all. The 37 million plus pounds of tobacco exported to Britain in 1700 had increased to 100 million pounds in 1771.[5] All was made possible by complex systems of trade and finance, with agents and brokers in the Chesapeake, major import and trading houses, notably in Glasgow (that city rising to its early modern prominence on the back of Chesapeake tobacco), and an elite of tobacco planters now able to flaunt their tobacco-based wealth in the mansions which dotted the river system of the Chesapeake Bay.

As tobacco was shipped east across the Atlantic, ever more Africans were shipped into the Chesapeake, though imports began to decline after the 1730s when growth of the local enslaved population provided local-born slaves for the planters. By 1776, some 120,000 Africans had been landed in the Chesapeake region.[6] These three elements were inter-related: the massive increase in tobacco exports, the rise of wealthy tobacco planters, and the arrival of large numbers of Africans.

It was a trade which also proved a fiscal bounty to the British state, with duties on tobacco (along with other imported goods) yielding enormous revenue. But the duties were so high that they also encouraged a massive smuggling industry in tobacco. From the first, then, tobacco was a sensitive political issue: its cultivation in the Americas, the slave labor required, its importation into Britain and the duties levied, all were issues disputed by a brew of conflicting economic and political interests. At first, London was the main center of tobacco interests, but as imports grew, as profits increased, commercial interests in a string of other port cities began to thrive on the tobacco trade. After the Act of Union in 1707, Scottish merchants had open access to the Chesapeake, and quickly made their commercial acumen and presence felt. By the mid-18th century, Glasgow had become Britain's major port for the tobacco trade to and from the Chesapeake. On the eve of the American Revolution, 47 million pounds of tobacco were imported through Glasgow, and Scots were a familiar social and commercial presence throughout the Chesapeake (as indeed they were throughout the British colonies, notably in the slave islands in the Caribbean). Scotland's distinctive literate and numerate class came into its own in the development of the tobacco industry and, in the process, Glasgow became a major driving force in Britain's wider economy.[7]

Not all these great volumes of tobacco were consumed in Britain, however, because a substantial proportion was re-exported, mainly to Holland and France. Britain's major export market was France – via the French state's monopoly. So huge were the volumes of tobacco produced in the Chesapeake that Europe's major merchants had to devise ways of passing on the commodity to the very edges of European trade. Merchants in London and Amsterdam were energetic in promoting the sale of tobacco throughout Britain (and her colonies) and across Europe. Promoting and selling tobacco became a major branch of European commerce in the 17th and 18th centuries, with all the commercial devices and strategies that were to become familiar in more recent times.

Tobacco moved back and forth, along all the maritime routes of trade and exploration. Brazil's healthy tobacco industry, for example in Bahia, became part of the South Atlantic slave trade, linking north-east Brazil to West Africa (the shortest and fastest of all the transatlantic slave routes). Curiously, the largest export market for Bahian tobacco was to the slave markets of West Africa. Merchants in Bahia developed a thriving trade to the

Bight of Benin, where Africans had developed a taste for Brazilian tobacco soaked in molasses: two commodities (molasses and
tobacco) cultivated by African slaves in Brazil were shipped in
large volumes across the South Atlantic, to become part of the
bargaining and exchange system for yet more African slaves destined for Brazil.[8] By the 1720s, two million pounds of Brazilian tobacco were being exported to the Mina coast, and were
also shipped to Angola, Sao Tome, Principe, and Benguela.[9] It
was if slavery had become a monster feeding upon itself. More
remarkable perhaps, slave-grown Brazilian tobacco was shipped
even further afield: tobacco from Salvador was exported to Goa
and Macao, and north to the St. Lawrence Valley. By the late 18th
century, Brazilian tobacco and snuff had become a fashionable
taste in the court of the emperors in Beijing.[10]

By the early 17th century, slave-grown tobacco had been
introduced into India, and to Malacca, Japan, and China. In
1710, a Jesuit remarked that tobacco had made Bahia famous in
"all the corners of the world."[11] Of course, tobacco was only one
of many crops transplanted from their indigenous locations to
distant places by the Portuguese (and other Europeans): part of
that remarkable 'Columbian Exchange' which was to transform
the social habits of people everywhere. Thus it was, by about
1700, that people in Asia, Europe, Africa, and India were consuming a leaf which had once been the preserve of indigenous
peoples of the Americas. Now, however, it was being cultivated
by African slaves.

It is perhaps easier to outline this dramatic rise of tobacco
than it is to understand *why* so many people found the commodity so irresistible. True, tobacco was not alone. A string of other
tropical commodities – as we have seen, coffee, tea, chocolate,
sugar – paralleled the story of tobacco. All of them underwent
the rapid transformation from exotic rarity to commonplace
essential. People on both sides of the Atlantic had, by the end of

the 17th century, come to regard tobacco as vital and pleasurable. They smoked, chewed, or snorted it (as snuff) and it had become a feature of everyday life. For years scholars have pondered the conundrum. How did an alien commodity become a commonplace necessity? Was there some biological craving that, quite suddenly, found satisfaction in tobacco (or sugar)? Or was it a process of commercialization: with merchants and their seductive commercial systems persuading more and more people to part with their cash (of which they had more to spare) on items their ancestors had not even known about?

Tobacco was yet another item which helped transform social life in the 17th and 18th centuries. It was one of the things people bought. People began to acquire ever more *objects* – things. Homes began to fill with artifacts which had previously been few and far between in very different corners of Western life. Clothing, furniture, linen, crockery, foodstuffs: essentials and luxuries began to appear in the inventories of people's personal possessions. What had once been luxurious became commonplace. Even the poor were affected. Working households of the late 18th century tended to own more items than their counterparts a century before. In Britain and in colonial America, the new luxuries were handed on, passing from the well-to-do into the hands of the poor. As we saw in Chapter 1, tea, and its associated tableware, the preserve of the rich in the early 18th century, had become common in the poorest of households. And all this in a mere two generations.[12]

A range of tropical produce, from the Americas and Asia, found a receptive and rapidly growing market in Europe and North America. But the rise of tobacco consumption was altogether more spectacular. Tobacco very swiftly became a feature of life of the alehouse and tavern, and established itself as a focal point for male sociability and camaraderie. It also spawned a clay pipe industry and, by 1730, hundreds of millions of clay pipes had been manufactured. They were, in effect, the first disposable consumer item, and their fragmented remains are to be found in archaeological sites in Europe, Africa, and the Americas.

Yet this massive consumption of tobacco had begun against a background of heated opposition, perhaps most famously expressed by James I in his tract *A Counterblaste to Tobacco* of 1604. Like other exotic commodities, tobacco arrived in Europe with some scientific and medical support, and was initially available in apothecary shops. The exotic items imported from Asia, and used as pharmaceuticals were, post-Columbus, complemented by goods from the Americas. Herbs, spices, roots, nuts, barks, plants, flowers, leaves, shrubs – these and more were now shipped to Europe to undercut the costly goods previously acquired from India and China. Although such American imports generally failed to dislodge traditional Asian medicines, many occupied a temporary place on apothecaries' shelves. Tobacco was similarly promoted for its medicinal properties, and there followed a lengthy and detailed debate, in print, about the alleged virtues of tobacco. Although that debate was conducted within the prevailing humoral theory of medicine, it formed the origins of a medical discussion about the impact of tobacco on health (and ill-health) that was to last, in very different forms, to the present day. European philosophers, scientists, and doctors argued about the medical pros and cons of smoking, chewing, or sniffing tobacco. Whatever the disagreements, many people turned to tobacco for a number of physical and psychological problems. In the summer of 1665, for example, Samuel Pepys – unnerved by the early signs of the plague – turned to tobacco;

> …I was forced to buy some roll tobacco to smell to and chaw – which took away the apprehension.[13]

Pepys also reported how coachmen and riders used tobacco to restore their tiring horses, blowing tobacco up the horses' noses when they flagged.[14] For all that, the rise of tobacco consumption took place, not in the apothecary shops, but in taverns and alehouses.

Once again it first took hold in fashionable circles, before quickly being adopted by middling sorts, then by laboring men. Barnaby Rich declared as early as 1614 that there is not "so base a groom that comes into an alehouse but he must have his pipe of tobacco." By the 1630s, tobacco was being sold throughout Britain. It was sold in shops, and by peddlers, but the alehouse was the principal and critical commercial and social outlet. Sellers acquired their supplies from traveling dealers, who often worked for wholesale merchants, and the end result was that tobacco was as familiar in the alehouse as ale itself. It provided male companionship, a hint of fashionable style, and its narcotic qualities made possible (in the words of a commentator in 1614) "the forgetting of all sorrows and miseries."[15] By the 1630s, it was also normal for the alehouse to sell tobacco, to the extent that when a man entered a tavern, the first greeting was

Sir will you taste a pipe of excellent and rare…tobacco?[16]

There were specialist tobacco shops in London and other major cities by the late 17th century, but the main outlet continued to be the alehouse, greatly helped by the fall in the price of tobacco, thanks primarily to the massive production and importation of tobacco from the Chesapeake. But the upsurge of tobacco also reflected rising levels of 'conspicuous expenditure' throughout society by 1700.[17] We have revealing 17th-century drawings – simple woodcuts – of smokers in alehouses. A century later, with taverns providing clay pipes for the smoker, alehouses were renowned for their permanent fog of tobacco smoke.[18]

If anything, the Dutch were more extreme than the British. Even heavy smokers visiting Holland were astonished by the amount of smoking, and the number of smokers, they encountered in Dutch taverns. In the words of Simon Schama, "The smell of the Dutch Republic was the smell of tobacco." One Frenchman claimed to have counted 300 smokers in a single Rotterdam inn. The Dutch seemed indifferent to the fog of tobacco smoke in confined places. Cartoonists liked to sketch an 18th-century Dutchman as fat, drunk, and lighting yet another pipe "with the smouldering embers of the last."[19] All this was greatly assisted by the emergence of an important tobacco growing industry in the Netherlands itself – and the remarkable story of Dutch pipe making, centered on Gouda, where 15,000–16,000 people were employed in the local pipe industry. Tobacco was, then, an integral aspect of Dutch social and domestic life. It was a common saying that "If a Hollander should be bereft of his pipe of tobacco he could not blissfully enter heaven."[20]

Dutch paintings regularly caught the local smoking habit in tavern life; of drunkenness, smut, coarse behavior, and general lewdness in all forms: poking fingers into pipes, blowing tobacco smoke into a woman's face. Smoking was not only dangerous but it was part of the feckless anti-social behavior which seemed to characterize tavern life and which drew condemnation from those who frowned upon taverns and their customers. If alcohol did not stupefy the customer, the tobacco would, numbing the body and the brain just like other narcotics.[21] Furthermore, time spent smoking a pipe of tobacco was itself lazy and frivolous (or so its enemies claimed). However much clerics, churches, and businessmen might decry tobacco, it became an endemic and apparently deep-rooted feature of Dutch social life. The hundreds of tobacconists throughout the country sported their distinctive trade sign above the door: 'The Smoking Moor.'

Another reminder, if any were needed, of the link between Africans and tobacco.[22]

As in Holland, so in Britain, tobacco caught the eye of contemporary novelists and cartoonists. Caricaturists in particular (those critical barometers of social life in the 18th and 19th centuries) regularly represented scenes of smoking and drinking as part of contemporary male social activity. Hogarth, Gillray, Cruikshank, and other lesser-known artists often represented the masculine world of tobacco, drink, and public camaraderie. Hogarth's 'Benjamin Read in 1757' portrayed a portly older man, fast asleep after a hard day's work (and a hard evening's drinking) with a pipe in each hand. Hogarth also portrayed men at breakfast; shaving, eating, smoking (and himself drawing).[23] As often as not, smoking was exposed as part of a raucous, boozy scene, with dancing, drunkenness, and sometimes general mayhem.[24] At times, though, smoking was represented as men sitting silently, quietly enjoying their tobacco – lost in their own thoughts – even when in the company of others.[25] Smoking provided graphic artists with yet another entrée into contemporary mores, and, in the hands of mischievous (sometimes outrageous) draftsmen, could be used to insinuate sexual liaisons, political intrigue, duplicitous politics – indeed the whole array of human vices and frailties.[26]

In the early medical debates about the benefits or dangers of tobacco, the question arose: was it good for women and children? At first there was little sense that gender was important, and initially both men and women smoked pipes. Visitors to North America were frequently struck by the universality of smoking. One man, writing in 1686, noted that worshippers would smoke both before and after a church meeting.

It was here I saw that everybody smokes, men, women, girls and boys from the age of seven.

A Swedish visitor to Canada and Pennsylvania in the mid-18th century made a similar remark. Tobacco, he wrote, is

> ...universally smoked by the common people. Boys of ten or twelve years of age, as well as the old people, run about with a pipe in their mouths... People of both sexes and of all ranks, use snuff very much.[27]

Though the evidence is mixed, smoking certainly became an overwhelmingly male preserve. By the late 18th century, women smokers were unusual in Europe. Contemporary pictures, in Holland and Britain, suggest a disapproval of female smoking. Women who smoked were generally portrayed as crones, or all-round low-life.[28] And that, clearly, reflected a changing etiquette of tobacco consumption. We know about the way people consumed tobacco because much of it took place in public places, especially in alehouses and coffee houses. And these were, overwhelmingly, male-dominated locations. Taverns were places where men met, throughout the day, or at the end of the working day, to rest, drink, meet friends, and enjoy themselves. They quaffed their ale and they smoked their pipes. Coffee houses offered a similar meeting place, but unmarked by the vices (and consequent disapproval) of alcohol consumption. Coffee houses were also places of work and business, as well as recreation – notably in London. But they, too, were shrouded in tobacco smoke, and as more men arrived, they filled their pipes as they filled their coffee cups. For centuries, in Arabic and Turkish societies, coffee had provided the occasion for masculine pleasure and business. Translated to Europe and North America, it now came alongside the more recently established habit of smoking tobacco. In addition was the development in Europe of smoking clubs, specifically devoted to pipe smoking. Again, contemporary pictures, especially by the caricaturists of the late 18th century, conjure up revealing images of choking, smoky conviviality.[29] Thus, the public places where men gathered, venues which were primarily for men and which, by convention or social pressure, had the effect of excluding women, were locations where men smoked tobacco.

A visitor to London in 1618 commented that "Gentlewomen moreover and virtuous women accustom themselves to take it as medicine, but in secret. The others do it as pleasure."[30] There are, it is true, numerous Dutch images of female pipe smokers in 17th century, and while a few convey an elegant, respectable image, it was more common to suggest disapproval of female smokers. It is hard to prove conclusively, but the evidence seems to show that women smoked less than men, though they became keen consumers of snuff.

Smoking was also widely spread through society. For a start, tobacco prices fell and smoking became a cheap, everyday habit. As tobacco got cheaper, distribution systems expanded and became highly efficient. Its popularity can be partly measured via the remarkable growth of pipe manufacture. In the 1630s, there were 7 pipe-makers in England, but that grew to 66 in the 1690s.[31] By then, smoking was everywhere, among all sorts and conditions, in town and country.

For long periods, consuming tobacco as snuff was more popular than smoking it. Snuff-taking seems to have originated in Spain, before spreading to Portugal, and then across Europe by the end of the 17th century. In France, on the eve of the Revolution, of the 15 million pounds of tobacco sold through the French state monopoly, 12 million was in the form of snuff. A similar pattern existed in other parts of Europe, notably in Italy and Austria. In Britain, snuff was common by the mid-17th century, but its popularity increased greatly in the following century. It may even have overtaken smoking in the late 18th century. Tobacco as snuff lasted longer than when smoked, and therefore worked out cheaper.[32] It was easy to prepare simple snuff, using a basic rasp, grating the tobacco leaves, then storing the snuff in a snuff box. And, as with all such commodities, complex and commercial developments produced a range of more costly versions, each with different additives, colors, fashions. In England alone, there would eventually be two hundred snuff manufacturers, each with their own secret commercial recipe.[33] Snuff gained a social respectability that pipe smoking lacked, and its popularity was not effectively undermined until the late 19th century.

Snuff-taking found early favor in fashionable and elite circles, especially among royals and the clergy. From the first, then, snuff had an aura of social respectability which pipe smoking lacked. It did not have the obviously anti-social qualities of smoking; there was no communal fog, no coughing and spiting. It created its own disadvantages of course, especially the exaggerated sneezing, and filling handkerchiefs with nasal contents, much to the disgust of non-snuff takers.

One significant off-shoot of the respectable snuff-taking fad in the 18th century was the development of the snuff box. At first, these were simple, basic items, suited to everyday usage. But as snuff-taking became more fashionable, the simple, wooden versions were augmented by expensive items which were themselves fashionable commodities. Crafted in porcelain, precious metals, and tortoiseshell, they often had the addition of elaborate decorative motifs and precious stones. Royalty confirmed the prestige of snuff-taking by giving and receiving expensive and elaborate snuff boxes. Large ones were used for ceremonial and communal snuff-taking (for example at formal meetings, or after dinner). So widespread and popular was snuff-taking that snuff boxes became a universal aspect of personal and social life in the 17th and 18th centuries, in all corners of Western society. Boxes were made from every conceivable kind of material: from wood, from the material remains of famous buildings, from timbers of bridges and churches. Snuff boxes were even fashioned into the handles of walking sticks. They were carved in the form of shoes (and became an important gift between lovers), in the shape of a ship, or a gun, in the form of a book, in human form, or as an animal head. Others were made in the form of hats, helmets, hands, carpenter's tools, and even (surely unconsciously) of coffins. Some had secret compartments; others elaborate imagery or portraits on the outside. But few collections could match the 52 gold snuff boxes given as wedding presents to Marie Antoinette when she married Louis XVI.[34]

Traveling tobacco salesmen in Britain embarked on their journeys with equal volumes of tobacco and snuff, hoping to sell both to shopkeepers and tavern keepers in their regions. Snuff had accompanied tobacco in the transition from the fashionable to the mundane. Working men took snuff, drinkers in taverns smoked pipes of tobacco *and* took snuff from the boxes of snuff available alongside other pleasures, while the rich paraded their snuff-taking via the most costly and exquisitely made snuff boxes. Meissen catered for the top end of the market by manufacturing beautiful porcelain snuff boxes.[35] Today snuff-taking seems unappealing, but at its fashionable height it attracted few critics, even at a time when smoking had its detractors. It was, throughout, respectable: practiced in the upper reaches of society (notably in France – the arbiter of taste in 18th-century fashion) in ways that gave it a stamp of fashionable approval. The spread of smoking was accompanied by a host of obviously unpleasant consequences (bad breath, blackened teeth, coughing and spitting). By comparison, the occasional sneeze from snuff (which, in any case, could be controlled and even directed into a fashionable gesture) was of little consequence. In addition, snuff did not require the complex equipment for lighting tobacco (flint and a tinder box); it was, far and away, the simplest and most socially acceptable means of ingesting tobacco.

In North America, though snuff was also popular, by far the most widespread tobacco habit was chewing, with all the obvious social and health consequences. Though Europeans had noticed Indians chewing tobacco in their early encounters, tobacco chewing was unusual in Europe. But the habit became an entrenched and growing custom in North America. Frowned upon by commentators, especially by European visitors to North America, chewing tobacco was popular with sailors and with others working outdoors (where it was difficult, if not impossible, to maintain the light in a pipe). Americans became infamous for their love of chewing tobacco. As late as 1900, almost half of the tobacco consumed in the USA was chewed.[36] The cultivation of tobacco specifically for chewing developed rapidly in the USA from the 1820s, helped by new industrialized systems of processing tobacco, notably in Virginia and North Carolina. A huge industry evolved, though it mainly consisted of small producers.[37] The social and health costs were incalculable: chewing tobacco generated a positive plague of men spitting in public.

Smoking had always involved a marked degree of coughing and expectoration, but chewing tobacco brought on a veritable epidemic of spitting. Spittoons had been introduced in the 17th century to cope with smokers' spitting habits, and those receptacles became ever more essential as tobacco chewing became widespread. Spittoons were available everywhere. In 1769 a Philadelphia tin-plate worker advertised among his wares "stool and bed-pans, spitting and chamber pots..."[38] In 1772, a New York City hardware store advertised a long list of imported items including 'spitting basins.'[39] And among Joseph Stansbury's stock of imported Chinaware available at Second St. Philadelphia in 1776 were blue and white 'spitting pots.'[40]

Spitting in North America grew progressively worse with the massive expansion of the industrial production of chewing tobacco in the 19th century. Men – always men – spat out wads of chewed tobacco, and tobacco juice (and anything that went with it), wherever they happened to be. Spitting on the floor, both indoors and in public, became a messy, unpleasant American habit which prompted a prolonged discussion in the press, and eventually led to local and state laws, and the introduction of practical efforts to control and stop it. Nineteenth-century newspapers were peppered with commentary about spitting. An article in *The Liberator* in 1847 complained,

Can a man be a gentleman who chews or smokes tobacco,
in the presence of ladies, and breathes his pestiferous breath
into their very faces?
These are the men who travel in the carts every day,
whose mouths are bulging out with tobacco, and
from the juice of which a constant *spitting* is kept up, – not
only to the injury of clothing and nerves, but to the injury of
carpets, runts, and seats.[41]

The early 19th century women's fashion for long dresses was dogged by problems created by tobacco spitters. Critics claimed that long dresses swept up all the dirt and mud in the streets and pavements, and acted as a mop for the ubiquitous pools of tobacco spit. Women traveling on public transport and steamboats complained that "The tobacco chewers cover the floors with saliva, which is wiped up by the long dresses now worn by women…." The answer was either a ban on spitting, or a change in fashion, and a decision to wear shorter dresses.[42]

Spitting was not a uniquely American vice of course, but it seemed more widespread and more evident on that continent than elsewhere. Americans chewed tobacco in such enormous volumes that Europeans traveling in the USA frequently made hostile comments on the habit – a sure sign of the difference between the two continents. Nowhere seemed safe from tobacco-chewers' spitting habits. Reporting on a debate in Congress in 1856, an Englishman described one elected representative with "one leg over the desk in front, the heel of his chair tilted back and his other leg flung over the arm of it, he chews his quid, and squirts his tobacco juice at his neighbors' spittoon, which he misses."[43] Charles Dickens, visiting the USA in 1842, complained that "this filthy custom" was everywhere. He thought that Washington DC was "the headquarters of tobacco-tinctured saliva."[44] The *Provincial Freeman* (an African-American newspaper published in Canada) printed a critical doggerel in 1856:

> Chewing in the parlor,
> Smoking in the street
> Choking with cigar smoke
> Every one you meet
> Spitting on the pavement
> Spitting on the floor,
> Is there such enslavement?
> Is there such a bore?
> In hotel and grocery
> Tobacco juice and smoke
> Defile the floor and air,
> And sicken us or choke.
> How we do detest it,
> How we do deplore
> On your vest to see the spit
> Trickle down before.[45]

Even the most unlikely of occasions were not spared. A temperance meeting in Baltimore in 1835 was punctuated by the sound of spitting: that society's new carpet was preserved when a spittoon was ordered for meetings.[46] Churches were not exempt. A New Orleans newspaper reported in 1867 that the instructions on a local church door to leave tobacco at the door meant that "worshippers could kneel and pray without disfiguring their clothes by getting into pools of tobacco juice."[47] Nothing seemed sacred; not the inside of shops, churches, Congress, trains, steamboats – not even Plymouth Rock.

Plymouth Rock (reported a Philadelphia paper in 1867) is becoming very unclean and unseemly, from the habit of pilgrims spitting tobacco juice and throwing tobacco cuds, and the remnants of luncheons upon it.[48]

Yet the American habit of chewing tobacco actually increased during the 19th century. Even as late as 1940 Americans chewed more than 100 million pounds of tobacco.[49] It was so serious a social (and increasingly a health) problem that politicians were eventually forced to issue ordinances and laws prohibiting spitting in public places.

What changed the pattern of tobacco consumption in North America and Europe, and eventually worldwide, was the development of industrialized cigar and later cigarette manufacture. Smoking rolled tobacco had been popular since the first days of European encounters with tobacco. Unlike smoking a clay pipe, rolled tobacco was easy to light, and it was easy to maintain the lighted tobacco. By the late 17th century, royal factories in Seville and Cadiz were producing cigars (which were smoked by both men and women), and the first factory in Germany opened in 1788. But the habit was not as popular elsewhere in Europe, and pipes continued to dominate until the early 19th century. Fashions changed quickly of course: new smoking fads prompted social curiosity and emulation (also inviting the mockery of critics). By the 1820s cigar smokers in London were caricatured for creating a veritable fog of tobacco smoke on the streets of London. Children – and even a pet monkey – appeared in cartoons as cigar smokers.[50] But the real expansion of cigar consumption took place after mid-century and was linked to the changes in cigar manufacture in the Americas.

Havana had long been a major center for cigar manufacture (and it remains, today, one of the city's major tourist attractions). Cubans became – and remain – avid cigar smokers. In 1950, for example, they smoked 350 million cigars: a very great bulk of all cigars produced on the island.[51] But political turmoil in Cuba persuaded Spanish manufacturers to move to Florida, first to Key West, later to Tampa. There, the world's biggest cigar factories, employing large numbers of Cuban and Spanish cigarmakers, churned out cigars by the millions. With such a massive industry now in the USA, the mighty power of North American commerce and advertising promoted cigars across the nation – and eventually round the world.

It was, however, the small, cheap cigarette which utterly transformed the story of tobacco. Cigarettes – fine-cut tobacco wrapped in paper – had been popular both in Turkey and Russia, and inevitably found their way into Western Europe. Yet it was the *mechanization* of cigarette production, in common with the wider story of mechanization, which revolutionized the manufacture and consumption of tobacco products. A machine for making cigarettes, displayed at the Paris World Exhibition in 1878, was able to produced 3,600 cigarettes an hour.[52] Cigarettes as we now know them spread rapidly thereafter. European workers, brought to the USA to teach Americans how to hand roll cigarettes, and a variety of companies, experimenting with different tobacco mixes, created new and rapidly expanding mass markets, though initially cigarettes struggled against pipe and chewing tobacco. The triumph of cigarettes was effectively secured by James Duke, who transformed an old family tobacco business into the giant it is today. He modernized production and lured good workers to his plants in Durham and New York. Then, in the 1880s, machinery began to replace the ranks of female tobacco rollers who had dominated production thus far. By the end of the 1880s, a machine could produce as many cigarettes *in a minute* as a female worker could in an hour.

Machines became ever more efficient, and the tobacco industry forged ahead into a massive program of mechanization, producing cigarettes more cheaply – and more quickly – than ever before. James Duke led the way: his cigarette factories became models for the highly mechanized, industrial future. Curiously, while the cigarette industry quickly mechanized, cigar production maintained its old hand-crafted mode, produced by large numbers of small companies. Cigarettes, on the other hand, sold in packs of ten and twenty and their rise was finally completed by the perfection of modern safety matches, sold alongside the cigarettes. Cigarettes became ubiquitous.[53]

For cigarettes, soon produced by the tens of millions, the problem was in fact *over-production*, and this led to the development of another familiar and very modern phenomenon: aggressive (and not always truthful) advertising. Again, James Duke was at the forefront, with his uncompromising promotion of products, using new printing systems, vividly colored and eye-catching advertisements, competitions, and free cigarette cards (about sport, adventure, fashion, famous faces, and heroes), all given away with the cigarettes. He aimed at young men, hoping to establish the habit of cigarette smoking at an early age; catch them young, and you had them for life. His opponents, especially in the press, quickly spotted Duke's tactics. "Every possible device has been employed to interest the juvenile mind," complained the *New York Times*. But Duke's advertising blitz went much further than the youth of America. He purchased furniture emblazoned with his name – and gave them to retailers: billboards and buildings were plastered with gaudy ads for his cigarettes, in both town and country. Duke also began to gobble up his smaller competitors. By the last years of the 19th century his 'Tobacco Trust' had created an effective monopoly of American tobacco production. However, as with a similar development under the Rockefellers in the American oil industry, such massive monopolies incurred the dislike of public and politicians alike. The stage was set for a new kind of political-commercial fight, about business trusts and monopolies.[54]

Duke dispatched senior executives round the world, looking for, and creating, new markets for his cigarettes worldwide. Thus, he opened up Australia, Japan, China, and Great Britain to his products, his advertising, and his promotional campaigns. By 1910, the Tobacco Trust was worth a dazzling $350 million.[55] When anti-trust legislation required him to dissolve the Tobacco Trust, the process proved long and complex, so cleverly had Duke devised and shaped his business affairs. Duke's achievements were extraordinary. He had laid the foundations for massive, global cigarette consumption, which today is measured in the billions of cigarettes. All major countries produce vast volumes of cigarettes, and all try to sell to the rest of the world. Newly emerging modern economies – China and Brazil, for example – similarly seek to create world markets for their produce. In 1990 the USA produced 695 billion cigarettes, Europe 631 billion, China 1,525 billion. Today, China has 300 million smokers: more than one half of all Chinese men are smokers, and seven out of ten of the world's top cigarette brands are Chinese.[56] The total economic activity of the world's tobacco companies amounts to $97,197 million.[57] And all this from what had once been an indigenous weed of the Americas that had first established itself as a major item of consumption via the labor of African slaves.

Cigarettes (and matches – later lighters) changed the entire global story of tobacco consumption. It was now easy to smoke virtually anywhere: at home, walking in the street, traveling, sitting in public places. The new cinemas of the 20th century, for example, built smoking into their architecture, providing ashtrays secured onto the seat backs. But the most striking development was the feminization of smoking. It seems to have happened spontaneously at first, but tobacco companies – again led by the American giants – realized the commercial potential, and began to advertise directly to a female clientele. New brands of cigarettes – household names to this day – were devised, each the product of careful experiments with tobacco mixing and treatment. And all were then marketed via massive advertising budgets. Women were persuaded that cigarettes were fashionable, good for their health, figure, and looks. Film stars were recruited to add their luster to the brand. (How many famous scenes in movies were accompanied by film stars smoking?) It was clear that women who smoked had joined the good life.

Behind the global rise of the cigarette lay the story of hard-hitting, modern advertising. Indeed, its onslaught caused outrage left and right, not least because it often bordered on the mendacious. (By the 1930s, one campaign had recruited family doctors to its side and tried to suggest that smoking was actually healthy.) The amounts of money invested by tobacco companies in such campaigns were staggering. As early as 1928, $7 million was spent advertising *Lucky Strike*, a sum that was second only to the advertising budget of General Motors.[58]

Cigarettes had, in the USA (and to a lesser degree in Europe) become part of a much broader consumer revolution driven forward by the new, imaginative, and sometimes utterly ruthless advertising industry. Between 1900 and 1925, the sale of goods in the USA increased by 400%, at a time when the population increased by only 50%.[59] The difference was the result primarily of advertising, and newly devised schemes of public relations with 'scientific' approaches to the manipulation of opinion and consumer taste. The creation of the now-familiar global desire for smoking cigarettes elevated tobacco consumption to staggering levels. By 1950, Americans were consuming 1.5 billion pounds of tobacco. In 1880 Americans smoked on average 50 cigarettes a year; by 1920 they smoked 500. Cigarette sales by the mid-20th century accounted for 90% of *all* tobacco sold in the USA. By then Americans were smoking 350 billion cigarettes each year.[60]

Cigarette smoking had, claimed its promoters, a host of virtues and qualities. For women it was associated with beauty and charm, for men, virility and strength. Smoking was alleged to bring pleasure for every smoker – a feature of modern sociability which, in the 17th century, had been a masculine monopoly in the alehouse. Indeed, by the mid-20th century, smoking had become a major feature of sociability itself: built into the workplace, transport, entertainment (in theaters and cinemas). It was also slotted into work, with breaks for a cigarette a recognized and sometimes legally guaranteed part of the working day. Tobacco was also a currency – widely exchanged in prisons and, during World War II, a much sought-after commodity in societies starved of resources.[61] In the postwar devastation in Europe and Asia in 1945, people traded their most prized possessions – even their bodies – for cigarettes.[62]

*   *   *

In this massive, global phenomenon – a worldwide addiction and epidemic – it is often hard to recognize the same habit which had once seen men huddle round their clay pipes in

17th- and 18th-century alehouses and coffee shops. The simple urge to light a pipe of tobacco, which had spread throughout the Western World from the 17th century onward, had, on the eve of World War II become a vast global business. We now know, of course, that tobacco had also created a modern plague, spawning a host of diseases, illnesses, and extreme levels of sickness and mortality worldwide. The medical arguments against smoking, and the equally fierce rear-guard action by the tobacco industry, were to become a feature of late 20th-century social and political life. While hundreds of millions of smokers may find smoking pleasurable, we now know that it is the cause and occasion of unprecedented levels of suffering and death. In a curious return to the pioneering days of tobacco consumption, tobacco once again lies at the center of a fierce medical and scientific debate. Is it good – or bad for you? Today, it is hard not to agree with the denunciation of tobacco by James I in 1604. Yet who, today, makes *the* fundamental historical link? That the origins of widespread tobacco consumption lay in the colonial cultivation and production made possible by enslaved Africans in the Americas?

Notes

1. For an important analysis of slavery and tobacco see T.H. Breen, *Tobacco Culture*, Princeton, 1987.
2. Philip D. Morgan, *Slave Counterpoint: Black Culture in the Eighteenth Century Chesapeake and Lowcountry*, Chapel Hill, 1998, p. 41.
3. Philip D. Morgan, *Slave Counterpoint*, p. 61.
4. Jordan Goodman, *Tobacco in History: The Cultures of Dependence*, London, 1993, p. 59; 134–135; Alan Kulikoff, *Tobacco and Slaves: The Development of Southern Cultures in the Chesapeake, 1680–1800*, Chapel Hill, 1986.
5. Jordan Goodman, *Tobacco in History*, p. 146.
6. David Eltis and David Richardson, *Atlas of the Transatlantic Slave Trade*, New Haven, 2010, p. 20.
7. T.M. Devine, ed., *Recovering Scotland's Slavery Past: The Caribbean Connection*, Edinburgh, 2015.
8. Jordan Goodman, *Tobacco in History*, pp. 162–163.

9. Jordan Goodman, *Tobacco in History*, p. 164.
10. Carol Benedict, *Golden-Silk Smoke: A History of Tobacco in China, 1550–2010*, UCLA, 2011, pp. 113–114.
11. A.J.R. Russell-Wood, *A World on the Move: The Portuguese in Africa, Asia and America 1415–1808*, Manchester, 1992, p. 140; 174.
12. Jan de Vries, *The Industrious Revolution: Consumer Behavior and the Household Economy, 1650 to the Present*, Cambridge, 2008, p. 152.
13. Robert Latham, ed., *The Shorter Pepys*, London, 1985, p. 494.
14. Robert Latham, *The Shorter Pepys*, p. 820.
15. Peter Clark, *The English Alehouse*, London, 1983, pp. 134–135.
16. Peter Clark, *The English Alehouse*, pp. 134–135.
17. Peter Clark, *The English Alehouse*, p. 228.
18. Peter Clark, *The English Alehouse*, p. 314.
19. Simon Schama, *The Embarrassment of Riches*, New York, 1987, p. 189.
20. Simon Schama, *The Embarrassment of Riches*, pp. 196–199.
21. Simon Schama, *The Embarrassment of Riches*, pp. 210–213.
22. Alison Blakeley, *Blacks in the Dutch World: The Evolution of Racial Imagery in a Modern Society*, Bloomington, 1993, pp. 57–59.
23. 'Benjamin Red, c. 1757.' 86. Catalogue 88. 'Hogarth's Tour. Breakfast at the Nag's Head.' 1732, 28, No. 29, In A.P. Opp, ed., *The Drawings of William Hogarth*, London, 1948.
24. 'A Whistling Shop. Tom and Jerry Visiting Logic. On Board the Fleet, July 1821.' In John Wardroper, *The Caricature of George Cruikshank*, Boston, 1978, p. 108.
25. 'Enjoying a Friend.' 1798. In *Isaac Cruikshank and the Politics of Parody*, Los Angeles, 1994 (Fisher Gallery), p. 121, No. 87.
26. 'The Mansion House Trust, Or Smoking Attitudes.' 1800. In E.B. Krumbhaar, *Isaac Cruikshank*, Philadelphia, 1966.
27. Quoted in Jordan Goodman, *Tobacco in History*, p. 63.
28. See, for example, Thomas Rowlandson, 'Cattle not insurable.'(1809).
29. 'A Smoking Club.' Author's collection.
30. Quoted in Jordan Goodman, *Tobacco in History*, p. 66.
31. Jordan Goodman, *Tobacco in History*, p. 65.
32. Rudi Matthee, 'Exotic substances.' In Roy Porter and Mikulas Teich, *Drugs and Narcotics in History*, Cambridge, 1995, pp. 38–40.
33. Jordan Goodman, *Tobacco in History*, pp. 72–75.
34. Kenneth Blakemore, *Snuff Boxes*, London, 1976; Malton Monroe Curtis, *The Book of Snuff and Snuff Boxes*, New York, 1935.
35. Residenzmuseum Munchen, *Meissen Snuff Boxes of the Eighteenth century*, Munich 2013 (Rockefeller Library, Colonial Williamsburg).
36. Jordan Goodman, *Tobacco in History*, p. 92.
37. Jordan Goodman, *Tobacco in History*, pp. 225–226.
38. *Pennsylvania Chronicle*, July 10–17th, 1769, vol. III, issue 25, p. 207.
39. *The New York Journal*, November 12th, 1772, issue 1558, p. 780.
40. *Pennsylvania Ledger*, April 20th, 1776, issue LXV, p. 1.
41. 'Tobacco,' *The Liberator*, September 29th, 1847.

42. 'Short dresses,' *The Lily*, April 1st, 1851.
43. *The National Era*, December 25th, 1856.
44. Allan M. Brandt, *The Cigarette Century*, New York, 2007, p. 25.
45. 'For tobacco lovers,' *Provincial Freeman*, July 5th, 1856.
46. 'Tobacco and spitting,' *Baltimore Gazette*, October 5th, 1835, p. 2.
47. 'Tobacco chewers,' *New Orleans Tribune*, May 17th, 1867, p. 3.
48. *Philadelphia Inquiry*, August 31st, 1867, p. 2.
49. Jordan Goodman, *Tobacco in History*, p. 92.
50. William Heath, 'Cigars, 1827.' In Mark Bills, *The Art of Satire*, London, 2006, p. 164.
51. Hugh Thomas, *Cuba. Or the Pursuit of Freedom*, London, 1976, p. 1158.
52. *Tabago: A Picture-Book of Tobacco and the Pleasures of Smoking*, Munich, 1960, p. 86.
53. Allan M. Brandt, *The Cigarette Century*, p. 30.
54. Allan M. Brandt, *The Cigarette Century*, pp. 38–39.
55. Allan M. Brandt, *The Cigarette Century*, pp. 25–38.
56. *The Guardian*, June 2nd, 2015, p. 13.
57. Jordan Goodman, *Tobacco in History*, p. 11.
58. Allan M. Brandt, *The Cigarette Century*, pp. 70–75.
59. Allan M. Brandt, *The Cigarette Century*, p. 75.
60. Allan M. Brandt, *The Cigarette Century*, pp. 96–97.
61. Allan M. Brandt, *The Cigarette Century*, pp. 99–101.
62. Tony Judt, *Postwar: A History of Europe Since 1945*, London, 2007, pp. 87–88; Ian Buruma, *Year Zero: A History of 1945*, New York, 2013.

4

Mahogany
Fashion and Slavery

Harewood House in Yorkshire is home to the Lascelles family and to an astonishing collection of family possessions. The 18th-century house itself, its landscaped settings and gardens, its magnificent collection of paintings, the building's interior design and attractions – all set Harewood apart as a place of incredible appeal and charm. It is not surprising, then, to learn that it is also home to some of the best Chippendale furniture. In fact, Thomas Chippendale's biggest commission was to furnish Harewood House with a variety of items, in bedrooms, halls, and dining room, and to bring the very best of late 18th-century craftsmanship to Harewood's domestic and social life. It was an opportunity to display to the eminent guests who frequented the house that wealth and good taste went hand in hand, and on a grand scale. The whole thing – the house, its contents, its grounds, and setting – formed a fitting and fashionable tribute to the family who lived there. In the space of a century, the Lascelles had risen from being humble Yorkshire farmers to major Atlantic traders, merchants, financiers – and planters. When Harewood House was completed in 1771, the family counted themselves among Britain's major grandees.

Slavery in Small Things: Slavery and Modern Cultural Habits, First Edition. James Walvin.
© 2017 John Wiley & Sons, Inc. Published 2017 by John Wiley & Sons, Inc.

Chippendale's most complete work is to be found in the State Dining Room, which is dominated by a large dining table surrounded by twelve dining chairs, and accompanied by beautiful side tables and wine cooler, and lead-lined urns for holding warm plates. In keeping both with contemporary taste and with Chippendale's work, those furnishings are all crafted from the most fashionable and sought-after timber of the period – mahogany. All the mahogany used had been felled by gangs of slaves working in the tropical rainforests of the Caribbean and Central America.

Thomas Chippendale's major workshop was located, suitably, at the heart of metropolitan life, in St. Martin's Lane in London. There, Chippendale and his craftsmen worked at the center of British power and wealth, close to the political and social elites who dictated fashionable taste, and who commissioned Chippendale (and others like him) to create the most lavish and costly of domestic fittings. The most fashionable of wooden items were those crafted from mahogany, and few craftsmen created items from that wood better than Chippendale. Inevitably, many late 18th-century portraits of the great and the good often showed individuals and families sitting around, leaning on, or simply close to their highly polished mahogany furniture. There were, of course, a variety of other woods used for the purpose, but in a country which had rapidly denuded itself of the timbers traditionally used in construction, ship-building and furnishings, by the mid-18th century the most fashionable woods were imported from distant sources.

English timbers had been in steep decline for centuries, even the famous 'Hearts of Oak' celebrated in the Royal Navy's marching song (the words written by Garrick in 1760). For centuries, monarchs and parliament had sought ways of protecting existing forests and developing new ones.[1] Despite this, attrition of the natural woodlands continued, and by the 18th century, the British were importing huge volumes of timbers, especially from the Baltic and Northern Europe. There was a voracious appetite for timber to fuel the astonishing expansion of commercial and Royal Naval ships. (The Royal Navy's 69 ships of the line in 1670 had grown to 126 a century later.[2]) Britain's global commitments, its colonies, trading stations, and empire, and the oceanic routes between them, needed a large and expanding maritime reach, both for its merchant ships and for the Royal Navy. Fortunately, the empire also provided many of the materials needed to expand and maintain that naval capacity.

At a more domestic level, craftsmen and joiners making furnishings for wealthy Britons had a variety of timbers to work with. But, as with other commodities from the far ends of the world which found favor in the 17th and 18th centuries, exotic timbers secured a place in domestic British taste. And none more so than mahogany, the demand for which developed quickly. It is a hardwood which was perfect for the craftsman's skills, allowing carvers to create elaborate shapes and patterns that were not possible using softer woods. Mahogany also yielded richly polished surfaces, and the whole process became an ideal accompaniment to the growing 18th-century taste for *chinoiserie* and rococo styles. By the late 18th century, the quayside of many British and North American ports were piled high with stocks of mahogany logs and planks awaiting sale and transfer to carpenters and craftsmen.

The trees themselves were found initially in Cuba and Jamaica, and had been used extensively by Spanish shipbuilders. The 17th-century expansion of British power and control in the Caribbean brought those trees to British attention, and small volumes were shipped home together with other local hardwoods. Larger cuts were also shipped as ballast alongside the (initially) more valuable logwood (which was used for making dyes for British textiles). Early settlers in the Caribbean had also used mahogany for house building, for floors and shingles, Caribbean craftsmen also used mahogany to make domestic furniture, and some of them took their affection for the wood to North America and Britain when they relocated. Others – officials, military, planters, traders, and sailors – returning from the slave islands in their thousands, brought back the fashions and tastes from the slave settlements. Mahogany and mahogany furniture slowly found their way into all corners of the Caribbean, North America, and Britain by the late 18th century. It was used for everything, from cradles to coffins.[3] *The Times* reported in 1787, that

> Modern refinement has substituted mahogany
> instead of walnut timber, for the purposes of furniture in
> the houses of the rich, and even of the middling orders of
> people...[4]

Demand had become so great that major deforestation took place in Jamaica and Cuba, though an enormous acreage of Caribbean woodland had been simply destroyed by the early 'slash and burn' system of land clearance to make way for sugar cultivation. Efforts were made to cultivate mahogany, to open up previously inaccessible mahogany-growing locations, and to explore new regions – notably the Mosquito Coast (Belize) where the trees were in plentiful supply.

What transformed the British demand for mahogany was a legislative quirk – a simple Act of Parliament, the Naval Stores Act of 1721, which removed the duties on imported naval stores. The powerful West India lobby persuaded government to include mahogany in that list, and thus, an item which they traditionally wanted to be rid of (to clear land for further sugar expansion) was cleared for entry to Britain and North America free of duty.[5] At a stroke, mahogany henceforth became

affordable for craftsmen working for the upper end of the
domestic market. There followed an extraordinary and voluminous production of that range of mahogany furniture we are
familiar with today and which, in many respects, has come to
characterize late 18th-century domestic and social life. Jamaica
exported mahogany in such huge volumes that, by the end
of the century, local mahogany was scarce and increasingly
costly. Thereafter the timber was logged and shipped from the
Mosquito Coast.

Ships heading home from the Caribbean (having delivered
their cargoes of Africans to the slave markets) returned with
a wide variety of slave-grown produce. Though we are familiar with ships loaded with sugar and rum, mahogany, too,
became an increasingly important and lucrative cargo in the
18th century, notably for the port of Lancaster, where traders
developed an early interest in mahogany. In 1720 a Lancashire
cabinet maker, Robert Gillow, had moved to Lancaster, and had
become familiar with town's trade to the Caribbean. Gillow may
even have served time as an apprenticeship to a ship's carpenter, but at some point in this early period he became familiar
with mahogany. Gillow formed his own cabinet-making business in Lancaster and by the 1730s had developed a thriving
Lancaster business, importing rum, sugar – and mahogany –
and exporting his furniture back to the slave islands. In this
Gillow had been greatly helped, like others, by the change in
the law in 1721. With the duties on mahogany slashed, from
1722 onward craftsmen in Bristol, Liverpool, and Lancaster –
ports to which the supplies of mahogany were now being delivered on the same terms as London – were able to acquire
supplies of the world's best timber for furniture makers. Gillow
in Lancaster was a prime illustration of an important point: that
the genesis and growth of the mahogany trade was as much a
provincial as a metropolitan business. In 1753, for example, a

Jamaican shipper of mahogany to London found that his timber was quickly snapped up by buyers in Sheffield, Newcastle,
Manchester, Leeds, and Hull.[6] From Lancaster, Gillow dispatched his furniture not only to British customers (in London
and throughout provincial Britain) but to the far side of the
Atlantic. The company sent large numbers of 'Windsor chairs' to
Jamaica, for example, all made from mahogany that had already
crossed the Atlantic in the opposite direction. Gillow's company,
continued by his sons trained in the craft, had agents in the
Caribbean, and by the 1750s had even branched out into the
slave trade itself. The company's ships sailed to Africa for slaves,
then to the Caribbean with a cargo of Africans, thence back to
Lancaster loaded with slave-grown produce: sugar, rum – and
mahogany.

What had begun as a speculative local trade developed into
a major international commerce. In the century 1700–1800, we
know of 122 ships leaving Lancaster for Africa and the Americas: they took on board 23,588 Africans and delivered 20,189 to
the slave markets of the Caribbean and North America.[7] Many
of those ships made the return leg freighted with mahogany
bound for Lancaster. After the *Thomas and John* delivered the
132 survivors of its original 150 Africans at Savanna la Mar
in Jamaica in1768, it took on board a cargo of sugar, rum,
cotton, pimento, logwood, and 36 planks of mahogany.[8] In
1785, the *Fenton* delivered 174 Africans to Kingston, returning to Lancaster filled with a large cargo of 541 planks of
mahogany.[9]

Other ships traded direct between Lancaster and the
Caribbean, returning with similar mixed cargoes, but many
loaded with planks of mahogany destined for the Gillow workshops. Like most traders, Gillow developed various lines of business to the Caribbean (using agents in Barbados and Antigua).
He ordered dyes and cotton (for the growing textile industries

of Lancashire), timbers for his own busy workshops, and dispatched the finished furniture to the prospering classes across
Britain, and even in the Caribbean. With a shop in London's
Oxford Road (now Oxford Street) which they maintained until
1906, the Gillows had, like Wedgwood, made the transition
from a provincial birthplace to a metropolitan showplace. The
company tried to keep abreast of changing furniture fashions (it
is thought to have helped promote the craze for billiard tables
from the 1760s, for example[10]). It's no surprise that the Gillows
eventually branched into the commerce on which so much else
hinged; the slave trade itself to and from their home town of
Lancaster.

This vogue for mahogany furniture also took root at much the
same time in British North America. Despite living on a continent abounding with an enormous variety of timbers, prosperous Americans also took to mahogany furniture for their homes.
North American forests were vast and plentiful, yet Americans, too, bought planks of mahogany from the Caribbean,
and American craftsmen (many of the pioneers having lived
and trained initially in Britain) honed their skills on local and
imported timbers. As early as the mid-18th century, visitors to
the North American colonies were puzzled that whenever they
visited prosperous American homes, in major cities and in the
grand homes of planters and landowners, they were confronted
by extensive mahogany furnishings that had so recently become
voguish in Britain. This was perhaps understandable among
those who knew, traveled, and periodically lived in Britain, but
much the same was true for affluent men who lived in remote
rural settings, far from British influence. American men and
women of taste and refinement (and money), like their peers
in Britain, responded enthusiastically to the growing taste for
mahogany furnishings.

Philadelphia was the center of mid-18th century North
American fashion and taste, its grand town houses boasting

the best furnishings produced by local and British-born crafts-men. Aided by books of designs (and by Thomas Chippendale's *The Gentleman and Cabinetmaker's Director* of 1754), Ameri-can craftsmen had the abundance of North American timbers at their disposal. But fashion dictated that the best, most desirable, and socially exclusive woods should be imported hardwoods. The most lavish and impressive of all such items were the fur-nishings crafted for the fabulously wealthy John and Elizabeth Cadwalader's Philadelphia home in 1769. (Even they – among North America's wealthiest elite – would doubtless have been stunned to learn that one of their chairs would be sold, two cen-turies later, for $2.5 million.) Under the guidance of Thomas Affleck, a Scottish-born, London-trained cabinet-maker, a team of craftsmen delivered what is widely accepted as the finest of 18th-century American furniture. Much of it – and certainly the best pieces – were made from mahogany.[11] The finest sur-viving pieces attributed to Affleck, now to be found scattered across the USA in the nation's major museums and galleries, are dominated by mahogany. In Boston, New York, Philadel-phia, and Washington, Affleck's mahogany pieces (dining and card tables, chairs, sofas, chests, and armchairs) provide tes-timony not merely to his craftsmanship, but to the American hunger for mahogany in the mid- and late 18th century. It was, yet again, a fashion which soon spread from the wealthy to the modestly prosperous. Robert Manwaring in 1765 claimed that the furniture he made was "calculated for all People in differ-ent stations."[12] For those unable to afford the costly imported mahogany, there were craftsmen willing to paint chairs and fit-tings to make them look like mahogany. George Washington could not afford mahogany for the hall paneling at Mount Ver-non, so he had it constructed from pinewood which was then painted to look like mahogany.[13]

At mid-century, evidence of mahogany was inescapable in colonial North America, yet within living memory it had been rare and unnoticed. The *Virginia Gazette*, North America's old-est continuous newspaper, published regular mentions of and adverts for the sale of mahogany throughout the 1760s and 1770s: items offered for sale or auction, imported mahogany and mahogany furnishings for sale. In July 1768, "…a quantity of HONDURAS MAHOGANY of all sizes, and esteemed to be the best ever imported in the colony…" was offered for sale in the port of Norfolk. Among the mahogany furnishings adver-tised in the *Gazette* were the following: a bed, bookcase, cabi-net, card tables, chairs, desks, dressing boxes, dressing glasses, dumbwaiters, knife case, looking glass, plate glass, prints, *sec-retaires*, tables, tea board, tea chest, and tea tray. The *Gazette* also reported regularly on the price of mahogany in Jamaica, the volumes of that timber imported by particular ships in the James and York rivers, and cargoes of mahogany currently avail-able for sale in Norfolk, Petersburg, Portsmouth, and Prince George County. The paper also ran reports of mahogany lost in shipwrecks, of cargoes jettisoned to save a ship in distress, and mahogany lost to Spanish ships (or, after 1776, seized by British ships).[14] Similarly, inventories of the estates of recently deceased Virginians catalogue the widespread ownership of mahogany furniture. Among the personal effects left by Joseph Royle when he died in 1768 were twelve chairs, two dining tables, two card tables, and a tea table – all in mahogany. A house sold in Williamsburg, Virginia in August 1777 was offered along with its contents, which included a mahogany dining table and chairs, a mahogany plate case, a mahogany bureau, and a tea urn standing on a mahogany stand. In 1767, the notice for a sale of mahogany furniture in Williamsburg was printed alongside a sale of

> About twenty very likely Negro SLAVES among which is a carpenter, and seven very good sawyers…[15]

The coincidence here was remarkable, because *all* the mahogany devoured by craftsmen on both sides of the Atlantic in the 18th century had been logged, dragged, and floated to the nearest outbound sailing ship by slaves.

The North American interest in mahogany may have started when colonists moved north from the Caribbean to settle in North America. Settlers from Barbados, for example, moved to the Carolinas, taking with them distinct architectural styles which can still be seen in buildings in those two regions. It seems clear enough that the use of mahogany in the Caribbean, in construction and for furnishings, was also carried north in the movement of peoples and cultures which characterized the early years of European settlement in the Americas. Jonathan Dickson, born in Jamaica in 1663 and owner of two plantations on that island, later settled in Philadelphia where he worked as a merchant. In 1698 he ordered from Jamaica a "Few finewoods for ye Joyners & Some Mahogany…in board or Plank for Chest of Drawers & Tables." When he died in 1718 he left 18 items of furniture made from mahogany, and a large supply of mahogany timber.[16] However, the main impetus behind North American demand and fashion, and the substantive rise in importation of mahogany, derived from the British connection. In this particular case, the metropolitan tail wagged the colonial dog. It was fashion and taste, emergent prosperity, and conspicuous consumption, on both sides of the Atlantic, which drove forward the North American demand for the hardwood.

Demand grew quickly and at first there seemed to be plenty of mahogany available. As the British secured their own Caribbean possessions in the course of the 17th century, and as they experimented with different crops and systems of labor (and as they struggled to find suitable commodities for export), mahogany was just one of many indigenous timbers (and other flora and fauna) which caught the settlers' eye. But it also proved a major

obstacle when they wanted to convert dense Caribbean woodlands and forests into manageable and cultivable land for tropical crop production (tobacco initially, then, most importantly,
sugar). How much native timber was lost to the slashing and
burning of the settlers will never be known, but it seems likely
that, for all the trees felled for use as timber, many more simply
went up in smoke.[17]

After the British ousted the Spanish from Jamaica in 1655,
they followed earlier Spanish habits of using mahogany for construction and furnishings. In the words of Edward Long, a major
planter and important historian of the island, writing in 1776,
"...most of the first-built houses were of this wood."[18] The trees
were in plentiful supply along the south coast where settlements
were concentrated, and formed a basic component in private
homes and civic buildings in early colonial Jamaica. Churches,
government buildings, planters' homes, and merchants' retreats
from the bustle of Kingston all made extensive use of mahogany
in construction, for floors, doors, roofing, paneling, and wain-
scots. Much of the furniture was also made from the same
wood.[19] At first there was no problem securing the timber
because, again in the words of Edward Long, "This graceful and
valuable tree...grew formerly in very great abundance along the
coast..."[20] All that changed, however, and within little more
than half a century mahogany had effectively vanished from its
early Jamaican sites. Edward Long bemoaned the fact that the
trees had been "almost exterminated from those parts in process
of time, it is at present found chiefly in the wooded, mountainous recesses, where vast quantities of it still remain...."[21] Once
the commercial value of mahogany as an *export* crop was fully
appreciated (although the timber had been carried in bulk as
ballast on returning slave ships) and the trade given the boost
of duty-free entry to British markets after 1722, it enjoyed commercial take-off.[22] As ever greater volumes found their way to

British and North American markets, the mahogany 'frontier' was pushed back from the coastline into Jamaica's mountains and into inaccessible, difficult locations which, even with slave labor, proved too costly to extract profitably. Though there was still plenty of mahogany in Jamaica, by the last quarter of the 18th century it was locked away in the fastness of mountainous retreats. The range of mountains to the east of the island were, in Long's words, "covered with a forest of mahogany and other gigantic trees."[23] The problem remained accessibility.

These were not the kind of trees familiar to Europeans. Mahogany trees were enormous. There were two basic types. The short-leaved West Indian and the big-leaved Honduran mahogany. The former dotted the Caribbean islands; the latter were to be found in great profusion on the coast of Central America, and along a coastal littoral which stretched from Mexico to the Amazon. But the timber belonged to the world of Spain and Portugal, and the English-speaking world had to find its supplies on its own Caribbean possessions, and, later, on disputed lands on the Mosquito Coast. Fully grown trees were upward of 100 feet high, with a correspondingly large circumference. Even when they were found in accessible and manageable locations, mahogany trees posed enormous difficulties for the loggers. Logging *specifically* for mahogany meant targeting and selecting the trees within the forests, and that involved arduous, intensive, and often dangerous labor. The hard work began even before the loggers picked up their axes and saws to tackle the mahogany. Roads and paths had to be cleared to gain access to the trees, and then to remove the downed timbers, ideally to a nearby waterway so that the massive logs could be floated away, down to manageable riverside locations. There were small numbers of loggers and joiners scattered among the white populations of the Caribbean – ex-soldiers and sailors, convicts, transportees, indentured laborers, and others who formed the miserable white populations of the early Caribbean colonies. But the key workers in the logging industry, as in all other forms of colonial manual labor and cultivation, were the enslaved from Africa. The mahogany furniture which Americans and Europeans found so appealing was derived overwhelmingly from the sweat of African slaves toiling in the rainforests of the Caribbean and Central America.

The Naval Stores Act of 1721, and the subsequent massive expansion of mahogany imports into Britain and North America, coincided with the peak years of Caribbean slavery. Indeed, the massive expansion of logging for mahogany in Jamaica in the half century following that Act was made possible by the population of enslaved Africans already imported into the Caribbean. The relatively small number of slaves logging mahogany in Jamaica formed just one (and largely invisible) group among hundreds of thousands of Africans working throughout the Americas as slaves. Though sugar dominated the Jamaican slave economy, and has come to define the popular image of slave work in the Caribbean, slaves worked at a host of tasks. Whatever work was required, slaves were expected to do it, from the simplest of domestic chores to the heaviest and most brutal of field work. For some of them, after 1722, that meant logging for mahogany. Woodcutting was as strenuous, arduous and as dangerous as any form of slave labor we care to study. It has, however, been overshadowed by the other major forms of plantation slavery – from sugar to cotton – and has been largely ignored by historians. Although we have no firm statistics, it is clear that logging involved only small numbers of slaves. They worked in small gangs, hidden from view for months at a time in the depths of the tropical forests, in the charge of a small band of white men, and exposed to the dangers and risks both of their work and of the jungle. On the islands, and later on the Central American coast, slave owners and merchants pushed inland, up rivers, or forging new paths, to find mahogany when the coastal supplies had been depleted, as they very quickly were. Logging was not only among the most strenuous of slave work, it was also perhaps the most isolated. At the turn of the century, George Pinckard described one such logging team in a remote district of Demerara:

> a party of naked slaves, male and female, the act of dragging the trunk of an immense tree out of the forest with ropes. They were conducted by a driver with his whip: and pulled on the load by mere strength of arm, having no assistance from any machinery, and only availing themselves of placing billets of wood under the tree, at short distance from each other, in order to prevent it from sinking into the dirt, and doubling their toil.[24]

Small gangs of cutters set up camp in the forest. There they built simple dwellings and corralled a few livestock. Some gangs included female slaves, but most woodcutters lived apart from their womenfolk. The key man, at first, was the 'huntsman': an experienced slave who spotted and chose which trees to tackle. He did this by climbing to the top of a tree, surveying the land, and spotting which mahogany tree within reach seemed the best target. The huntsman

> …cuts his way through the thickest of the woods…and climbs
> the tallest tree he finds, from which he minutely surveys the surrounding country…[to locate] the place where the wood is most abundant.[25]

He would then lead the others to the chosen site. These huntsmen were the key figures in the entire operation: they knew the ways of the forests, how to spot the best mahogany, and where other trees had been left behind as they moved on, but which they might return to later. These men became their owners' eyes in the lucrative business of locating and logging the most valuable trees. Naturally enough, they were rewarded for their skills (with free time, better food, bonuses of one kind and another), rewards which slave owners everywhere handed out to their elite or favored slaves.

Having targeted a tree, the cutters then constructed a working platform, about twelve feet from the ground, from which the slaves set about felling the tree with axes, hacking at it from two sides until they produced that image so familiar in the popular mind; a large tree, hacked into a narrow 'V' shape at the bottom and ready to topple. They repeated the process on a number of trees and when they had felled enough of them they switched their efforts to clearing pathways and tracks, attacking the undergrowth and trees with axes, machetes – and fire – and clearing away rocks and rubble with pickaxes and hoes. In Belize, some of the tracks from the felled trees to the nearest river stretched for ten miles, and the road clearing accounted for two-thirds of the entire operation. The timbers, marked with the owner's initials, were then 'cross-cut' and dragged, on bigger operations by oxen and carts, to the water's edge, to be floated downstream. (Again – similar images are familiar from modern lumberjacks at work in North America.) Removing the logs to the water's edge was so strenuous that it was often undertaken by torchlight at night to avoid the oppressive heat of the day.[26] In Central America, the logs were floated enormous distances – sometimes upward of 200 miles – with gangs of slaves following in canoes to deal with any problems *en route*. On reaching the ocean, the floating cargoes were halted by chain booms, the logs lashed together to form rafts, then steered towards the wharves and quaysides.[27]

The slaves' punishing work did not end at the dockside. Loading mahogany logs onto the outbound ships involved another strenuous and dangerous exercise. First the floating logs were drawn to smaller craft by a process known as 'kedging', flinging ropes attached to a small anchor around the logs, and drawing the logs towards the boat using iron clamps ('dogs'), then sailing out to the awaiting ships. Hauling them on board and storing them below deck involved yet more brute, dangerous labor, but at this point the ship's crew took over. The storage below deck, or on deck, was supervised by the ship's captain and mate, their prime concern being the careful loading of the timber. Loose or shifting logs at sea spelled danger and possible disaster in a storm.

The size of the slave logging gangs varied greatly. The smallest gangs seem to have been about twelve strong: others were as big as fifty (those this was still nothing compared to the numbers involved in sugar). Some were hired out by their owners – part of the 'jobbing gangs' of slaves who moved from one task to another (field work, road building) earning money for the slave owners who rented them out for labor on whatever task that came along.[28] The early 19th-century logging industry in Belize and Demerara involved bigger, more organized gangs, working to a well-developed seasonal timetable. The levels of cruelty and punishment doled out to the slaves also varied. It was more difficult, in small and isolated groups, for the white supervisor or manager to be as ready with a whip as his counterpart might be on plantations. An isolated white man, trying to manage a team of slaves in a violent fashion, in a remote location – and where the slaves were all armed with an array of dangerous tools – was to invite trouble. Logging slaves were chosen for their strength, and their working lives, in such remote locations, bred an independence which was quite different from the lives of many other slaves.

Theirs was also a lonely life, far removed from the main slave communities and, for many of them, far away from the companionship of women. In bigger camps, there was a coterie of slaves gathered to service the needs of the woodcutters: cooking and feeding, caring for the vital tools, looking after the livestock used for hauling, for slaughter and food. For slaves in the cutting teams – the men who spent their days hacking at the vast base of the mahogany trees – it was the brute realties of woodcutting and removing the logs which made their lives grueling and dangerous in the extreme. Drawing up a table of comparative slave hardships, i.e., establishing which slaves fared worse than others, is a pointless exercise, but it is hard to spot many redeeming features in the lives of slaves logging mahogany trees in 18th-century Jamaica or in Honduras in the early 19th century. Theirs was a stark and dangerous existence. Camped out, away from the company, and from normal foodstuffs and cooking of a slave community, the enslaved woodcutters lived off rations they carried out to their camp, whatever they could cultivate or rear locally, and whatever edible materials they could find or kill in the forests and rivers. In addition to the natural dangers of the forests – snakes, insects, disease, and oppressive heat – there were the very real dangers of logging with saw and axe. A weary or careless swing of an axe or saw, a momentary lack of attention close to falling timbers, and serious injury and death could easily result.

Slave owners everywhere faced the persistent problem of slave resistance and runaways. Getting enslaved people to do what was required under oppressive conditions was no easy task. Slaves developed a sharp sense of what they could or could not get away with; always treading a risky line between doing what their owners and superiors demanded and holding back in ways that suited their own interests. In the forests, however, the logging teams led an independent working and social life that was rare among slaves on the plantations. Their drivers and masters, the men working with them in the forests, always outnumbered by people in possession of dangerous tools, recognized the limits of their control in such isolated locations. Help was very far away. There had to be compromises – an understanding – of how much could be expected of the enslaved labor force: push too hard, behave too aggressively or violently, and the slaves might flare up.

Slave owners throughout the Americas were plagued by worries about the control they exercised over their enslaved labor force: they worried about the slaves' obedience, and feared slave resistance, ranging from outright violent revolt to sullen and obstinate foot-dragging. The men who managed the logging gangs lived with such concerns more intimately than many planters. After all, they lived and worked cheek by jowl with the slaves, sharing their working and daily lives in a sweaty jungle intimacy. Their lives were quite unlike those of most planters on the bigger, more mature plantations. What's more, while the masters in the jungle knew their slaves more closely than most other masters, their enslaved laborers, in turn, knew their superiors very well indeed. They were, after all, camp mates, living in close proximity for months on end. In a curious, if vicious, fashion, in what is one of the great paradoxes of slavery, both needed each other.

The prospects for slaves to succeed in running away were perhaps greater in Central America, especially in those regions disputed by Spain and Britain, and where slaves recognized the possibilities of escape. Whole gangs of cutters sometimes disappeared, though such mass escapes were unusual. Slaves everywhere knew what awaited them if they rebelled, and were subsequently caught. The draconian process of law – the physical violation and execution of slaves, the public displays of bodies and body parts, the litany of lashings and tortures inflicted on rebels (and often on the innocent) – was the gory substance of slavery in the tropical Americas. But for those logging in the forests the question remained: where could they run *to*? The wilderness itself posed enormous and lonely risks. What sort of freedom was it to live in such inhospitable and dangerous environments? Many no doubt wanted to return to loved ones, left behind in the trek into the forests, and escape would not necessarily bring them closer.

There was an irony behind the story of slaves cutting down mahogany trees. Though theirs was just one aspect of the oppression endured by slaves everywhere, their harshness and miseries resulted in a commodity of great cost and luxury. There is a vast chasm of incomprehension – an issue which is hard to grasp to this day – between the crashing sound of a massive felled mahogany tree in the rainforest of Jamaica or the Mosquito Coast and the highly polished beauty of a costly table in the home of wealthy people in London or Philadelphia. Indeed, the chasm was so great, in both geographical and metaphorical terms, that it is unlikely that people saw the link. When John Singleton Copley painted Mr. and Mrs. Isaac Winslow in 1773 he chose to present that rich Massachusetts couple leaning on a richly polished mahogany table: so polished that the table acted almost as a mirror for the elderly pair.[29] But who, even today, when looking at that portrait, considers the gangs of slaves whose efforts delivered that mahogany in the first place?

Within the space of a mere fifty years, a tree that had once provided durable timber for early settlers in Jamaica, and for the naval requirements of Spain, had become an object of great taste and discernment in Europe and North America. During his visits to London after 1757, Benjamin Franklin had learned to appreciate the beauties of mahogany and to judge the qualities of different species. He made specific requests when he ordered craftsmen to make furniture to be dispatched to his elegant Philadelphia home. He even chose mahogany for his printing press. His son continued the tradition, asking his father to order and dispatch mahogany chairs from London, because the craftsmen and wood in Philadelphia did not quite suit his taste – or pocket.[30] Another of America's revolutionary heroes (and silversmith), Paul Revere, was also painted by John Singleton Copley. Revere can also be seen holding a silver teapot, both he and the tea pot vividly reflected in the burnished surface of a mahogany table. It was "the very picture of refinement."[31]

A number of prominent mid- and late 18th-century Americans, famed in commerce, politics, and wealth, chose to have themselves painted close to mahogany furnishing. The 1767 portrait of Jeremiah Platt, a New York merchant, has the man standing next to a Chippendale chair.[32] Men and women of refinement, taste, and wealth in America projected themselves surrounded by all the trappings of contemporary fashion: the best objects that money could buy. Their clothes and hats, their jewelry, their silver ware, their furniture, all spoke of their status and self-regard. The rise of American prosperity is an astonishing story: of hard work, skill, and commitment (plus the necessary luck). But behind that story, so often and so vividly reflected in contemporary portraits, there lay another, much deeper saga: the history of African enslavement across the Americas. The precise impact of slavery on the rise of Western material wellbeing continues to be a historical conundrum, but there is no doubt that many of the artifacts which Western people came to rely on, for pleasure and for ostentatious display, derived directly from the efforts of African slaves. It was – and still is – easy not to notice. Who even thinks of slavery when admiring Chippendale's mahogany furniture in the State Dining Room at Harewood House?

Notes

1. Keith Thomas, *Man and the Natural World*, London, 1985, pp. 195–199.
2. N.A.M. Rodger, *Command of the Ocean: A Naval History of Britain*, London, 2006, pp. 607–608.
3. Jennifer L. Anderson, *Mahogany: The Costs of Luxury in Early America*, Cambridge MA, 2012, p. 12–13.
4. Quoted in Jennifer Anderson, *Mahogany*, p. 19.
5. Adam Bowett, *The English Mahogany Trade, 1700–1793*. A thesis submitted for the degree of Doctor of Philosophy, Department of Furniture, Faculty of Design, Buckinghamshire College, Brunel University, November 1996.
6. Jennifer Anderson, *Mahogany*, p. 76.
7. 'Lancaster. 1700–1800.' *Slavevoyages.org*.
8. '*Thomas and John*,' Voyage 24634, 1768. *Slavevoyages.org*; Melinda Elder, *The Slave Trade and the Economic Development of 18th-century Lancaster*, Halifax, 1992, p. 96.
9. 'Fenton,' Voyage 81440, 1785. *Slavevoyages.org*; Melinda Elder, *Lancaster*, p. 99.
10. Judith Dunn, 'Gillows of Lancaster: Two centuries of English furniture,' *New England Antiques Journal*, 2008.
11. See items under 'Thomas Affleck' in Philadelphia Museum of Art, Collections, www.philamuseum.org (retrieved 30/12/2015).
12. Jennifer Anderson, *Mahogany*, pp. 58–59.
13. Author's visit to Mount Vernon, November 2015.
14. 'Mahogany,' in Index to *Virginia Gazette*, 1736–1780, vol. 2, by Lester J. Cappon and Stella F. Duff, Institute of Early American History and Culture, Williamsburg, Virginia, 1950.
15. *Virginia Gazette*, August 8th, 1777: November 12th, 1767. Today, the storage facilities of Colonial Williamsburg are piled high with 18th-century mahogany furniture.
16. Quoted in Jennifer Anderson, *Mahogany*, p. 18.
17. David Watts, *The West Indies: Patterns of Development, Culture and Environmental Change since 1492*, Cambridge, 1987, pp. 393–394.
18. Edward Long, *History of Jamaica*, London, 1776, 3 vols.: I, p. 278.
19. Edward Long, *History of Jamaica*, I, pp. 278; 313. II, pp. 21; 124; 205.
20. Edward Long, *History of Jamaica*, III, p. 842.
21. Edward Long, *History of Jamaica*, III, p. 842.
22. Adam Bowett, *The Mahogany Trade, 1700-1793*. Ph.D. thesis, 1996. University of Buckingham.
23. Edward Long, *History of Jamaica*, II, 205.
24. Quoted in B.W. Higman, *Slave Populations of the British Caribbean 1807–1834*, Baltimore, 1984, p. 177.
25. Quoted in Jennifer Anderson, *Mahogany*, p. 162
26. Jennifer Anderson, *Mahogany*, p. 162.
27. B.W. Higman, *Slave Populations*, pp. 177–178.
28. Jennifer Anderson, *Mahogany*, pp. 160–161.

29. Mr. and Mrs. Isaac Winslow, *John Singleton Copley: The Complete Works*, www.johnsingletoncopley.org (retrieved 30/12/2015).
30. Jennifer Anderson, *Mahogany*, pp. 189–190.
31. Jennifer Anderson, *Mahogany*, pp. 55–57.
32. Jennifer Anderson, *Mahogany*, p. 57.

5

Stately Homes and Mansions
The Architecture of Slavery

Three grand homes – two in Virginia, one in Yorkshire – were built or remodeled at much the same time and form an unlikely trio of architectural gems. Today, all three – Mount Vernon, Monticello, and Harewood House – are major tourist sites, visited by armies of tourists keen to enjoy the buildings, their manicured surrounds and gardens, and the exquisite family possessions which adorn room after room. George Washington's Mount Vernon (1758–1778), a few miles south of Washington D.C., and Thomas Jefferson's Monticello (1770–1809), the magnificent neoclassical structure with its commanding hilltop view in Virginia, share obvious links. Both were homes of US presidents, and both were also homes to gangs of slaves: skilled and laboring people who helped to construct the very fabric of those Great Houses and grounds. At Monticello the slaves even levelled the mountain top on which their master planned to build his home. They, like George Washington's slaves one hundred miles to the north, all toiled not only to construct the owner's dwelling but also to make those plantations profitable concerns for their masters. Harewood House (1759–1771), 4,000 miles away, seems the most removed, unconnected even, from slavery, standing as it does in a beautiful stretch of

Slavery in Small Things: Slavery and Modern Cultural Habits, First Edition. James Walvin.
© 2017 John Wiley & Sons, Inc. Published 2017 by John Wiley & Sons, Inc.

Yorkshire countryside. Harewood House looks like the odd man out. But it isn't. In 1833, when Britain abolished its slave empire, the owners of Harewood House received almost £27,000 compensation for the emancipation of the 1,277 slaves they owned in Barbados and Jamaica. All three magnificent homes, Harewood, Monticello, and Mount Vernon, trace their modern origins and purpose to the world of African slavery.

One of the great curiosities of the modern-day remembrance of slavery is the inordinate (and largely admiring) attention paid to the mansions and Great Houses of slave owners. Many of the fashionable homes of planters (their former plantation houses, their town houses, or their European rural retreats) have been preserved, restored, and rendered desirable both as luxury residences and as attractive tourist destinations. Some – notably Mount Vernon and Monticello – have become shrines to the nation's great leaders. Many are indeed immensely attractive; some are regarded as classics of their kind and have become historical monuments in their own right. Tour operators offer commercial bus tours for visitors keen to drive along the Mississippi, or the streets of Natchez, and cruise past the lavish homes of people who made their fortunes on the back of African slaves. Still, for all the obvious aesthetic appeal, it seems odd that we have come to admire the homes of the planters and slave owners, not least because we have, at the same time, almost totally forgotten or ignored the homes of their slaves. Indeed, there has been a marked tendency to recall slavery through the domestic architecture of the slave owners. Perhaps this is not so surprising. After all, relatively few slave dwellings survive. While the physical structures of slave life have largely disappeared, many of their owners' homes have survived. In the tropics, however, even the most substantial building quickly succumbs to tropical decay. Even lavish Great Houses are quickly overgrown by luxuriant bush and undergrowth.[1] More troubling, though, is the way the concentration on planters' homes has served as a smoke screen for slavery itself. We admire the Great Houses and often overlook the very people who made everything possible there.

Millions of people lived out their lives as enslaved people in the Americas, in a range of simple (sometimes basic and primitive) and often temporary dwellings. In the main, theirs were crude, meager abodes, even in the most developed of slave communities. Surviving buildings, and contemporary illustrations of slave homes – sketches, drawings, maps, and plans – all convey a similar impression; slave homes that were basic at worst, and rustic at best. Much the same, of course, could be claimed for the dwellings of the rural laboring poor the world over. And there, too, we remember the extensive dwellings of their masters, but forget the homes of the poor – again because so few survive.

Slave dwellings were generally given little contemporary attention, even by men who took great pains to give precise and detailed accounts of land, factories, and workplaces. When we scrutinize plans, maps, and sketches of plantations, we find that slave houses tended to be added more for decoration than accurate representation.[2] Even so, and despite the romantic gloss often added to many images of slave housing, we can glean a great deal from such meager evidence: Slaves disliked the early communal dwellings – barracks – built for them, much preferring the privacy of their own home, however simple or crude. In time, masters came to respect that privacy (for instance by not entering slave dwellings unless necessary). In tropical colonies, those cabins and cottages were constructed from simple wattle and daub with palm frond roofing. In time, and as communities evolved, the dwellings became more substantial, with brick outdoor cooking facilities. Slave houses, of course, varied in quality and substance. Privileged slaves, for instance, were often given better housing, along with other perks that went with their status. But on the whole slave housing was easily removed, relocated, or simply abandoned when economic activity and work – and therefore human habitation – moved on. Slaves were easily relocated, even on the same property, part of the physical upheaval and relocation that formed the transient and disturbing disruption which haunted their lives.

Slave housing in North America tended to be in the form of simple cabins located some distance from the planter's home. Contemporary artists and commentators were struck by the contrast between the homes of the owners and of the slaves. Though slaves made great efforts to enhance their domestic lives by improving the interiors of their cabins (and by cultivating gardens and plots close by), their living conditions remained simple and largely unadorned.[3] Again, all this was true of laboring people in general. The story of slavery, however, offers an even sharper irony, because the very people who fashioned and directed a system of great brutality – the slave owners – are often remembered for the refinement, style, and taste of the way they lived. The appealing architecture of plantocratic living has often, in modern times, become a decoy to camouflage the brute reality of slavery itself. Having said that, major efforts are underway today to reconstruct slave homes and communities. But no serious observer is under any illusion that, say, Thomas Jefferson's slave cabins on Mulberry Row are in any way comparable to Jefferson's dazzling home, only a few hundred feet away, on the hilltop at Monticello. A simple, basic point remains: even where there are good examples of slave houses and communities, we continue to remember slavery – to see slavery in our mind's eye – through the attractive homes of the slave owners, not the slaves. Slaves *dominated* the human and physical landscape.[4] Yet we remember not the string of cabins housing the enslaved laboring force, but the planters' mansions. Only recently has serious attention been paid to the importance of slave dwellings.[5] Yet without those poor homes, and without the labor of their inhabitants, there could have been no grand neo-classical porticos, no lavish tree-shaded driveways. Above all, there could have been no crops – tobacco, rice, sugar, or cotton – to transform aspiring white farmers into planters of great substance and style.

*　*　*

Many African slaves on American plantations had first encountered Europeans in the daunting confines of a very different kind of European building: the infamous slave forts on the Gold Coast of Africa (Ghana) (See Chapter 6). In the very years that both Mount Vernon and Harewood House were under development, the British were undertaking a massive reconstruction of their military and commercial base at Cape Coast Castle. Today, that building and Elmina close by, as well as other forts like them on that stretch of coast, also attract hordes of tourists from all corners of the world, but especially from Europe and North America. Tens of thousands of tourists descend on the major slave forts of West Africa, now UNESCO World Heritage Sites, which dot Africa's slave coast. The tourist experience of those forts is, however, utterly different in every respect from a visit to Harewood House or Mount Vernon. For all the splendors of the location – with magnificent views from the ramparts of the African coastline, of the crashing Atlantic rollers, and of the teeming, bustling communities of fishermen who live and work in the immediate shadow of the fort, visiting Cape Coast Castle and Elmina is not a pleasant or uplifting experience.

Tourists to the slave forts can undergo the chilling experience of being locked in the cold dark cellars which once housed untold numbers of Africans awaiting dispatch to the slave ships, riding at anchor off shore. A visit to the forts is often a searing experience for people of African descent. Visitors simply stop and weep. Some are led away in distress. Even people with no direct family link to the horrors that unfolded in those forts (and in a myriad other places along that coast) can find such visits deeply troubling. The local tourist industry (which ranges from major government departments through to legions of hawkers selling their wares, as dozens of tour buses disgorge their passengers) does little to diminish the sense of terror and misery that unfolded inside the slave forts.

The contrast between a stately home in Yorkshire, a Virginian Great House, and the slave forts of Ghana could not be greater. Harewood House, beautiful, refined, luxurious; Cape Coast and Elmina Castles raw, brutal, and visceral. Yet all *were* linked, and all shared a defining experience: the enslavement of Africans. And they stand as major structural and architectural reminders that the slave system of the Atlantic left behind a host of physical remnants of a world that has long disappeared.

It may seem a perverse twist of historical fate that slavery has now become a major tourist attraction. Nonetheless, on both sides of the Atlantic, millions of people queue and pay to enter major sites of slave memory. The range of such sites is quite remarkable; European stately homes, slave forts, plantation Great Houses, museums, merchants' town houses. At one extreme, they form an aspect of 'dark tourism'; sites of painful memories which have been refashioned and designed to elicit maximum emotional stress and pain from the visitor. It is impossible to visit the major slave forts in Ghana without being struck – overpowered even – by the claustrophobic terror of the place. Yet even here, tourism rules. In Senegal, Gorée Island's slave fort proclaims itself to its hordes of (largely Francophone) tourists with greatly inflated data about slave numbers (which owes more to the local tourist board than it does to historical evidence).

At the other extreme, many buildings associated with slavery are presented to the visitor as delightful gems of contemporary fashion and taste: the finest examples of their architectural and cultural times, to be visited and admired for their astonishing beauties. There are many such buildings whose very physical existence, though rooted in African slavery, manages to convey a public demeanor which is totally divorced from slavery itself.[6] Who would even *associate* the beauties, say, of the James River Great Houses with the crowds of African slaves whose labor underpinned their very existence?

* * *

In early colonial North America, water was the main means of communication, and plantations and homes were generally found close to the waterside. They also tended to be isolated from each other, but close to the jetties and wharves which were vital for the importation of goods (and people), and the export of local produce. In the early phase of settlement, planters' homes were necessarily simple. But by the last years of the 17th century, planters who had prospered, notably in tobacco, later in rice, were able to devote more money and thought to constructing elaborate dwellings. Influenced by contemporary British Georgian tastes, they often opted for substantial brick buildings which proclaimed their owners' status and wealth. Surrounded by elaborate gardens and grounds, such homes were an effort to copy what they had learned of their social counterparts in Britain itself, 4,000 miles removed. Visitors to colonial Virginia were frequently struck by the similarity between what they encountered in the Tidewater region and what was common in Britain. To this day, tourists visiting the tobacco plantations which fringe the James River, between Williamsburg and Richmond, will be immediately struck by the fact that they seem very British. More striking still is the minimal attention paid, on many of those plantations, to the African slaves whose labor in the surrounding tobacco fields was vital to the property's well-being. On some plantations, slavery is not even mentioned.

Using designs borrowed from contemporary British architecture, prosperous Virginian planters built brick homes that reflected the prosperity yielded by the tobacco fields. To this day, the string of plantation houses which dot the James River road stand as monuments both to the wealth generated by tobacco and to the domestic styles affected by their owners.[7] Though this Tidewater architectural heritage is impressive, it pales in comparison to the slave-based legacy of South Carolina. Charleston was the entry point for the importation of 180,000 Africans, most destined to work as field and plantation slaves. On the eve of the American Revolution, Charleston had become the fourth largest seaport in North America, and its African labor force, and their local-born offspring, brought forth a string of export crops – rice, indigo (for dye), and naval stores. A substantial proportion of the population of Charleston was black and enslaved, and was instrumental in transforming the city into a bustling and sophisticated port. Today it is perhaps the prettiest and most eye-catching city in the USA, flaunting an array of 17- and 18th-century town houses and neighboring plantation Great Houses, all much gentrified and renovated, but again, architectural reminders of the city's slave history. Only a few miles outside Charleston, Middleton Place is perhaps the most striking proof of the wealth spawned by slave-grown commodities (in this case, rice). When Middleton Place was transformed into its current remarkably appealing landscaped form, the change coincided with the development of Harewood House and Mount Vernon. And, like Mount Vernon, Middleton Place now attracts busloads of tourists who wander round the house, admire the furnishings, and explore the magnificent grounds and their gardens (when in bloom, the azaleas fringing the lake are stunning).

Today, Middleton Place – like Harewood House – is, quite simply, a sumptuous place, with clear and unmistakable links to a British architectural model: it is grand, elaborate, and beautiful. Its owners seemed as keen to impress the visitor as they were to turn its fertile lands to profitable cultivation – courtesy of the resident African slaves. Middleton Place was both a thriving plantation (mainly in rice) and also an attractive seat for a prosperous gentleman and his family. Such images of what constituted a planter's life – the essential domestic and social trappings of a planter seated in the center of his property – proved enormously influential, and were contagious. Men who moved on, men who, in the early 19th century, rode and sailed south and west to new American frontiers, to establish themselves as planters in their own right on the new expanding lands of cotton plantations in the US South, recalled the architectural splendors of the Old South. The Plantation Great House proved to be an infectious concept, and it quickly took root wherever slavery thrived in the new Cotton Belt, and wherever slave owners began to accumulate enough money from their speculation to create a domestic and social lifestyle that befitted the cotton planter. The Old South offered an architectural model which translated from Tidewater Virginia to Kentucky, then much further south to Louisiana. But in the transition, the plantation house had been greatly transformed, both in the Chesapeake and the Carolinas, from a relatively simple farm into an *estate*, a property which projected fashion, taste, and good breeding. It became a social and architectural haven of style and flair in the American countryside. The land itself had been subdued and brought into productive use by people (the slaves) who had themselves moved – but against their wishes. Here were the historical foundations for the image of *Tara*, the plantation mansion, established by Margaret Mitchell's *Gone with the Wind*.

On the eve of the American Civil War, plantations were scattered across the US South in their thousands. For all the grandeur of the most extravagant, most slave owners did *not* live like that. After all, there were 46,274 plantations in the entire South, and the great majority of them functioned thanks to the labor of between 20 and 30 slaves. There were only 2,300 major plantations that used large numbers of slaves. The typical slave owner was a small farmer who owned only a handful of slaves and who often worked alongside them.[8] But again, the ones we remember are the more lavish plantations and their mansions. Some of the most lavish, the most striking, and most complex were those to be found in the coastal area stretching from the Chesapeake Bay down to Florida. Another group spanned the middle sections of South Carolina, Georgia, and Alabama to eastern Mississippi. But the most luxuriant and memorable of all were the relatively new plantations dotted along the fertile lands of the Mississippi Valley, roughly between Memphis and New Orleans. Yet the popular and abiding image of the Southern plantation remains *Tara*. True, more modest planters were keen to ape the style of their planter superiors, and to build homes and fill them with items which defined their taste and sophistication. And everyone hoped that the next cotton harvest would yield the material bounty to allow them to renovate, improve, and enlarge. With luck and hard work, they might even be able to move to that epicenter of good taste and fashion – New Orleans itself.

Right across the South the undoubted appeal and beauty of a lavish home came at a price. Both Middleton Place and the grander homes in the city of Charleston present us with a history so entangled in slavery that it is hard to see one without looking at the other. But it remains a highly contested history, though this is true of the history of the entire South. What to one side appears to be an aesthetically pleasing old colonial city, or a delightful rural mansion, is, at one and the same time, when seen through different eyes, the heartland of slavery. Charleston – a beautiful city – was the port where tens of thousands of Africans exchanged the misery of the slave ships for a lifetime's bondage in North America.[9] For those with eyes to see, the architectural beauties of Charleston, and of the Old South in general, mask a darker story.

Travel north from New Orleans, along the 'Great River Road,' along the meandering trail of the mighty Mississippi, north towards Baton Rouge and Natchez, via its many tributaries and bayous, and you will be spoiled for choice. Dozens of properties proclaim their architectural style – French, Spanish, Creole, even Caribbean – many with astonishing neoclassical facades. Approached along stunning driveways, shaded by a canopy of trees (oak and cypress) which cut through manicured gardens and grounds, the houses announce their social grace and taste through their sumptuous interiors, with sweeping staircases, alongside costly 18th- and 19th-century furnishings and household contents.

The tourist literature thrust into visitors' hands addresses the beauties and taste of the properties.[10] A few boldly confront their enslaved past. Whitney Plantation (previously *Habitation Haydel*) presents itself to visitors as a slave plantation: interpreting its history through the eyes of the enslaved labor force. But that is exceptional and unusual.[11] More often, such places do not even mention the missing feature in the entire opulent scene. The contrast is stark and often hard to grasp: refinement and fashion living cheek by jowl with the crude and often violent reality of life in the neighboring slave quarters. Only recently, and that largely because of modern movies (notably *Twelve Years a Slave*), has the public been confronted by the glaring incongruity.

Most slave owners did not, however, live in lavish, *Tara*-like Great Houses. On the eve of the Civil War, 250,000 Americans owned slaves – but the average slaveholding numbered only ten. Being a slave holder did *not* automatically bring prosperity and opulence and the magnificent planters' homes were the exception, not the rule. Nor was the extreme luxury of the biggest and most successful slave owners mirrored in the older slave societies in the Americas. Even so, slavery generated material prosperity for those in command of the Africans, for those who owned slaves, and for the merchants managing the trade between the slave economy and the US North, and Europe. Many such people sought to create for themselves a domestic environment which was both fashionable, and sometimes grand. But it was always, and everywhere, in sharp contrast to the crudities of slavery at large.

The rapid and widespread growth of the slave-grown cotton industry in the USA transformed a huge swathe of the South. The Cotton Belt stretched from South Carolina through Georgia, Alabama, Mississippi, Louisiana, Arkansas, and into Texas. Cotton created an industry with an enormous geography, stretching from the American frontier, via the booming towns and cities of the South, through the ports of New Orleans and Mobile, to the damp industrial towns of Lancashire and Germany. And the cheap goods manufactured from that slave-grown cotton were exported, through Liverpool, to dress the wider world in cheap cotton goods. By 1850, the US South was disgorging 2.5 million bales of cotton each year (each one weighing 181 kgs). In the process, the population of the South (both black and white) boomed: in 1810 there were 1.1 million slaves; by 1860 this had increased to almost 4 million. Small towns grew into major urban centers, linked by steamboats, then railways, to more distant cotton lands. And both plantations and towns acquired ever more elaborate homes and communities as cotton wealth spilled out from the slave fields into the purses of the slave-holding classes. Many of those who worked in the cotton fields saw their efforts transformed, before their very eyes, into the luxuries of elaborate plantation Great Houses.

The new cotton barons, the newly enriched cotton planters and traders, hastened to announce their wealth, and to flaunt their good taste, by building elaborate homes both on their plantations and in local towns. Styles varied; some were traditional American, others greatly influenced by French designs and ideas (especially in New Orleans)[12], but large numbers adopted the neoclassical Greek and Roman style which took root in North America by the early 19th century. Town houses in New Orleans, mansions on the bluffs above the Mississippi at Natchez, and Great Houses on plantations across the South – all spoke to the wealth created by slaves in the cotton fields. The modern visitor, however, often has to scratch around, or ask direct questions, to find mention of the slaves. Natchez boasts some of the grandest and most elaborate of early 19th-century mansions in the USA – *Rosalie, Longwood, Melrose, Stanton Hall, Magnolia Hall* and others – yet most stand in historical isolation: architectural beauties divorced from the bondage that underpinned them. One tour company claims, in its glossy brochure, that "The history of Natchez is fascinating. Here every American can find a part of his heritage…," naming the French, English, Spanish, and Indians. But no Africans.[13] When Africans and slavery are mentioned in local tourist literature they tend to be noises off stage: what is clearly an irritating descant to the hymn of praise being sung to the good taste and refinement of the properties' owners. It is, yet again, hard to escape the shadow of *Tara*.

Tara's classical façade and sweeping staircase, its elaborate and ornate furnishings and draperies, were all redolent of the newly acquired wealth created by cotton. It was also an architectural style which went far beyond the cotton plantations. Civic and federal buildings, urban architectural centerpieces (churches, libraries, banks, universities, assembly rooms – even post offices), all were constructed in the new American classical style. And all represented the astonishing rise of North American economic power; that confident physical and human expansion that was the USA in the early 19th century, and which was driven forward by trains, canals, urban growth, massive immigration, and movement westward. And of course by slavery.

At the heart of all this lay the cotton fields of the South, and the millions of slaves working the rich soil of the Delta, to enhance the wealth of their owners and of society at large – though rarely for themselves.[14] Armies of slaves toiled in the broiling heat of Southern summers, in the shadow of some of America's most impressive plantation mansions. Mississippi and Louisiana came to boast a multitude of elaborate classical mansions, approached though triumphal archways and drives flanked by guardian lines of trees. The mansions had grand colonnades, porches, and galleries, all designed to maintain coolness in the sapping humidity of the Southern summers, and also intended to confirm the planter's wealth. No such comfort was afforded the ranks of slaves cultivating, picking, and transporting the cotton.

The most fashionable extreme of Southern plantation life was characterized by a luxury and material consumption that would have made 18th-century British aristocrats sit up and pay attention. What accentuated the extremes – slave poverty on one hand, the well-being of masters and their families on the other – was the harsh discipline of slave life and work: the physical pressures and punishments deemed necessary to keep the slave gangs at work. Corporal punishment, cavalier attacks, brute intervention, and the most ugly and degrading violence in the fields (not to mention the pervasive sexual threats to slave women) all stood in sharp contrast to the genteel refinement of the Great House, and the social life it offered to friends and visitors. Today, and unlike with the slave forts of Ghana, the mansions of the South have been purged of their dark tourism and given a patina, even the odor, of good taste.

*   *   *

The most obvious architectural traces of slavery survive (and in places thrive) on the African coast, and in the heartlands of plantation slavery across the Americas. But what about Europe? Here we face a real conundrum. Slavery flourished far away from Europe – in Africa and the Americas, and on the high seas. Yet Europe was the very engine which drove forward the entire system. The Atlantic slave system was devised, perfected, and brought to profitable fruition by Europeans. From their palaces, counting houses, merchants' offices, and shipping agencies, it was the Europeans who pulled the strings of this massive global system. But those people lived and worked many thousands of miles away from the focal points of their commercial empires. They planned, financed, and orchestrated a slave system that remained distant: literally over the horizon. It would be wrong, however, to imagine that, because of distance, slavery failed to leave its physical and architectural influence in the European heartlands. The architecture of slavery lies scattered across Europe itself.

Few planters had homes on the scale and splendor of Harewood House, one of England's great stately homes. It nestles in gentle rolling hills, far removed from the geographic center of slavery. Located on the road between the industrial town of Leeds and the fashionable spa town of Harrogate, Harewood enjoys a stunning location, set in magnificent grounds and gardens, and housing an astonishing array of paintings and furnishings. In many respects it is a perfect Yorkshire location, and the house and grounds form a very Yorkshire treasure, with commanding views across farmland towards Wharfedale, and all perfectly placed for access to the beautiful Yorkshire Dales. Even for those familiar with the history of Harewood House, it is sometimes difficult to grasp that the place emerged from a family's complex dealings in the slave empire of the Atlantic. In fact, Harewood is just one, albeit a spectacular, example of a building and location whose slave connections tend to be masked by the accident of distance. Though many thousands of miles from the slave coast of Africa, and from the plantation colonies of the Americas, Harewood House has direct links to the world of Atlantic slavery.

Harewood House was built for Edwin Lascelles between 1759 and 1771. By a remarkable coincidence, on the far side of the Atlantic in almost exactly the same period (1758–1778), George Washington was re-modelling his own family residence at Mount Vernon. He also abandoned tobacco for varied agriculture on the property. That property stands on land owned by his family for a century, on a bluff overlooking the Potomac River, a few miles south of the town that was to bear his name and was to become the capital of the USA. Today Mount Vernon is a major tourist attraction. It is, after all, the home of one of the most revered figures among the Founding Fathers. But George Washington had also been a slave owner from the age of 11 (when he had inherited ten slaves). By the time of his death in 1799, 318 slaves lived and worked at Mount Vernon. Today, and in contrast to other Great Houses and plantations, the story of those slaves is fundamental to the narrative which greets every tourist to Mount Vernon. In talks, displays, through the words and actions of interpreters, in the physical fabric of that much-reconstructed plantation property, slavery is exposed and debated in all its complexities and contradictions. There can be no clear understanding of George Washington, of his home at Mount Vernon, without confronting the troubling matter of American slavery. At both Harewood House and Mount Vernon great pains are now taken to integrate the story of slavery into the broader narrative of their respective properties.

Though Harewood House was (and is) exceptional, the British landscape is strewn with private, commercial, civic, and religious buildings inspired by or rooted in the trade to and from the slave colonies. Planters from the Americas con-structed European homes – sometimes palaces – from slave-based riches. In the last years of British slavery we know of twenty-six such homes, scattered across Britain, the property of slave owners from one small corner of the Caribbean: the tiny islands of St. Vincent and the Grenadines.[15] The major ports which serviced the slave ships are marked by the profits of that commerce. Commercial and dockside premises, homes of the prosperous merchants and sailors, warehouses and fac-tories devoted to the slave trading business, all have survived in the years since slavery ended. They stand, today, as physical monuments to the Atlantic trade. Small ports which grew fat on the Africa trade expanded, and often adopted the names of the commerce which yielded their prosperity. Bristol's 'Guinea' St., Liverpool's Penny Lane, Tarleton St., Rodney St., Gorée Piazza, Great Newton St., Cunliffe St., and Earl St. In Scotland, Glasgow thrived on its trade to and from the Chesapeake, its warehouses and elaborate homes surviving as architectural reminders of the impact of slavery. Glasgow has its Virginia, Jamaica, Tobago, and

Antigua streets; other Glaswegian streets are named after the city's 'tobacco barons'.[16]

We are accustomed to the most lavish end of this spectrum of wealth; the stately homes of returning planters who did their best to outshine returning Indian nabobs with the elaborate style and splendor of their stately homes. They sought, in fact, even to outstrip local aristocrats in the extravagance of their style and spending power. More common, though, were men whose local, less exuberant homes enhanced the streets and squares of Britain's port cities. Men who owned, or part-owned, slave ships, factories which processed slave grown produce, and trading houses which bought and sold to and from the ships bound for Africa, alongside families who retired from their slave properties on the far side of the Atlantic.[17] In some of the more fashionable squares in Bristol, slave-based prosperity was the dominant theme among a string of neighbors and friends. Men with interests in the slave ships, in trade to and from particular points of the slaving compass, all lived cheek by jowl in Bristol's more stylish quarters. And as the city expanded, similar cohorts of wealthy men moved out into newly developed squares and communities. Indeed, it seems clear enough that much of the urban expansion of Bristol was grown on the back of and was sustained by the city's profitable Africa trades. Shippers, merchants, manufacturers, industrialists, planters, and colonial officials all rubbed shoulders in Bristol's desirable quarters, and created the physical fabric which survives, to this day, among the more attractive places to live in Bristol.

Those with grander ambitions, and deeper purses, moved out of town completely, settling in their own rural retreats. Rich merchants and returning planters became part of this distinctive 18th-century pattern: of settling into fashionable, sometimes spectacularly lavish, stately homes. By the mid-18th century a sizeable group of men with commercial interests in slavery, and trading to and from Africa, had established homes in the rural hinterland of Bristol. By 1769, at least 44 people lived in fashionable homes within a ten-mile radius of the city. Sometimes, these prosperous men took over much older estates and modernized them: others started from scratch to build a grand residence to reflect their wealth and status. In the process they also sought to improve *themselves*, adopting the styles and fashions which characterized people of gentility, through education, book collections, and attending fashionable social gatherings. Such gentility was, however, more characteristic of neighboring Bath, and Bristol maintained a reputation for its calloused, rough-necked style. Bristol slave merchants who failed to effect a more genteel style at least had the satisfaction of knowing that they had paved the way for their offspring to enter more refined and polite society. In the words of Madge Dresser "luxury followed riches, then, refinement followed luxury."[18] This remarkable progression (from quayside counting house to fashionable rural retreat) succeeded in hiding the African slaves packed onto Bristol's slave ships, or toiling in American properties – and all serviced and maintained by Bristol traders. Here was just one regional example which could be replicated across the face of late 18th-century Britain. Prosperity and luxury, dominant social themes of 18th-century British life, which, once again, had their roots thousands of miles away, on the slave coast of Africa and the slave colonies of the Americas.

A similar tale could be repeated for Liverpool, a city manifestly shaped and created by its sea-faring history. Many of its major squares, lined by rows of splendid Georgian houses, and many of its civic and public buildings have origins in the city's heyday as a slave trading port. African faces and heads adorn a number of civic and private buildings, carved in stone as a lasting physical reminder of Africa's contribution to the development of the city. Two hundred of Liverpool's major traders in the slave era invested in properties in the city itself and, in many cases, in the rural hinterland surrounding it. As in all forms of commerce, there were casualties along the way: men whose dealings in the African trades led to ruin. More striking, though, were those whose successes were confirmed in the homes they acquired in the city and its environs. As they prospered, they moved: from the old city center to new suburbs and into the country. Some acquired country mansions and estates, others improved themselves by marriage, and some confirmed their rise in the world by dispatching their sons to Oxford or Cambridge.

We know that there were lots of *small* investors in Liverpool's slave ships, people whose minor investments yielded relatively small returns. Equally, not all successful businessmen in the city derived their prosperity from the slave ships, and many diversified their business interests into other activities. Even so, there were large numbers of local people who rose to prosperity and propertied substance on the backs of the slave ships, their success now to be counted in real estate in and around the city of Liverpool.[19]

*   *   *

The most lavish and extensive injection of slave-based money into the British system came, ironically, as a result of slave emancipation in 1833. The £20 million (brokered by Rothschild's) which the British government used to compensate slave owners to secure the freedom of slaves was an astonishing confirmation, at the death, of slavery's financial importance to Britain. For more than a half century following the establishment of the Abolition Society in 1787, arguments about slave freedom had washed back and forth. In the end, the question was resolved by financial compensation. The British *bought* the slaves' free-dom. The complexities of the scheme need not detain us, but the general point is clear enough. Each slave was, once again, assigned a monetary value (this time by a government official) and that value was paid to the former owner. All came courtesy of the British taxpayer. In effect, it was a massive, final act of slave trading. Yet there was no hint in the process that the slaves themselves should be compensated. If there was any doubt that slavery had lost its economic vitality and utility, the compensation of 1833 blew that augment apart. British slave holders prof-ited hugely from slavery, merely by accepting the value assigned to their human property. Claims for compensation expose just how extensive slave ownership was *in Britain*. More than 6,000 people living in Britain claimed compensation for the loss of their slaves in the colonies.[20] Slavery had seeped into the heart and soul of the British people – and was not merely restricted to its wealthy elites. There were any number of humble people who by marriage, inheritance, or sheer personal happenchance had come into the possession of slaves in the Americas.

The £20 million compensation that was paid for the slaves' freedom was channeled into a host of British and imperial investments. Compensation allowed Britons to fund invest-ments at home and abroad, from Scotland to Sydney. It invig-orated and enhanced colleges, universities, museums, galleries, and private cultural collections. It found its way into bricks and mortar, as former slave owners used their compensation to buy, renovate, or extend estates and town houses, castles, churches and public buildings, or simply create monuments to themselves. It was, in many respects, a fitting and symbolic way of bringing Britain's formal association with slavery to an end. After all, from the earliest days, merchants and planters had created physical tributes to themselves in the guise of ever more elaborate homes and mansions. Now, after 1833, in an era marked by rising anti-slavery sentiment and a revulsion at the very concept of slavery, those who had benefitted most from the system consolidated their wealth and status, once again on the back of the slaves. This time, after 1833, it came glossed with altruism and high principles.[21] Emancipation in 1833, like abolition before it in 1807, came garlanded with self-congratulation – and the nation rejoiced in its high principles. But both abolition and emancipation were underpinned by material interests and rewards – not for the slaves; that largely passed unnoticed.

* * *

The Atlantic slave system was so massive, so pervasive, that it became part of the warp and the weft of Western life itself. Atlantic slavery was a vast economic enterprise which involved hundreds of thousands of sailors, tens of thousands of voyages, millions of Africans, centuries of economic activity, scores of commodities and goods, complex financial dealings – over a period spanning more than three centuries. How could so vast a structure, so pervasive a system, *not* intrude into the very fabric of Western life? And yet....

In the case of Europe, lying as it does geographically removed from the centers of slave activity, it was easy not to spot the slave connections. Moreover, many of the physical traces left by slavery seem detached, unconnected to slavery itself. How is one to make the link between the splendors of a British stately home and the slaves whose labor was integral to that property? Here lies one of the great paradoxes of slavery. The people who profited from slavery often distanced themselves from it. They often sought to confirm their rise to material and social eminence by surrounding themselves with the elaborate, physical trappings of wealth. Luxuries and ostentatious dwellings were, of course, all part and parcel of the much broader social transformation from the 17th century onward – the rise of luxury and refinement on both sides of the Atlantic (though not all of it slave related).[22] Complex social and economic changes flowed from distant parts of the globe (most notably, for the British, from India) to feed the wider development of Western material consumption. Indeed, this Western urge to luxury was fed by an integrated global economy. All the same, the Atlantic slave system was fundamental, and if we require proof, we need only glance at the physical landmarks which today survive in all corners of the slave trading compass; stately homes in Yorkshire, forts on the African coast, town houses in Liverpool, Bordeaux, and Natchez, and the rural and urban mansions of merchants and planters across the Americas. The bald truth is that the shadow of slavery is inescapable.

Notes

1. Roger Leech, 'Lodges, gardens and villas.' In Madge Dresser and Andrew Hann, eds., *Slavery and the British Country House*, Swindon, 2013.
2. For a masterly study, see B.W. Higman, *Jamaica Surveyed: Plantation Maps and Plans of the Eighteenth and Nineteenth Centuries*, Kingston, 1988.
3. John Michael Vlach, *Back of the Big House: The Architecture of Plantation Slavery*, Chapel Hill, 1993, Chapter 11.
4. John Michael Vlach, 'The plantation landscape.' In *American Architectural History: A Contemporary Reader*, Keith Eggener, ed., New York, 2004, Chapter 5.
5. See *Slave Dwellings Project*, Second Annual Conference, Charleston, S.C. Oct 8–10th, 2015.
6. See the various essays in Madge Dresser and Andrew Hann, eds., *Slavery and the British Country House*, Swindon, 2013.
7. Leland M. Roth, *American Architecture: A History*, Cambridge, MA, 2000, pp. 73–77.
8. John Michael Vlach, 'The plantation landscape.'
9. James Walvin, *Crossings: Africa, the Americas and the Atlantic Slave Trade*, London, 2013, p. 125.
10. Bobby Potts, *Plantation Country along the Mississippi*, New Orleans, 1996. I possess a collection of plantation brochures and tourist literature from these plantations.

11. www.whitneyplantation.com (retrieved 30/12/2015).
12. Ron Katz and Arielle de la tour d'Auvergne, *French America: French Architecture from Colonization to the Birth of a Nation*, New York, 2004.
13. *Natchez on the Mississippi*, Pilgrimage Tours, Official Guide Book, n.d.
14. For a recent account placing cotton slavery at the heart of US development, see Edward Baptist, *The Half Has Never Been Told: Slavery and the Making of American Capitalism*, New York, 2014.
15. Simon D. Smith, 'Slavery's heritage footprint: Links between British country houses and St Vincent, 1814–1834.' In Madge Dresser and Andrew Hann, eds., *Slavery and the British Country House*, pp. 59–60.
16. T.M. Devine, ed., *Recovering Scotland's Slavery Past: The Caribbean Connection*, Edinburgh, 2015.
17. Madge Dresser, *Slavery Obscured*, Chapter 3.
18. Madge Dresser, *Slavery Obscured*, p. 118.
19. David Pope, 'The wealth and social aspiration of Liverpool's slave merchants in the second half of the eighteenth century.' In David Richardson, Suzanne Schwarz, and Anthony Tibbles, eds., *Liverpool and Transatlantic Slavery*, Liverpool, 2007, Chapter 7.
20. *Legacies of British Slave-ownership*. UCL. www.ucl.ac.uk/lbs/legacies (retrieved 30/12/2015).
21. *Legacies of British Slave-ownership*. UCL. www.ucl.ac.uk/lbs/legacies (retrieved 30/12/2015).
22. Simon Gikandi, *Slavery and the Culture of Taste*, Princeton, 2011.

6

Maps
Revealing Slavery

Malachy Postlethwayt, an employee and arch defender of the Royal African Company, published four editions of his massive study *The Universal Dictionary of Trade and Commerce* between 1751 and 1774 (he died in 1767). Those volumes formed an extraordinary compendium of evidence about the world at large. Compiled from a host of (largely French) sources, and openly derivative in nature, the *Universal Dictionary* provides an important mine of contemporary evidence. Postlethwayt was, for example, an advocate of trade to Africa – and not simply for slaves. Africa, he argued, was a continent brimming with abundant resources and commodities, from timber to gold, and which offered unimaginable scope for normal trade. At the time he was writing, however, the continent's pre-eminent attraction for European traders was humanity: filling the slave ships which were destined for the plantations of the Americas.[1] Although also an apologist for and proponent of the slave trade, Postlethwayt recognized that the commercial potential of Africa went far beyond that trade in slaves.[2]

The third edition of his *Dictionary* (1766) incorporated the massive geopolitical changes agreed to between France, Spain, and Great Britain at the *Treaty of Paris* which had concluded

Slavery in Small Things: Slavery and Modern Cultural Habits, First Edition. James Walvin.
© 2017 John Wiley & Sons, Inc. Published 2017 by John Wiley & Sons, Inc.

the Seven Years War in 1763. At the back of the *Dictionary*, the author appended a series of up-to-date maps which reflected the changes brought about by the peace treaty: chunks of whole continents handed from one European power to another, and a scattering of tropical islands ceded from France to Britain (the victor). It was as if the European colonial powers were playing a gigantic game of chess with the entire world as their playing surface. Postlethwayt's maps (mainly French in origin with British alterations) form a series of snapshots of the physical world as it was known in 1763. They also provide revealing assessments of the world of slavery in the Atlantic. Look closely at the maps, and the contours of Atlantic slavery leap off the page. Postlethwayt's maps explain, to people who could read them, the very nature and significance of the wider world. They offered a glimpse into the power, the global reach, and the commercial muscle of the Western world in the late 18th century. The maps also provide a series of cartographical snapshots of slavery.

The maps of Africa are essentially maps of the African coastline (though that was true of other continents which remained under-explored and sometimes even unknown to the Europeans). But the sub-Saharan Atlantic coastline of Africa teems with activity and is portrayed as a crowded crossroads of shipping and commerce, notably of the trade in African humanity. Though the distances involved are immense (almost 4,000 miles from Mauritania to southern Angola), the European interest in the African coast was heavily concentrated in those regions which yielded the best returns for the slave ships. Postlethwayt's maps of West Africa convey the sense of a crowded littoral, with images of forts, settlements, and national flags – and ships – dotting the coastal landscape and the ocean.[3] There are sketched hints of some of Africa's other commercial attractions: gum forests in Senegambia, 'redwood trees' in Angola. The map also specifies geographic features – hills, even 'A great

Tree,' and it pinpoints African settlements and peoples. Revealingly though, it tells us that "their most populous Towns" were "generally further inland." By and large, however, the African interior is empty: a geographical void, largely unknown to outsiders, except where it could be penetrated by river. Yet the author – and those he relied on for his information – clearly knew a great deal about Africa, via traders and merchants who had links between the coast and the interior, as well as from traditional and ancient geographers. Nevertheless, Postlethwayt's knowledge of the African interior seems sparse compared to his knowledge of the coast.

Postlethwayt's map of Africa is, in simple outline, the story of Europeans trawling for Africans on the Atlantic coast. At critical points, the map displays a series of forts: almost medieval in their outline, capped by European flags announcing the forts' national identity. Here were European outposts on the very edge of Africa. The Portuguese had led the way exploring that coast, but they had soon been followed by all the other major European maritime powers, exploring, navigating, and charting the coast, both for its own potential and as an important pathway towards the Indian Ocean and the riches of Asia. Those small groups of Europeans also needed security, against the dangers of Africa. 'Phipp's Tower' on the Gold Coast was described in Postlethwayt's map as being "built for the defence of Cape Coast towards the land."[4] Above all, however, these forts were protection against the threats posed by other European powers. Forts sprouted at a number of strategic locations: at trading posts, commanding entrances to rivers, or deep up an African river at a trading location. These African forts were one version of the structures which European constructed in all corners of their emerging empires. To this day, their surviving remnants speak to the strategic and commercial importance of the spot they commanded: on the African coast, in the Indian Ocean and India, at a host of settlements in China and Southern Asia, throughout the Caribbean and North America. From Quebec to Elmina (Ghana), from Galle (Sri Lanka) and onto Batavia (Jakarta), Europeans constructed a string of major (and lots of minor) forts.

Today, the forts on the Atlantic coast of Africa are infamous for their incarceration of countless African slaves. Elmina, Cape Coast, and Gorée Island attract huge numbers of modern tourists, notably of people of African descent from throughout the diaspora (see Chapter 5). Though the forts represent the inhumanity and suffering of the slave trade itself, their historical reality is more complex than local tourist guides would have visitors believe.

The most famous, and the most numerous forts (some sixty in all) were built along a relatively short stretch of the coastline on the Gold Coast. The name is a giveaway. Gold from the inland gold fields initially lured the Europeans to that region. Their early slave trading was up and down the African coast (trading slaves to and from other Africans), or from Africa to Portugal. The forts grew, in size, complexity, and numbers, as plantations developed in the Americas and came to depend on imported African slave labor. It was in the era of slave trading that forts proved their worth as secure bases, holding pens for large numbers of slaves, and centers for local and regional trade and business.

Europeans applied their centuries of experience of constructing forts to build their African outposts. In time, those massive constructions developed into communities in their own right, housing (within the fort and hugging its walls) mixed communities of Africans, Europeans, and people born of both. Some forts even became the center of new towns and settlements. But from first to last the Europeans who manned them (along with the growing numbers of Africans – and the offspring of local women and European men) had little more than a toehold on the African coast. They were unhealthy places for the Europeans who lived in and around them: they died in large numbers from tropical diseases (as did the crews on the slave ships lying off-shore and slowing filling with African slaves).

Europeans also constructed forts at strategic points on rivers (James Island, Gambia), at offshore islands (Gorée, Senegal), and at major island way-stations (Sao Tome). Some were lit-tle more than squalid (and dangerous) trading posts. But all were highly prized by European politicians and traders and were fiercely protected, fought over, seized, and exchanged (in warfare and treaties). Though some were indeed important for the transit and sale of Africans from land to sea, many more Africans – millions more – passed into European hands by other means and via routes other than the slave forts. Nonetheless, to this very day, those daunting, but in some cases stunning, struc-tures proclaim the importance of the Atlantic slave trade.

The forts also bear testimony to the Europeans' fear of each other, and of the threat posed by European rivals to the supplies of gold and, later, of African slaves. Forts were also developed by monopoly trading companies, though monopolies quickly fell out of favor largely because they failed to supply African slaves in sufficient numbers. Planters needed more Africans than a monopoly could supply and in the early 18th century the Atlantic slave trade was opened up. The forts survived, however, because they were useful bases of military and national strength, despite the cost of maintaining them in the face of tropical wear and tear, and against continuing European rivalries on the slav-ing coast. The forts, on maps as in reality, sported their national flags, but those flags changed hands just as the forts changed hands. Yet what did all this mean to local Africans, as they saw ownership, and the flags, change from, say, Portuguese to Dutch and then to British? And what possible difference did it make to the shackled slaves waiting to pass through the 'Door of No Return' onto the canoes and thence to the slave ships? The forts, whatever their nationality, had one brutal thing in common: they were prisons for Africans in transit to the ships.

By the early 18th century, as American demand for slaves reached new heights, the African forts managed to retain their strategic importance, even though supplies of Africans were reaching the slave ships via other routes. Slave traders learned how to locate the best supplies of Africans, which African middlemen to approach, and which cargoes those Africans demanded in exchange for slaves. Slave trading on the coast varied from once place to another, and as trade dried up or boomed, the slave captains (and their European backers) shifted their attention and efforts accordingly. Africans were acquired from barracoons on beaches, in small handfuls from local traders, from specific ports. We now know that of the 12 million Africans loaded onto the slave ships, 4.7 million came from four slave ports: Loango, Cabina, Luanda, and Benguela.[5] Some towns, notably Ouidah in Benin (which dispatched 1 million Africans to the ships), were actually *inland*, and the slaves were marched to embarkation on the shoreline (by African guards). All this, and the supplies of Africans arriving at the final transfer point on the coast, depended ultimately on conditions in the African interior.

Europeans had some, largely imprecise, knowledge about the interior of Africa, much of it acquired from traditional and classical sources. Postlethwayt's map of Africa depicts "this great Region as described by Ptolemy, joined with the knowledge of Edrissi the Nubian Geographer and Leo the African, agrees with several new Discoveries, all uniting to verify their Accounts."[6] The land north of the Cape of Good Hope is merely described in Postlethwayt as 'The Land of the Hottentots.'[7] Huge swathes of the interior are marked only by the occasional landmark: rivers, trees, hills, human settlements. The very great bulk of all references to Africa are *coastal*, and are a reflection of outsiders' contemporary knowledge of the continent. Europeans knew that Africa yielded a host of important commodities (the very items which the seaborne traders sought on the coast). They knew of distant inland people, many of whom reached the coast in the shape of slaves sold by African slave traders. But much more striking are the *gaps* and the *spaces*. While the African Atlantic coastline bristles with names of locations, and geographic features seen, recorded, mapped, and charted by Europeans, the interior (the massive heart of Africa) remained beyond the ken of Europeans. It appeared on maps as it did in reality – a void. It would remain relatively undocumented to any precise degree until the mid- to late 19th century. Yet it was from those areas of uncertainty – the mysterious interior – that Europeans derived many of their slaves. Nevertheless, Europeans also realized that the unknown interior offered enormous untapped commercial scope. As Postlethwayt's map noted of the Gold Coast, "The English here have great opportunities to extend their inland Commerce."[8]

At the major slaving locations on the Atlantic coast, Africans could look to the ocean and see various sailing ships riding at anchor. They lay offshore taking on board more Africans until the captain decided that he had enough to make a profitable voyage across the ocean. In minor locations, when Africans saw a vessel clearly in search of cargo, they lit a fire to tell the ship that slaves were available for sale and barter. At the major trading points, from Ghana south to Angola, Africans were ferried to the ships in small craft: African dug-out canoes, and small sailing or rowing vessels lowered from the European ships. The European (and ever more Brazilian and North American) sailing ships were (and looked) complex machines, quite unlike anything Africans were accustomed to. It was virtually impossible, when African slaves rebelled and succeeded in over-whelming the crew at sea, for the slaves to sail and navigate such alien contraptions.[9] For Africans who had been marched as slaves from interior locations, and who had not seen the ocean before, sailing ships were utterly unknown and bewil-dering entities. Yet they were the key to the entire enterprise – 12 million people departed West Africa on such vessels.

Images of those sailing ships figured prominently on maps drafted in the slave-trade era. Sketches and drawings of sailing ships, at anchor, under sail, heading east, west, and south, pep-per the imagined coastline of the cartography. In some respects, they are stylized representations, not unlike ships drawn on maps of all corners of the world.[10] But they were also *real*: sails and flags unfurled, the ships' bows pointing towards African destinations, their guns visible and ready for any eventuality. The greatest danger faced by the slave ships, when fully loaded, was from their African prisoners. At least one slave ship in ten suffered a slave revolt, and the ships employed swivel guns that could be pointed inward, directed at the African captives.[11] Such drawings of sailing ships were also used to fill up the void that was the vast expanse of the Atlantic Ocean. Map-makers every-where filled up the empty oceanic space on their maps by litter-ing the seas with sailing ships.[12]

The Atlantic was not merely a vast expanse of water. It was the place, a series of routes, where millions of Africans spent months on end, in transit, between Africa and the Americas. Many Africans spent longer waiting on board their floating prison, off the coast of Africa, than they did crossing the ocean. Many were at sea, but remained within sight of Africa longer than they were out of sight of land, apparently lost in the watery vastness of the Atlantic. What happened on those ships was the stuff of individual and collective nightmares, from the first moment Africans came on board, to the last one stepping ashore in the Americas (though they had no idea where they were). It was an inexpressibly terrible experience: alien, from the start, filled with physical dangers, awash with filth and sickness, buffeted by the unpredictable twists and turns of the ocean itself, and assailed by the moods and fears of their jailors – the sailors. Nothing could have prepared an African – anyone for that matter – for the experience of the slave ship.[13]

The Atlantic Ocean was, at one and the same time, a complex oceanic system of currents, winds, and of seasons; of shoals, reefs, banks, and doldrums, a place of howling gales and gigantic waves. It was a complexity of physical and natural dangers and risks which could perplex and terrify even the most experienced of deep-water sailors. African slaves were not alone in the terror they often experienced as their ships plunged and twisted their way between the mighty forces of the Atlantic Ocean.

Many 18th-century maps of the Atlantic, and of other oceans, were adorned with images of faces. Often they were cherubs, with cheeks puffed out, blowing vigorously onto the surface of the sea. Those faces were more than mere ornamentation: they represented perhaps the most important element sailors needed – and feared; the wind, and wind systems, to push their vessels across the ocean but which, in an instant, could turn into a violent gale – or worse. The rise of the compass saw the decline of these images from maps, but for years navigators looked to those round-cheeked cherubs for guidance. They needed to know about the direction of prevailing winds, where and when they changed. Just as important, sailors needed to know of the currents which carried ships in their powerful and sometimes irresistible flow. Entries on maps sometimes made the specific point. Postlethwayt's map of Africa describes "A strong Current sets to Eastward, except in the Hermiton Season (about January) when it sets the contrary Way." To reinforce the point, strong lines – pointers and arrows – are slashed across the ocean in the direction of the flow. An arrow heads south-east "In March-April and May" but "During the rest of the Year" the arrow points north-west, in the parallel but opposite direction.[14]

For all the major improvements in ship design, in navigational instruments, in charting and mapping the ocean and coastlines (and the simple accumulation of experience over the years), mariners were always at the mercy of the elements. The Atlantic had two weather systems which dictated the direction, timing, and seasonality of the flow of shipping. The North Atlantic was dominated by a system that moved clockwise; vessels from Europe were helped on their way to West Africa when they joined warm currents off the north-west coast of Africa. The South Equatorial currents then helped ships leaving the African coast and heading towards the Caribbean (and onward to North America). In the South Atlantic, the major currents flowed anti-clockwise: the Brazilian current was joined by the Benguela current and propelled ships to Brazil. In both the North and South Atlantic, these currents were assisted by prevailing wind systems.

Sailing *within* one of these systems enabled vessels to make the quickest of Atlantic crossings (the swiftest being those leaving west-Central Africa for Brazil). But ships which passed from one weather system to another took longer: the longer a ship was at sea, the worse the levels of sickness and death among the Africans incarcerated below deck. But even the most experienced of masters faced the unpredictable twists and turns of Atlantic weather. Moreover, throughout much of the history of the slave trade, navigation remained an approximate science (until the ability to fix a vessel's longitude became available) and ships, sometimes entire fleets, sailed many miles off their intended course. Poor navigation, miscalculations, mistaken sightings, all could lead to disaster. An error in navigation was the origin of the disaster which led to the murder of

132 Africans on the *Zong* slave ship in 1781.[15] Africans trapped on slave ships which ran aground on reefs, sandbars, or rocks faced certain death: the crew was unlikely to release them (and become greatly outnumbered by them). Africans drowned in wrecks because they were manacled below on a sinking ship. We know of slave ships that were blown apart (fire was a permanent risk on sailing ships), whether by accident or in the course of a slave revolt. In total 148 slave ships vanished completely, lost with everyone on board, victims of storms, shipwreck, or revolt.[16]

The sufferings of Africans cannot be measured simply by tabulating the obvious casualties (more than one million Africans did not survive the Atlantic crossing, their corpses cast overboard to the following sharks), because even among those who survived, and who stumbled ashore in the Americas, sickness was rife. Indeed, the high levels of mortality among Africans in their first few years in the Americas was as much a consequence of the slave ships as it was of adjusting to the new environment on the other side of the Atlantic. Crossing the Atlantic was a time of intense suffering for *all* the Africans concerned, especially when the weather turned violent, or the ship was becalmed. Whenever the crew (their numbers diminished on many voyages by tropical sickness) were fully pressed simply sailing the ship, they could not be spared to tend to the Africans manacled below deck. Clamped together, in a pitching, rolling ship, unfed and untended, the living and the dead endured days on end in the filth of the slave decks. Those cherubic cheeks we see on maps, puffing the wind, and the simple arrows on the map, meant something utterly different for the ranks of Africans shackled below, the air vents shut against the storm. The Africans were in effect abandoned until the storm had blown over. Then, even men with the strongest of stomachs found it hard to climb below deck to help them when the weather improved. Of course, not all ships were tossed around like this. We know of some voyages that were relatively swift and untroubled – especially across the shorter voyages in the South Atlantic to Brazil. Even so, for *every single* African, the Atlantic was a new, terrifying, and utterly bewildering experience. Nothing in their lives could have prepared them for the months on board the ship as it rode at anchor off the African coast, followed by weeks – sometimes months – ploughing west or north-west to the Americas, with no land in sight, just the immensity of a heaving ocean and its waves, the noise of the wind and the accompanying sounds of timbers and sails straining against the elements. And all this punctuated by the terrible cries of distress and of sickness issuing from the ranks of African prisoners.

We know that the mood of the crew changed, they were cheered, by the first sight of land – often heralded by the arrival of birds even before land could be seen. Sometimes, landfall came quickly. Barbados (the most easterly of the Caribbean islands), or the refuge of All Saints Bay, with Salvador initially hidden from view, might bring a relatively swift transfer back to *terra firma* (after local authorities had cleared the vessel to discharge its human cargo). But for many, approaching land must have seemed little more than a mirage. For a start, many could not see it, unless they were brought up on deck for exercise and cleaning. And often, the ships sailed on with their Africans destined for a more distance port or landfall. Or the slaves were transferred to another vessel for onward travel.

The sight of land did not bring an end to a ship's navigational difficulties and dangers. The Caribbean, for example (where four million Africans were landed), presented its own distinct problems. Maps clearly show that arc of islands – but each one had its own inshore risks, with reefs and cays lurking dangerously in apparently deep water. Sailing between the islands brought its own complex navigational and weather problems, and the captain needed local charts and expertise.

A simple glance at a map of the Caribbean gives an instant impression of the difficulties of sailing through those waters. The region consists of thousands of islands, islets, keys, and mere dots of land which form a great 2,000-mile chain that arcs from Cuba to Trinidad. The Bahamas (not strictly part of the Caribbean) similarly consist of hundreds of other islands (thousands if we include the sand banks and cays that simply jut out of the ocean). Postlethwayt's map of the region included an inset in the Bahamas describing local cays as "small rocky Islands with ouzey Shores, where Boats or little Sloops, if run aground can easily run off."[17] Here was an enormous expanse of ocean – a critical area for ships sailing between North America and the Caribbean – which invited disasters. The Bahamas attracted resident 'wreckers': ships that cruised the waters looking for any profitable salvage that might come their way when they chanced upon a new shipwreck. Olaudah Equiano was a famous example of a shipwrecked victim in the Bahamas, finally rescued by the crew of a small hoy. The roving 'wrecker,' a salvage ship, was already packed with survivors of a wrecked whaling ship. The rescue ship, teeming with survivors both from the whaler and from Equiano's ship the *Nancy*, was itself almost lost to a sudden storm as it headed to New Providence.[18]

Storms apart, among the myriad islands of the Caribbean and the Bahamas it was easy to mistake one small island for another, or to confuse a point on one island for that on a different island. Someone on board the *Zong* confused reference points on Jamaica and St. Domingue (Haiti), with the infamous murderous results. Such difficulties, common to all sailing ships, were made worse by death and disease on the slave ships. When experienced sailors and navigators died on the Atlantic crossing (as many did), navigation fell into inexperienced hands, and the ship's navigational problems multiplied, compounding existing dangers and risks. In 1738 the Dutch slave ship *Leusden*, sailing to Surinam, was driven onto inshore rocks in a storm: the crew and 14 Africans survived – but 702 slaves perished.[19] As late as 1838 an 'illicit' Spanish ship was wrecked on the Pedro shoals south of Jamaica; 300 Africans died.[20]

Ships leaving the Caribbean and traveling north towards the Bahama chain thence to North America could take a number of routes. The most common was the Windward Passage between Santo Domingo and Puerto Rico and is one of the most notoriously difficult sailing passages, characterized by sudden and unpredictable shifts of currents and winds. The entire region is plagued by a number of natural hazards, on land and at sea. The hurricane season was only the most spectacular danger facing ships transporting Africans into the region and shipping slave-grown produce to the markets of Europe and North America.

Sailing through the Caribbean Sea was a dangerous task even for the most experienced and alert navigator. When danger loomed – an attack, a navigational error, a devastating storm and impending disaster – the Africans were abandoned to their fate. All the evidence suggests that the crew feared the ranks of Africans as much as the weather: freeing the Africans, in the course of a shipwreck, would merely multiply the dangers facing the crew. Thus, the Africans remained locked in, entombed below deck, to await a terrible fate.

In addition to these natural dangers, there lurked the unpredictable threats of piracy and wartime disruption. Caribbean islands switched national hands in the process of the prolonged wars that characterized the 18th century, and vessels had to be alert not to fall victim to enemy navies and privateers. Wartime attacks at sea endangered crew and slaves alike, as competing European maritime powers fought for imperial possessions and all the hardware – including ships – that went with them. The 244 Africans already on board the Dutch slaver the *Zorgue* (and renamed the *Zong*), found themselves transferred to British control when the vessel was seized by a British warship, part of struggle between the British and the American colonists and their European friends – with all the disastrous consequences that followed.[21]

When Africans landed in the Americas, they must have felt that their seaborne torments were over. Many, however, were simply transferred from one ship to another. Sometimes Africans traveled onward relatively small distances: from Martinique to Guadeloupe, for example. Others, however, endured prolonged onward journeys. The small Dutch islands, notably Curacao, became major transit points for Africans changing vessels and being shipped to other Caribbean destinations. Spanish colonies in particular relied on other nations to provide their African labor force, and huge numbers of Africans were transferred to Spanish colonies via other islands, notably Jamaica, Curacao, and Barbados. Some, having endured massive sea journeys, were then marched enormous distances, across South America, to Bolivia, Peru, and Chile. The precise figures for these onward movements of Africans remain uncertain, but we know that 1,679,000 Africans were shipped to a new destination *after* their initial arrival in the Caribbean. In total 21,525 Africans eventually found themselves in North America, having first landed in the Caribbean.[22]

The seven major American destinations for Africans (Rio, Salvador, Kingston, Recife, Barbados, Havana, and St. Domingue's Cap-Français) were also transit points from where Africans were moved on, to other locations.[23] Many of course simply trekked into the interior of the colony, on a Caribbean island, in North America, or Brazil. Others found themselves in smaller vessels heading along rivers and waterways towards a final destination (unknown to them, of course). Some found themselves back at sea, trans-shipped from one island to another, or sailing on to a more distant location. Some locations were too remote, or their demand for slaves too small, to sustain a direct trade from Africa, and instead they acquired Africans who were transferred from other, major ports. The numbers involved were huge: perhaps one quarter of all Africans landing in the Americas were shipped on again, sometimes on journeys that lasted longer than the Atlantic crossing itself.[24] All this, on ships, river craft, or by foot reinforces the sense that the trade in Africans forms one of history's most remarkable, and most remarkably punishing, mass movements of people before the modern era.

We know in great detail the story of this enforced mass movement of Africans, from the African coast to the Africans' final destination in the Americas (which all too often was soon their final resting place). But we need also to add to the epic geography of their travels an element which is much less well known: the Africans' movement *to* the Atlantic coast. The *total* journey, from the Africans' initial point of capture in Africa (generally far from the Europeans' gaze or knowledge), is to be counted at best in many months, at worst, in years. Each stage, but especially the protracted seaborne nightmare, took a savage toll on all concerned. In addition to those who did not survive the Atlantic crossing, every African endured incalculable distress, from the crossing, and from the overland travels in Africa and the Americas. The immensity of those travels can be captured, after a fashion, by a glance at a map. But any map – 18th century or modern – is merely a signpost to a much deeper story. The maps provide no more than a skeletal framework for a monumental saga of human suffering.

* * *

The maps of the Americas tucked into the back of Malachy Postlethwayt's volumes are, for obvious reasons, more detailed that those of Africa. Whereas Europeans merely clung to the Atlantic coast of Africa, by the mid-18th century they had taken major strides to settle and contain large tracts of the Americas. Even so, the European presence was thinly settled: on the coastlines, and along the waterways and rivers which led deep into the interiors of North and South America. Postlethwayt's map of North America was marked overwhelmingly by outlines of mountains, lakes, and rivers, but scattered with the names of Indian settlements or areas of Indian dominance – and a few European communities. Some of the most deceptive (but revealing) details are about the fishing grounds located far to the north, close to the shoreline of Newfoundland and Nova Scotia. At first sight they do not seem linked to the world of Atlantic slavery. In fact the fisheries of the North Atlantic, the Grand Banks and a collection of some twenty other fishing banks, were important economic assets which represented a key negotiating issue in the Peace Treaty of 1763.[25] Spanish fishermen had been among the first to exploit the natural riches of the North Atlantic and had developed a large fishing industry on the Grand Banks, processing the fish on the nearby coasts. Cod was in such abundance that the fishermen could hardly cope with their voluminous catches.[26] The saltfish produced there was shipped back to the consumers of Spain (and elsewhere in Europe) but also transported south, to feed the slave populations of the Caribbean. By the mid-18th century barrels of saltfish proved ideal for feeding the armies of slaves in the Caribbean. (Following the introduction of the African ackee in the 1720s, the two came together to form what is, today, a national Jamaican dish – ackee and saltfish; the one from Africa, the other from Newfoundland.) Cod, fished from the Grand Banks then gutted, salted, and dried on the coast of

Newfoundland, thus became an essential feature of the slave diet in the Caribbean. Hence the fishing grounds located to the far north, and apparently unrelated to the maritime ebb and flow of the Atlantic slave system, were important assets for those nations keen to sustain their enslaved populations in the tropical colonies, working to produce important export crops.

* * *

Until winter sets in, the St. Lawrence River forms a major route into the northern heartlands of America. Similar arteries were available along the other great rivers of the eastern seaboard. People and goods traveled along the Hudson, Delaware, Susquehanna, and Ohio rivers, and via the complex system which fed into the Chesapeake Bay and the waterways leading inland from Charleston. Most memorable of all, of course, were the routes north from the Gulf of Mexico, up the Mobile and the mighty Mississippi, thence deep into the distant heart of the continent.

Like the Atlantic Ocean itself, these major rivers, and the smaller systems that fed into them, offered pathways to distant places. Until the coming of the railways, it was the rivers and waterways (and coastal waters) of North America (what became the USA) which were the key routes along which people traveled, migrated, and traded. It is true that in places, Europeans had also penetrated into Africa along the rivers, but there the problems they faced were not so much physical obstacles as medical, and the inroads of African tropical disease. But there, and in the Americas, all this had to be explored, charted, and mapped: transforming the natural, physical world into graphic and cartographical format. The waterways of the Americas were also vital in the history of slavery. They not only delivered Africans to their new homes but were equally essential for the movement and export of slave-grown produce. Throughout the Chesapeake, slaves loaded tobacco at the water's edge onto ocean-going ships, or transferred it to those vessels from smaller boats. Logging gangs of slaves, felling huge mahogany trees in Cuba, Jamaica, and the Mosquito Coast, dragged the timbers to the water's edge, whence they were floated downstream, to vessels destined for British and North American markets (see Chapter 4). Most striking of all in the course of the history of US cotton after 1800 were the river systems of the Mississippi Delta. Millions of tons of cotton from the slave plantations of the US South were transported by the steamboats and barges which plied their trade: along the rivers of the Delta.

The extraordinary rise of American cotton in the early 19th century was made possible by yet another mass movement of slaves. This time, however, it was not from Africa, but from within the USA itself, from the old slave states, to the new boom-ing cotton-based states of the 'Cotton Belt.' The phrase 'sold down the river' belongs to this era, when upward of one mil-lion people traveled along *internal* US slave trade routes to work as cotton slaves. They traveled by sea (from Norfolk to New Orleans, for instance), by steamboat up the Delta (boats which totally transformed the society and economy of the USA before the coming of the railways), or overland, from North Carolina to Alabama. Here was yet another massive movement of people of African descent, this time to revive North American slavery itself. Slaves worked the land, and steamboats removed the cot-ton they cultivated. In 1817 there were only 17 steamboats in the region. By mid-century there were 700. In 1813, 21 steam-boats delivered 70,000 tons of freight to New Orleans: by 1860 more than 1,500 steamboats shipped two million tons of cotton valued at $2 billion.[27]

By then, the city of Liverpool, the late 18th-century capital of Britain's slave trading empire, had become the major *entrepôt* for American slave cotton. Indeed, 80% of Britain's imported cotton, before 1860, was slave grown and Liverpool's merchants and shippers prospered on the back of it. So, too, did the Lancashire textile region. Liverpool and Manchester, so often rivals today, were drawn together in the early 19th century by mutual economic interests. Manchester, the first city of the industrial revolution (and that meant cotton), needed the port of Liverpool for its imported raw cotton, and for the export of finished textiles which then traveled to all corners of the globe on Liverpool ships.

Imported slave-grown cotton and exported textiles defined Manchester and American slave cotton was the basis for the Lancashire textile industry, and therefore a major element in Britain's industrial system. In 1860, half a million people worked in Britain's cotton mills, and close to 4 million people (one-fifth of Britain's working population) worked directly or indirectly in the cotton industry.[28] In 1860, Britain exported goods to the value of £164 million. Of that, £55 million was accounted for by cotton textiles. In 1800, Britain imported just over 16 million pounds of cotton from the USA (28% of the imported total). On the eve of the Civil War, the USA accounted for 88% of Britain's imports of cotton – a grand total of 1,230,607,000 pounds.[29] These astonishing figures were, naturally, reflected in the transformation of shipping in and out of Liverpool. The volume of goods leaving Liverpool in 1801 stood at 459,719 tons. Sixty years later it had risen to 4,977,272 tons. In the late 18th century, Liverpool ships had carried one African in five across the Atlantic. Now, its ships thrived on the industry made possible by slaves working on cotton plantations of the US South. Yet when Postlethwayt published a 1763 map of Britain, the port of Liverpool (named 'Leverpool' on the map) seemed merely another of Britain's ports, its name writ small onto the map itself.

More significant still, Manchester did not even appear on Postlethwayt's mid-18th century map.[30] Yet a century later, it had become *the* city of the industrial revolution, thriving, expanding, and making a global name for itself as the manufacturing hub of cheap textiles. What is easy to overlook, however, is Manchester's link to slavery. The city had become one axis in a new commercial and trading system which, like the Atlantic trading system of the 18th century, hinged on slavery. Transported Africans produced crops – primarily sugar – which were shipped from the Americas to Europe to satisfy an expanding market for sweetness in a wide variety of drinks and foods. Now armies of plantation slaves toiled across the US South to produce astonishing volumes of cotton destined for European markets. That cotton was initially packed onto the latest and most powerful machines to date: the steamboats, whose revolutionary significance has, again, often been overlooked. Their powerful technology was well in advance of the technology at work in the cotton mills in the north-east of the USA, most dramatically in the cotton town of Lowell, Massachusetts, or in Lancashire.[31] The massive new mills in Lowell were the largest integrated mills in the world (though based on Lancashire designs) and by mid-century, 52 mills employed 10,000 workers (many of them, as in Lancashire, young women and girls.[32]) That cotton, trans-shipped in the Gulf ports (and in Charleston), was then transported direct to Europe or, as likely, to New York for yet another transfer, this time to transatlantic ships heading for Liverpool (and other European ports). But who, even today, thinks of slavery when considering the industrial revolution, and the rise of British and American industrial, commercial and global power? Who makes the link between Lancashire's textiles and the descendants of Africans toiling in the slave South? Slave-grown cotton, like slave-grown sugar, had incalculable consequences. But few were as disastrous as those endured by the Africans and their descendants.

Manchester hardly mattered in the mid-18th century. Map-makers could ignore it – leave it off their maps of Britain – because it was of little importance. But maps which excluded Manchester included key locations on the African coast and in the recently settled Americas. They even cited parts of the oceans: the fishing grounds of Newfoundland, for example, were more important than Manchester in the 1760s. So, too, were the slave settlements scattered among the colonies of North America, the Caribbean, and Brazil. Even the Atlantic winds and currents attracted greater cartographical prominence than Manchester. But all that changed – and quickly. No map of Britain in the early 19th century could ignore the city. It was the future. Yet even Manchester continued to rely, in ways we often overlook, on slave labor in the Americas. Slavery continued to cast a long shadow over the Western world.

Notes

1. The Dictionary was published in parts, 1751–1755, and then in four subsequent editions to 1774. I have used the 1766 edition, housed in the Special Collection of the Rockefeller Library, Colonial Williamsburg. Malachy Postlethwayt, *The Universal Dictionary of Trade and Commerce*, 3rd edn., 2 vols., London, 1766.
2. 'Africa.' In *The Universal Dictionary*, vol. I.
3. *A New and Correct Map of the Coast of Africa from Cape Blanco…to the Coast of Angola*. This includes an inset map 'A Separate Map of the Gold Coast.' In *The Universal Dictionary*.
4. Malachy Postlethwayt, vol. II , 'A New and Correct Map of the Coast of Africa….' Point 20.
5. David Eltis and David Richardson, *Atlas of the Transatlantic Slave Trade*, New Haven, 2010, Table 5, p. 90.
6. Malachy Postlethwayt, vol. II, Africa, Plate First. 'The Northwest part.'
7. Malachy Postlethwayt, vol. II, Plate IV. 'The Southeast part.'
8. 'The Gold Coast,' A Separate Map of the Gold Coast,' Malachy Postlethwayt, vol. II.
9. We know of only one slave ship conquered by Africans and then sailed safely to port. See Greg Grandin, *The Empire of Necessity*, New York, 2014.

10. Dennis Reinhartz, *The Art of the Map: An Illustrated History*, New York, 2012, p. 42.
11. Eric Robert Taylor, *If We Must Die: Shipboard Insurrections in the Era of the Atlantic Slave Trade*, Baton Rouge, 2009.
12. Dennis Reinhartz, *The Art of the Map*, p. 52.
13. Marcus Rediker, *The Slave Ship: A Human History*, London, 2007.
14. Inset 'A Separate Map of the Gold Coast.' In *A New and Correct Map of the Coast of Africa...*, Malachy Postlethwayt, vol. II.
15. James Walvin, *The Zong: A Massacre, the Law and the End of Slavery*, London, 2011.
16. James Walvin, *Crossings: Africa, the Americas and the Atlantic Slave Trade*, London, 2013, p. 98, n. 23.
17. Malachy Postlethwayt, vol. II, Plate IV, 'The Southeast part.'
18. Vincent Carretta, *Equiano, the African: Biography of a Self-Made Man*, Athens GA, 2005, pp. 129–130.
19. James Walvin, *Crossings*, p. 98.
20. James Walvin, *Crossings*, p. 98.
21. See the account in James Walvin, *The Zong*.
22. James Walvin, *Crossings*, pp. 132–134.
23. David Eltis and David Richardson, *Atlas of the Transatlantic Slave Trade*, p. 198.
24. David Eltis and David Richardson, *Atlas of the Transatlantic Slave Trade*, pp. 198–199.
25. Malachy Postlethwayt, vol. II, 'Map of North America.'
26. Mark Kurlansky, *Cod: A Biography of the Fish that Changed the World*, London, 1998.
27. Walter Johnson, *River of Dark Dreams: Slavery and Empire in the Cotton Kingdom*, Cambridge MA, 2013, pp. 5–6; 256–257.
28. Gene Dattel, *Cotton and Race in the Making of America*, Chicago, 2009, p. 36.
29. Gene Dattel, *Cotton*, p. 37.
30. 'A Correct Map of Europe,' by Thomas Kichin, Geographer, in Malachy Postlethwayt, vol. I.
31. Walter Johnson, *River of Dark Dreams*, pp. 6–7.
32. Sven Beckert, *Empire of Cotton: A New History of Global Capitalism*, London, 2014, pp. 147; 407.

7

A Portrait
Pictures in Black and White

From his base in Boston, John Singleton Copley (1738–1815) established his name as one of the great portrait painters of colonial America. After a year studying in Italy, Copley moved to London in 1775. Thereafter, his portraits of the good and the great, and his ability to capture major historical moments (at a time when the British were at their peak of 18th-century imperial pride), brought him great success. In America and Britain, Copley's portraits captured the luxuries and costly artifacts enjoyed by powerful and newly enriched people of substance who surrounded themselves with the best of contemporary taste and fashion. In London he painted eminent people draped in the costly clothes and uniforms of the powerful, often surrounded by classical reminders of their claims to historical importance. Admirals and generals, peers, politicians, and judges, all and many similar are presented in sumptuous pictorial likeness in Copley's portraits.[1] One of them was William Murray, 1st Earl of Mansfield, the Lord Chief Justice, painted by Copley in 1783. Mansfield is shown surrounded by the full panoply of his legal authority. Wrapped in a lavish red gown with mink trimmings and sporting an elaborate legal wig, with frilled cuffs round his wrists, Lord Mansfield is seen clutching a

Slavery in Small Things: Slavery and Modern Cultural Habits, First Edition. James Walvin.
© 2017 John Wiley & Sons, Inc. Published 2017 by John Wiley & Sons, Inc.

legal document in his left hand, his right arm stretched across a table teeming with legal books and papers.[2] The most casual of glances leaves no doubt that here was a man of substance and great importance: a man who seemed to hold the very law in his hand. In that same year, 1783, the Lord Chief Justice was called upon to make a judgment in a case, about the slave ship, *Zong*, that proved infamous even in the history of Atlantic slavery.[3]

Mansfield had established his fame, both before and after his elevation to Lord Chief in 1755, as a master of the complexities of English law. He drove through a long overdue modernization of the law and its often arcane processes, and had developed a specialized expertise in the convoluted difficulties of commercial law, notably the law of insurance. All this at a time when overseas trade and maritime commerce were expanding globally at an astonishing rate, with intricate and sometimes curious effects for the law itself.[4] Nowhere was this more obvious (and legally complicated) than in the story of the Atlantic slave trade. A number of major slave-related cases came before English courts in the course of the 18th century, and it was inevitable that Mansfield would be called upon to make judgment on the legal complications raised by the slave trade.

Of all the cases which came before Mansfield, two stand out. In the Somerset Case of 1772 the core issue was the question of slavery in England: could a slave owner remove an enslaved person, against his/her wishes, from England, back to the slave colonies of the Americas? The *Zong* case of 1783, grotesque and inhuman, raised the question of whether the cost of Africans, killed when jettisoned from an English slave ship, should be borne by the insurers or by the ship's owners? Mansfield's handling of both cases was beadily scrutinized by Granville Sharp, who was among the first to agitate for an end to the slave trade, and who was keen to give wide publicity to the murderous inhumanity involved. Sharp was an adept publicist, and broadcast the details of the killings on board the *Zong* throughout England's political and social elites. As a result, Mansfield found himself subject to the kind of adverse publicity he clearly did not like, not least because his support for Roman Catholics had infuriated the London mob as recently as 1780. In the Gordon Riots of that year, the mob proceeded to torch Mansfield's elegant town house in Bloomsbury Square. His library, legal papers, judicial dress, and wig had been tossed into the street and burned. A chimney sweep danced before the mob dressed in one of Lady Mansfield's dresses. Along with the house, a priceless library of more than one thousand books (many of them autographed editions by contemporary authors), along with two hundred books filled with Mansfield's trial notes, were destroyed. It was a devastating personal (and historical) loss.[5] The fury of the mob – and the terror of respectable society – remained vivid sixty years later and became the center of Charles Dicken's novel *Barnaby Rudge: A Tale of the Riots of '80.*

Lord and Lady Mansfield narrowly escaped the mayhem, beating a retreat to their beautiful rural home at Kenwood (originally Caen Wood) on Hampstead Heath. At the time Hampstead was far from the city, and Kenwood House stood in rural isolation, commanding a splendid view south towards St. Pauls. Waiting for the fleeing Mansfields was a coterie of relatives and servants who lived at Kenwood, among them Dido Elizabeth Belle. She was a great niece of the Mansfields, and she presented an individual (and very beautiful) example of the complexities of slavery, right under Mansfield's roof.

Belle's mother was an African slave, her father an officer in the Royal Navy. We know very little about Belle, and for years our main source of information about her was her portrait which is periodically hung in Kenwood House, but which normally resides at the Mansfields' ancestral home in Scone, Scotland. Previously thought to be a painting by Zoffany, Belle's portrait is, at one level, just one of many which captured the black presence in Europe in the era of Atlantic slavery. Like so many others, it is a painting which reveals a person of African descent in the company of a white person. But Belle's portrait was very different from many of the other portraits of black people.

The Kenwood/Scone painting is a joint portrait of two young women who lived in Mansfield's home. At the center of the portrait is Lady Elizabeth Murray, Mansfield's great niece, raised at Kenwood from childhood after the death of her mother. The other, a black woman, was initially thought to be a household domestic. However, the sumptuousness of her dress and jewelry, and her coquettish pose in the picture, clearly suggest an altogether different rank. The two women were in fact related, to each other and to Lord Mansfield. They were, in effect, surrogate daughters for the childless Mansfields. Though Belle's background was very different from that of Lady Elizabeth Murray, her origins were not uncommon in the world of Atlantic slavery. Born about 1763, Belle's father was Sir John Lindsay, a captain in the Royal Navy, and the son of Mansfield's sister. Belle's mother was an African slave. In the slave islands, white men (planters, their employees, officials, and the military) were greatly outnumbered by slaves, and with few available white women, those men inevitably turned to African women for partners. Whatever the nature of those relationships (and they ranged from the most brutal and exploitative through to a lifetime's mutual affection), the results were generations of children born to white fathers and African slave mothers. What made Belle unusual was that she found a home with England's Lord Chief Justice.[6]

The most striking and visible feature of Belle's portrait is her beauty. Although she stands slightly off-center, to the left of the portrait, she is the one who catches the eye. Her finger points to her face, as if to invite the viewer to study her closely. She is dressed in dazzling satin fabric, her décor completed by a string of pearls, ear-rings, and an attractive headdress embellished with what look like precious stones. Her companion in the portrait also wears a string of pearls, and is dressed in an equally alluring pink dress. She – not Belle – is definitely center-stage: the prime object of study and the person we are supposed to look at immediately. Yet it is Belle, to the side, who catches the viewer's attention today.

For more than a century it was thought that one woman was handmaiden to the other: black servant to a white mistress. The way the two women are arranged in the picture underlines that relationship: the white woman is central, the black women marginal, yet the two women had been raised together as little girls in Mansfield's home. They were cousins, but we now know that their relationship was more complex than that. Lord Mansfield was clearly fond of Belle, increasingly so as he aged, and especially after the death of his wife in 1784, and the marriage and departure of Elizabeth Murray the following year. Thereafter, Belle cared for the aging judge, and he rewarded her in his will. For all that, she posed tricky social problems for fashionable society, even in so elevated a household as Mansfield's Kenwood House. Belle was both illegitimate and black, and in a society with sharp attitudes to status (and race), her rank was confused.

There were, of course, plenty of black servants in fashionable 18th-century European households, but Belle was no ordinary servant. Though her mother was enslaved, her father was a prominent sailor, born to parents from two major Scottish clans, and closely related to the Mansfields. He sent his daughter to Kenwood where she became the childhood and early adult companion of Lady Elizabeth Murray (whose own mother had died). The Mansfields were in effect fostering their relatives' children, though Belle's position was unusual. She did not dine with the family, instead joining the company after dinner (presumably eating with other servants). Periodically, however, she was included in the wider family circle at social events: visitors thought she was part of the everyday routines of household life. She also worked in and around Kenwood, taking charge of the dairy and managing the poultry. Eventually she cared for Lord Mansfield in his last years. Despite these chores, she joined guests for coffee after dinner, and walked together with women of the house round the grounds, as an equal. It would have been inconceivable that other servants enjoyed the same social privileges with their master and mistress. It was, then, clear enough that Belle's role and position was special, and that she and Mansfield were extremely fond of each other. Just like father and daughter.

Through all the years these two people – the Lord Chief Justice and the young woman of African descent – spent in each other's company, Mansfield was periodically concerned with the legal problems spawned by slavery. Was slavery legal in England? What rights did black people enjoy in England (as opposed to the slave colonies)? Were Africans on slave ships mere cargo and chattel (like other items in the cargo) to be disposed of as circumstance demanded, or should they be treated *as people*? And what compensations should be paid to slaves whose rights had been denied or refused (when, for example, husbands and wives had been separated and sold against their wishes)? In the very years when Mansfield was pondering these and similar weighty questions, when he had to make decisions which might strike at the material well-being of the entire slave empire, Belle lived under his roof: a single, living reminder of the issues he had to resolve.

It was clear enough (certainly to Mansfield himself) that the legal problems around slavery, in England, on the high seas, and in matters of commercial law, had not been fully resolved. (As late as 1834, 49 people claimed to be held as slaves in England.[7])

And if any evidence confirms that slavery continued to trouble Mansfield it was his will, drafted in April 1783. Then, and in the subsequent nineteen codicils he added over the following decade (he died aged 88 in 1793), he made financial provision for Belle. She received £100 a year for life (another lump sum of £500 was added in 1786), sums that were very similar to the money bequeathed to other close servants. Mansfield's most trusted manservant and accountant, for example, received £1000 and an annuity of £500. There was, then, nothing lavish or extraordinary about Belle's inheritance from Lord Mansfield. Critically, in what is surely an important move, Mansfield made sure Belle was *free*.

I confirm to Dido Elizabeth Belle her freedom.[8]

Why would Mansfield, a stickler for legal precision and niceties, so much as *mention* Belle's freedom, unless there were some doubt about it? Despite his own judgments – especially in the Somerset case of 1772, which was widely but wrongly assumed to outlaw slavery in England – Mansfield realized that the legality of slavery in England was not a clear-cut case. As long as slavery existed in the American colonies, and as long as British slave ships continued to ferry huge numbers of Africans into bondage in the Americas, small numbers of Africans would continue to arrive in England and Scotland *as slaves*. True, after the 1772 Somerset decision, black people living in England took matters into their own hands by simply walking away from their owners, securing their freedom among friends and sympathizers, especially in London. Nonetheless, violations of black freedom periodically took place. To ensure than Belle did not fall into a similar legal morass, the Lord Chief Justice guaranteed her freedom. It was to be a further forty years before Britain emancipated slaves throughout the British Empire.

In December 1793 (eight months after Mansfield's death), Belle married a Mr. Davinier in fashionable St. George's church, Hanover Square. Both bride and groom were registered as resident in the parish. Twin boys were born a year later (one survived) and a second son was born in 1800. Belle died in 1804 as Mrs. John Davinier and was buried in St. George's graveyard. Her husband later remarried and eventually returned to his native France. (Their last known descendant died in South Africa in 1975.)

Belle's grave, along with many others in St. Georges' graveyard, was removed in the 1970s as part of a redevelopment of the Bayswater area of London, and we do not know where her mortal remains now lie. In that she finally shared the fate of millions of others. Africans and their off-spring, born in the Americas who were consigned to unknown graves: mere human flotsam and jetsam of a brutal slaving system, cast ashore in the Americas and beyond, their lives and deaths unremarked except in the account books of the slave traders and planters. Along with only a handful of the millions of Africans transported, however, Belle is remembered primarily because we have her portrait. She and others were preserved for posterity by having their faces and persons captured on canvas. We now remember Belle because of her famous patron and relative. But she was only one of numerous African people who, over the centuries, found their way into European portraits and images. Belle's picture takes us into a broader story of Africans in Western art.

Long before the development of the Atlantic slave trade, Africans had been familiar in Europe, and had regularly appeared in contemporary imagery.[9] Commerce and empires around the Mediterranean had long used links to the trans-Saharan routes (many of which were slave based) and Africans traveled, as slaves, to the heart of Western Europe. Roman legions, for example, had scooped up manpower from the far edges of that vast empire – including Africa. But the story of this black presence in Europe changed dramatically in the 15th century. As European maritime nations began to explore the West African coastline, as they settled the Atlantic islands, and established direct maritime trading links to Africa, more and more Africans found their way to Europe itself. Ground-breaking Portuguese traders and explorers returned to Europe with the exotic produce and commodities of Africa: they also returned with enslaved Africans acquired in routine trade, via exchange and barter for goods on the Atlantic coast. The Portuguese led the way, not only in slave trading on the African coast, but in shipping enslaved Africans back to Europe. In August 1444, for example, about 250 manacled Africans were landed at Lagos in the Algarve – for sale.[10] By 1500, upward of 1,500 Africans had been landed in Lisbon for onward movement and sale to markets in the Mediterranean.[11] Africans were slotted into distinctive social and economic roles in Europe, especially in Portugal, though this intrusion of African slaves into various European societies created a perplexing mix of legal issues. As early as 1548, the High Court of Admiralty in London had to determine whether the evidence of Jack Francis, 'an infidel,' was permissible in an English court. Francis was the African diver – and slave – owned by an Italian merchant commissioned to discover the wreck of the *Mary Rose*. The court determined that Francis's word was as good as a Christian's.[12] By then, African laborers, servants, and court employees were to be found scattered across Europe, but especially in Portugal. Their presence reinforced a complexity of European stereotypes, mainly about color, about African nakedness, and African 'heathenism,' all of which drew on ancient and traditional cultural values about color and human rank that reached back centuries. It was, however, this *living* black presence in Europe which gave substance and solidity to those views, and which formed the basis for the many toxic attitudes which emerged in succeeding centuries.

The early African arrivals were objects of great curiosity. Contemporaries described their physical appearance, their markings and scarring, their clothing and decorations. Africans who now found themselves living and working in Europe were notable above all for their visual exoticism. Here were black people effectively marooned in white communities: small numbers of Africans in a sea of white faces. And this is how contemporary artists captured them, in their various roles: exotic black individuals who stood out from the crowd for the most obvious of visual distinctions. They were black in a world that was white. Their presence offered scope for Europe's elites to make play of the color (and cultural) differences, using Africans both to reflect European power and wealth and to give contrast to their own self-images of beauty and splendor. This was a theme that was to characterize the graphic portrayal of black people in Europe for centuries afterwards: they could be presented as a reflection of the wealth of the people who owned and employed them and at the same time represent the polar opposite of prevailing concepts of beauty and charm.

Africans quickly found their way into all corners of fashionable Portuguese life, in palaces and courts where they worked as servants, pages, cooks, and domestics. In 1526, for instance, King João III gave his queen an enslaved black pastry chef. In her turn, the queen gave black slaves as gifts to her friends and favorites.[13] Artists naturally made the most of Africans working in a host of eye-catching capacities. And Africans thus became an established image in European art, not merely as an artistic device, but as a reflection of the social reality of European courtly circles.

Sometimes, Africans were portrayed with the markings and facial scarring of their African origins. More often, however, they found themselves draped in new European attire and styles. They entered European iconography as kings (in scenes of the adoration of the Magi) and in other biblical settings and stories. Few artists used them to greater effect than Veronese (1528–1588) in his representation of the opulence of Renaissance Venice. He depicted Africans as a child in *The Miracle of St. Barnabas* (1565–1570), and again in *The Martyrdom of St. George* (c. 1565). We also find Africans in Veronese's *The Finding of Moses* (1575–1580), and African kings similarly appeared in his *Adoration of the Kings* (1573). More commonly, though, Africans were portrayed in simple, representational form, bedecked with jewels and with the refinements of people who worked in elite and courtly circles. Elaborate clothing and styles were of course a reflection of their master's or owner's status, rather than the Africans' own wealth and rank. Yet many Africans came from the gold belt of West Africa, and it was striking that many of them were painted wearing items of gold in Renaissance Europe. Nonetheless, however high the Africans' rank in their homelands, they entered Europe as unfree people, and were accordingly given the badge and trappings of slavery. We sometimes see them clad in leg irons and metal collars.

Africans were frequently shown laughing: an early example of a persistent image – the amiable, carefree person whose innocent folly was to become one of the most persistent caricatures in Western culture for centuries to come. Laughter was a suggestion of the Africans' lack of civility, one of the distinguishing features which distanced them from sophisticated Europeans. This, along with the view that Africans were promiscuous and not bound by prevailing European conventions of sexual and family behavior, occur time and again in commentary and portraits. Paintings also depicted them as indolent: people who would never work unless compelled to, a theme which was, again, to become basic to the institution of slavery and how to manage it. African slaves would only work under duress. Compulsion, in all its forms, from brute violence to cajoling and persuasion, was the necessary ingredient in Atlantic slavery. This caricature is to be seen, from the 16th century onward, in the way artists portrayed Africans living in Europe.

Despite the fact that the majority of Africans shipped into early modern Europe worked as laborers at various manual tasks, contemporary painters were struck more by their role as favorites and pets of Europe's royals and wealthy. Africans appeared as horsemen, swordsmen, swimmers, and divers and, most striking of all perhaps, as musicians. Trumpeters and drummers, in royal courts and military groups, dressed in elaborate finery, can be found in written accounts and pictures from as far afield as Scotland, Italy, and Spain. Africans were also used as court dancers, where, again, they were striking because of their exotic difference. Europeans liked the way African dance differed from its more sedate European counterparts, and Europeans widely assumed that Africans had a natural instinct and propensity to dance, and to dance in ways that were quite alien to Europeans. From the early days of the black presence in Europe, Europeans also believed that Africans were naturally musical, and that they expressed themselves through music-making and dance. Here was another early theme that was to persist to modern times. In essence it was an aspect of the broader relegation of Africans to a species of mankind that was utterly different from white people: different and greatly inferior. They were ignorant, illiterate, pagan – but good at music. Even Africans with high status (kings and ambassadors, for example) who visited Europe in the pre-modern world, though accorded the respect demanded by their position, were ultimately consigned to an inferior rank – thanks to their blackness.

* * *

All the major and aspiring European slave-trading powers became hosts to African visitors and settlers, and naturally those Africans were described in contemporary written and printed materials, social commentaries, and legal records, in verse, prose, and in theater. In the process, the earlier imagery of Africa and Africans, often rooted in ancient myth and fantasy, gave way to starker physical representations which people could see with their own eyes. Shakespeare had no need to reach back to the mythology of Africa when he wrote *Othello* in 1603; he had only to look at Africans living in London at the time.[14]

The black presence in Britain took longer to register than in other European nations. Though there were, as we have seen, Africans in Britain from early times, they were nothing like as numerous as Africans in Portugal, Spain, or Italy. These, after all, were the countries and city states which were the pioneers and financiers of the new seaborne trade into the Atlantic. But the rapid expansion of British trade to Africa and the Americas in the 17th century saw the growth of a significant black presence at home. That, too, was soon reflected in contemporary art. The use of black servants, common in Europe, caught on in Britain, with Africans flaunted not so much for their economic utility as for the prestige they bestowed on their employer. All this was now made easier by changes in the Americas. The rapid development of African slavery in British colonies in the Americas, especially following the introduction of tobacco cultivation in the Chesapeake and sugar throughout the Caribbean, also encouraged the widespread use of African domestic servants. Indeed, it became a caricature of colonial life that African servants catered for each and every aspect of domestic and social life of white people in the slave colonies, especially for the planter elite. From cooking to sex, from childcare to household chores, slave owners came to rely on their slave domestics, and the habit of employing black domestics inevitably found its way into graphic images, especially in the caricature and vulgar cartoons that characterized mid-and late 18th-century life.

Africans were occasionally featured in the press, and were sometimes offered for sale in English newspapers. In 1768, *The Liverpool Chronicle* offered,

> A Fine Negro Boy, of about 4 feet 5 inches high, of
> a sober, tractable, humane Disposition, Eleven or Twelve
> Years of Age, talks English very well, and can dress
> Hair in a tollerable way.[15]

The previous year, a Manchester newspaper had carried a similar advertisement, for "a Black Boy, 12 years of age, with a good character, who had had the smallpox and measles...."[16] Africans were more frequently caught in advertisements for slave runaways. This from the *London Gazette*, 1696:

> Run away from Capt. John Brookes of Barford near Salisbury,
> about the middle of August last, a middle-sized Negro Man,
> named Humphrey, aged about 30, in a dark brown Cloath
> Coat with hair Buttons....

By the late 17th century, black servants in livery were common enough to catch the eye of society gossip, and African faces began to appear in minor roles in portraits of prosperous or famous individuals and families. Such African faces on canvas (which generally remain anonymous) reflected both the ubiquity of Africans in Britain and the rank and status of the people they served and attended. These African portraits were, in human form, one aspect of changing fashion among the prosperous and governing elite. Although the custom of employing black servants was, in essence, an offshoot of what was happening in the American colonies, British royals, aristocrats, and the wealthy were emulating a social pattern long familiar to similar elites in Europe.

Painters who had captured the early African presence in royal courts, in Italy, Spain, Portugal, and the Low Countries, "transmitted this form of visual culture to their European neighbours...."[17] By the late 17th century, the relationship between white master/ mistress and black servant/slave had become an established feature of British portraiture. At its simplest it represented the social reality of life in courtly and wealthy circles, and by, say, 1700, the liveried black servant was a familiar feature of portraits hanging on the walls of the good and the great in Britain.[18]

The process was greatly helped by the royal patronage given to major European artists who were already accustomed to incorporating black people in their work. Charles I, a major patron of the arts, commissioned work by Van Dyck, Rubens, and others whose earlier work had *already* depicted black pages and servants. They in their turn had drawn on an even older Venetian tradition (best expressed by Titian), and their pupils and followers established what was quickly to become a major British tradition: portraits of local elites posing in the company of African attendants. There was a clear line of descent, from Titian through to the great British portrait artists of the 18th century (and indeed right down to the famous caricaturists of the late 18th century). It was an intellectual and artistic inheritance which embedded itself in the British cultural landscape. However, it was much more than a simple tradition handed from one generation to another. It also reflected British social life, because Africans and their local-born descendants could now be found scattered across the face of British society, and paintings portrayed the commonplace presence of black servants in prosperous and influential British households.[19]

This artistic fashion was greatly extended and promoted by artistic innovation, notably by the new trade in mezzotints, which helped to promote and expand the fashionable market for images of blacks. By the mid-18th century, however, we can begin to put names to many of the black faces lurking in the corner of such portraits. We sometimes know who they were, and how they came to be in the company of the man or woman portrayed. Dido Elizabeth Belle is, then, just one example. Like many others, she has been rescued from her artistic and social anonymity by careful research in recent years.

After generations of neglect, images of Africans in Western art now attract a growing and sophisticated scholarly interest. Indeed, those images have become a new prism for a fundamental reappraisal both of the specific paintings and of the world that spawned them.[20] Black children attending royals and aristocrats, and adult Africans side by side (though normally off-center), with white contemporaries remain largely anonymous, but research has sometimes restored lost names and identities. And yet, as with the millions of Africans scattered across the Americas, the anonymity of black people in British portraiture is symptomatic, and speaks to a major characteristic of African life throughout the enslaved diaspora. The very great majority of Africans had been deracinated both from their homelands and from their basic social origins. They had lost their African names, had been renamed, numbered, and named again. The importance of Africans in the slave system lay not in their names, however, but in their physical strength and endurance. Equally, what mattered in the fashionable world for which these portraits were designed was the Africans' beauty and their appeal, or the exotic contrast they offered to the subjects of the painting: black and white, domination and submission, authority and supplication. At one and the same time, such paintings presented the faces and ranks of two individuals;

white master/mistress, black servant/slave. Such individual representations could – and do – stand as a *leitmotif* for the wider world of Atlantic slavery.

The rise of British portraiture from the late 17th century onward was also a reflection of the massive expansion of British material prosperity. Ever more people were enjoying the fruits of Britain's expanding commercial and imperial wealth. The growth of trade and commerce, to and from Europe, the expansion of trade and dominion on the coast of Africa, in India, and the Americas, generated extraordinary prosperity for new commercial and trading classes. It also created unparalleled wealth among those who found their landed assets augmented by the riches from Britain's massively expanded merchant fleet. It was no accident that the elite of Caribbean planters became known as the 'plantocracy' – the name modelled around the very people (the aristocracy) whose landed and metropolitan styles the returning planters aped and adopted. Among the newly enriched, and those whose existing wealth was enhanced still further, luxury goods became symbols – the litmus test – of good taste and refinement.[21] What better way of displaying a family's status and wealth than by capturing their faces, individually or *en famille*, in a painting? Such portraits, of course, came with a specific agenda. They were intended to project not only the wealth and the status of the sitters, but, in the case of females, to present ideals of beauty. (It was to take the bravery of Velasquez and Goya to defy this trend and to paint the ugly realties of their royal Spanish sitters in the late 18th century.[22]) Women were portrayed clothed in the finest of exotic dresses and materials and lavished with dazzling jewelry – pearls were a favorite, with their traditional association with prosperity and fertility.[23] Time and again, women were pictured wearing necklaces which paralleled, in the most lavish fashion, the metal collars sometimes worn by the black slave in the portrait. In this parade of wealthy individuals no one doubted who was the dominant partner in the picture. Indeed, such portraits were designed as displays of mastery, of white over black, though that relationship might take a number of forms. This dominance could also be seen in ceramics and textiles, on trade cards, and advertisements, in commercial letterheads – even in public notices and signs. And, of course, on coats of arms. However, the dominance of white over black was best seen – at its most memorable and most costly – in the world of portraiture.

This development of British portraiture took place at a time when Britain had become the main engine behind slave trading in the North Atlantic, and when Britain was itself markedly affected by the fruits of the slave empire. The expansion of the British slave trade to the Americas took place, however, over the horizon, far from the British heartlands, and largely beyond the sight of the British themselves – (*except* of course for the thousands of sailors manning the slave ships, and those people living and working in the slave colonies). And yet, despite the vast geographic divide, few doubted the intimate involvement of Britain with the slave systems of the Americas. Anyone unaware of the intimate links between Britain and the world of slavery had only to glance at black people on the streets of Britain's major towns and cities, or at the black faces in contemporary imagery.

In the course of the 18th century, a series of distinct types emerged in the way black people were portrayed in British painting. They ranged from the parasol-bearing, dandy-like servant, the fop, through to the person exuding sexual menace. Best known, however, and most memorable, were portraits where black subjects were depicted alongside the good and the great. By the mid-18th century, however, those servants were no longer dressed as Africans. Now they appeared as black

Britons. They were dressed in contemporary Western styles and clothing. The prominent Africans who published memoirs or letters in late 18th-century Britain (and North America) chose as a frontispiece for their works images of themselves that were essentially Western. They were black, but they looked like any other person in Britain or the American colonies; wearing the clothing common among men and women of their class and status.

By the 1730s, such images of black and white captured together were no longer the monopoly of people who could afford costly portraits of themselves or their families. They now also belonged to the world of popular caricaturists, most famously William Hogarth. Hogarth's prints of contemporary London scenes regularly returned to the black presence, and he often based his images on specific places, people, and incidents. But Hogarth's blacks were not the subservient people of formal portraiture: they were disruptive and individual – people whose foibles and habits were recognizably human and normal. They also reflected the remarkable human diversity that was 18th-century London.[24] Hogarth also satirized the employment of black servants: a mocking of the social pretensions of people who wanted to enhance their own status via pictures of black servants. Hogarth's popularity and influence were enormous in his lifetime, and he established a tradition of graphic *criticism* of the employment of black servants which was to continue into the 19th century, notably by James Gillray, and Isaac and George Cruikshank. More important, perhaps, Hogarth's blacks were *different* from any who had gone before.

Despite their presence and significance, Hogarth's blacks were, until recently, virtually ignored by art historians. Today, and in common with the wider story of British black history, they are thought to represent critical issues not only in Hogarth's work but in providing an insight into London life in the 18th century. More critically, perhaps, Hogarth points to a simple truth that was too often overlooked or ignored: that a great deal of Britain's wealth in the 18th century traced its roots to the Atlantic slave empires. Today, is hard to dispute a basic but simple point, namely that there was an important link between wealth from empire and from the slave colonies, and the patronage of the domestic British arts.

It now seems obvious that blacks in 18th-century portraiture were 'figures of empire.' They were not only representations of imperial power and wealth but were the essential human constituents of that very empire. The chronology of the story offers a clue. From the 1660s onward, Africans began to appear in more and more portraits, *not* because of artistic traditions imported from Europe (though that played a role) but primarily because Europeans were shipping tens of thousands of Africans across the Atlantic as slaves. Rising prosperity at home created a growing demand for servants, and though there was no shortage of local, British-born people to train up as servants, they lacked the qualities that gave Africans their unique social cache. British servants were white and commonplace – effectively invisible. And they could not be enslaved. The American colonies established the widespread habit of using black domestic servants – who were also enslaved. Slave servants and other Africans were transported into Britain in small numbers. Thus black people became common sights on the streets, and appeared not only in portraits but in newspapers, church records, social commentary, and, most crucially, in courts of law, where runaways sought to secure their freedom, and where masters tried to maintain their grip over bonded labor. On a number of critical occasions, the one man charged with dealing with the legal ramifications of these problems was the Lord Chief Justice, Lord Mansfield. It was an extraordinary irony that, as he was pondering the problem of slavery in England and on the high seas, Dido Elizabeth

Belle, the beautiful daughter of an African slave woman, lived in his home.

Today, the portrait of Belle and her white cousin invariably prompts discussion about the beauty of the two women involved. Yet Belle's beauty (given massive, global publicity by a movie devoted to her in 2014) stands in stark contrast to the very system she had emerged from. The slave system that had brought her African mother to Jamaica, and which so haunted Lord Mansfield's courtroom, and dogged his reputation, was as ugly and repulsive as could be imagined. The portrait of Dido Elizabeth Belle stands in striking contrast to slavery itself: Belle and slavery – beauty and the beast.

Notes

1. Emily Ballew Neff, with William L. Pressley, *John Singleton Copley in England*, London, 1995.
2. William Murray, 1st Earl of Mansfield, National Portrait Gallery, London.
3. James Walvin, *The Zong: A Massacre, the Law and the End of Slavery*, London, 2011, Chapters 7–8.
4. James Oldham, *The Mansfield Manuscripts and the Growth of English Law in the Eighteenth Century*, 2 vols., Chapel Hill, NC, 1992.
5. Norman S. Poser, *Lord Mansfield: Justice in the Age of Reason*, Montreal and London, 2013, pp. 363–365.
6. Belle's portrait was even used as the front cover of a pamphlet issued by English Heritage: *The Slave Trade and Abolition*, English Heritage, 2007.
7. Simon D. Smith, 'Slavery's heritage footprint: Links between British country houses and St Vincent, 1814–1834.' In Madge Dresser and Andrew Hann, eds., *Slavery in the British Country House*, Swindon, 2013, p. 67.
8. Norman S. Poser, *Lord Mansfield*, pp. 392–393. See also Paula Byrne, *Belle: The True Story of Dido Belle*, London, 2014, pp. 170–171.
9. The full story is covered in detail in the ten volumes, *The Image of the Black in Western Art*, 10 vols., David Bindman and Henry Louis Gates, eds., Harvard University Press, Cambridge MA, 2010.
10. K.J.P. Lowe, 'Introduction.' In *Black Africans in Renaissance Europe*, T.F. Earle and K.J.P. Lowe, eds., Cambridge, 2005, p. 10.
11. Etienne Bourdue, Antonio de Almeida Mendes, et al., *La Peninsule Iberique at le monde, 1470-1650*, Neuilly, 2014, pp. 167–171.
12. James Walvin, *Crossings: Africa, the Americas and the Atlantic Slave Trade*, London, 2013, p. 15.

13. Annemarie Jordan 'Images of empire.' in T.F. Earle and K.J.P. Lowe, eds., *Black Africans in Renaissance Europe*, pp. 157–158.

14. Kathleen Chater, *Untold Histories: Black People in England and Wales during the Period of the English Slave Trade, c.1660–1807*, Manchester, 2007.

15. Gretchen Gerzina, *Black England: Life before Emancipation*, London, 1995, p. 7.

16. William E.A. Axon, *The Annals of Manchester*, Manchester, n.d., p. 97. [Available in Manchester Central Library.]

17. Catherine Molyneux, *Faces of Perfect Ebony: Encountering Atlantic Slavery in Imperial Britain*, Cambridge MA, 2012. p. 26.

18. Catherine Molyneux, *Faces of Perfect Ebony*, p. 27

19. Catherine Molyneux, *Faces of Perfect Ebony*, p. 28.

20. An important pioneer, opening up the field, is David Dabydeen, *Hogarth's Blacks: Images of Blacks in Eighteenth Century English Art*, Manchester, 1985.

21. See the essays in John Brewer and Roy Porter, eds., *Consumption and the World of Goods*, London, 1993.

22. Gwyn Williams, *Goya and the Impossible Dream*, London, 1976.

23. Catherine Molyneux, *Faces of Perfect Ebony*, p. 36

24. Vic Gattrell, *The First Bohemians: Life and Art in London's Golden Age*, London, 2014.

8

The *Brooks*
Slave Ships

In 2007, the British indulged in a prolonged and nationwide commemoration of the bicentenary of the 1807 abolition of the slave trade. Many major institutions, from parliament to the Church of England, most national galleries and museums (notably the British Museum, and the National Portrait Gallery), publishers by the dozen, the BBC, the national media, right down to small village schools, all commemorated, in their own distinctive fashion, the British ending of the slave trade. The Heritage Lottery Fund (HLF) handed out upward of £15 million, to 285 different bicentenary projects.[1] The range of projects was astonishing: from the refurbishment of Wilberforce House in Hull through to an oral history of Congolese people in Liverpool, from workshops for schools in Winchester to a project exploring links between Bexley and the slave trade. The HLF gave more than £25,000 to a project exploring the slave trade in the north-east of England, and in July that year 274 schoolchildren from the north-east donned red tee-shirts, each bearing the image of an African drawn from the 1788 picture of the slave ship, *Brooks*. They were corralled into the outline of that vessel on the Palace Green, between Durham University and the Cathedral.[2]

Slavery in Small Things: Slavery and Modern Cultural Habits, First Edition. James Walvin.
© 2017 John Wiley & Sons, Inc. Published 2017 by John Wiley & Sons, Inc.

One of the most remarkable displays of that year was the installation *La Bouche du Roi*, exhibited at the British Museum and five other British sites, but which toured a host of locations, beginning in Benin in 1999. Created by Romuald Hazoumè, it took the form of the famous 1788 image of the slave ship, the *Brooks*, but this time constructed from 302 'masks' made from petrol cans. A complex image, it represented the slave trade, modern West African petroleum, and government, and the squalid crowding – and smell – that accompanied all slave ships. As much a refrain on the problems of modern West Africa, *La Bouche du Roi* was, above all, in 2007, a stark visual and aromatic reminder of a slave ship.[3] It was, however, only the most spectacular version of an image, a picture, which dominated all other impressions of the slave trade in that year.

Certain images have been repeatedly used to convey an immediate impression of slavery and the slave trade. A chain (preferably one split asunder), a kneeling, supplicant slave (preferably with broken chains dangling from his wrists), and, more recently, a portrait of Olaudah Equiano: all these have been used, *ad nauseam*, as visual short-cuts to slavery. But *the* most visible, inescapable, and almost ubiquitous image has been that of a crowded slave ship. Most of these are versions of the original picture of the *Brooks* slave ship, first issued by Quaker abolitionists in Plymouth in November 1788.[4] Two centuries later, that image, and a myriad adaptations and versions of it, tumbled off the presses or flashed onto the computer screen. It was as if that single ship, built in Liverpool in 1781 and destined to carry more than 5,000 Africans on its eleven Atlantic crossings, represented the entire history of the slave trade itself. The *Brooks* had become the best known, most widely used, most recognized symbol of the slave trade. The original image had been designed to inform, educate – and appall. Quakers hoped it would win people over to the side of abolition by projecting the stark inhumanity of crowded slave decks. But who, among those pioneering abolitionists, could possibly have imagined that they were promoting an image that would continue to provoke, to cause outrage, and to inform opinion two centuries later? Though often used today in ways its creators could never have envisaged, the image of the *Brooks* has been more widely employed, and has developed a more popular base, than ever before. The *Brooks* has achieved a notoriety in the 21st century which it did not have even in its own time.

Designed to promote the abolition of the slave trade, the *Brooks* has lived on long after that trade vanished, revived for a host of reasons long after its initial purpose had been forgotten. The British and American abolitions of 1807–1808 did not, of course, terminate the transatlantic trade. More than four million Africans landed in Brazil *after* British and American abolition.[5] We also know that the conditions on board slave ships for Africans caught up in the 'illicit' 19th-century trade were, in many respects, *worse* than in the previous century: worse 'packing,' excessive violence (and 'jettisoning'), and, in many cases, much longer voyages (from Mozambique, for example).[6] But the potency of the *Brooks* survived – thrived even – not because of the slave trade but because it was absorbed into the world of print culture throughout the English-speaking world. As long as slavery itself survived – as it did in the USA until the Civil War – the *Brooks* was on hand to offer a simple and quick *entrée* to a broader debate.[7] Today, it is a picture which offers commercial as much as emotional appeal.

In recent versions, the *Brooks* has been used to adorn dust jackets and endpapers of books and on record sleeves. During and after 2007, the modern-day descendants of the *Brooks* appeared on posters and commercial advertisements, and were even used on a British postage stamp. Indeed that year, the *Brooks* was everywhere: it was a particular favorite for pamphlets issued by various departments of the British government.[8] In locations as far apart as Hamburg, Australia, and Rio, the *Brooks* has been adapted by artists and film-makers. It was even worked into sand models by artists on Copacabana Beach. In keeping with the digitization of the modern world, the *Brooks* can now be found on a multitude of websites: the BBC, the British Library, the US National Archives, The Royal College of Surgeons, County Archives, Museums and universities – all have used it. It has even been used, in caricature, for a commercial advertisement for vodka and (hard to believe) tastelessly employed to serve as a comparison with aircraft seating arrangements. It is, in short, inescapable: always on hand for an endless string of adaptations. Those who use it *know* that it will instantly prompt a particular memory and thought. We see the *Brooks*, and we think immediately of the pestilential horror that was the Atlantic slave trade. The *Brooks* has thus been transformed from a simple historical artifact – a stark black-and-white picture promoting a specific political campaign in the late 18th century – into a globally recognized icon of the modern world. It also attracts criticism as a tired, hackneyed image which conveys African passivity, not resistance. Even so, it is now so commonplace and recognizable that it is hard to know if anything new can be said about it.[9] Yet its origins were humble and single-minded.

Pictures of the *Brooks* were widely promoted by Quakers and the early British abolitionists, and had an immediate and stunning effect when first published in 1788. The shipboard conditions were so obviously wretched, the Africans' available space so cramped, and the condition of the Africans so vile, packed sardine-like between decks, that the picture shocked and revolted all who saw it. Yet, by the 1780s, the slave trade itself was such a major business, employing tens of thousands of people from Europe and the Americas, that the grotesque stinking reality of life (and death) for armies of Africans on the ships was no secret. Huge numbers of people were acutely well-aware of the terrifying nature of life on board a slave ship: sailors on board, the men who traded in Africans on the Atlantic coast, and others who greeted them in the Americas – the agents, merchants, planters, and officials who bought and bargained for the slaves on arrival, men who inspected the Africans (in the most hideous, intimate fashion), to say nothing of the European and American merchants and traders in a number of slave trading ports who masterminded the entire system from their distant offices. Despite all this, the early images of the *Brooks* had a profound and seismic impact among people *not* involved in the slave trade. People found the picture profoundly shocking.

Early in 1790, when Thomas Clarkson, the outstanding campaigner for British abolition, was in Paris on abolition business, he showed his picture of the slave ship the *Brooks* to the French statesman and finance minister, Jacques Necker. The Frenchman was so appalled that his instant reaction was to show the image to King Louis XVI. On reflection, however, he felt the king's health to be too delicate to be confronted by such a horrible sight.[10] Even allowing for royal sensitivities, this one incident exposes one of the most enduring qualities of the *Brooks*. It appalled as much as it informed, establishing a sense of outrage among those who saw it. Even today, the image repels. Which other picture, designed as a piece of graphic propaganda, has maintained its ability to shock for more than two centuries?

* * *

The *Brooks* was a Liverpool slave ship which, before it came to public attention, had already made four voyages to the Gold Coast between 1782 and 1787. It continued trading until 1804, making eleven slaving voyages, taking on board 5,122 Africans, and delivering 4,729 survivors (mostly to the Caribbean, with 322 to Spanish America).[11] Its wider fame, however, began in an unlikely location – Plymouth. There, in November 1788, William Elford, a banker, friend of the prime minister, and prominent member of the local branch of the Abolition Society, was instrumental in the decision to print 1,500 copies of a drawing of the *Brooks*. The original Plymouth print showed the lower deck viewed from above, along with a picture of the London abolition committee's seal, and some remarks which spelled out the ship's dimensions. The Plymouth prints were circulated across the West of England, and copies sent to London. The London committee promptly issued their own version, still based on the *Brooks*, though now with the addition of a plan of the quarter deck and a cross-section of the vessel. The London version also contained extra information about a slave ship which had been extracted from Alexander Falconbridge's *Account of the Slave Trade on the Coast of Africa*, also published in 1788. Within a year, more than 8,000 copies of this revised version had been printed, and copies were soon to be found in every city in the land; pinned up in coffee shops, on street corners, and even displayed in private homes.[12]

In the words of Thomas Clarkson, the purpose of the print was "to give the spectator an idea of the sufferings of the Africans in the Middle Passage...." The print "seemed to make an instantaneous impression of horror upon all who saw it...." The London committee, Quakers to their fingertips, also wanted precise figures – hard, statistical data – which they could use to reinforce the visual shock conveyed by the image. The exact measurements of the *Brooks* were thus provided by Capt. Parrey of the Royal Navy, who had recently been sent to Liverpool by Prime Minister William Pitt the Younger to secure the measurements of local slave ships. He inspected twenty-three vessels, took down detailed measurements of nine, and decided that, though the *Brooks* did not provide the smallest space per slave, it seemed, on the whole, to be *the* most typical slave ship.[13]

When abolitionists in London and Plymouth acquired this data, they realized it provided ideal grist to their mill. Henceforth, it was no longer a matter of offering the public, or parliamentarians, a generalized denunciation of the trade: they could simply point to the picture and to the facts and figures of this one slave ship. It was also data which could be used in a variety of ways. It was ideal for a direct appeal to the public, and it suited the arguments which abolitionists, led by William Wilberforce, were preparing to deploy in parliament itself. The *Brooks* fitted the bill in every respect. Named after its first owner, the *Brooks* was bigger than most other slave ships and had carried an average 512 Africans on her various Atlantic crossings. On the eve of the ship's public recognition and fame, the *Brooks* had transported 740 Africans to the Americas. Even by contemporary standards these were enormous numbers – with all the inevitable dangers and traumas for the incarcerated Africans. Perhaps more telling, however, is the shocking fact that these numbers were greatly in excess of the numbers allowed *after* the limitations (the ratio of Africans per ton) imposed by the Dolben Act of 1788. The familiar image of the *Brooks* – the one which has remained in the popular mind from that day, is of a human cargo *after* those restrictions had been imposed. It may be hard to imagine, but the crowded packing of Africans in the popular images we all now recognize represented an *improvement* on the grotesque scenes on board the *Brooks before* 1788.

All this evidence, factual and visual, was placed on the table in the House of Commons during the slave trade debates held between 1788 and 1789. Abolitionists had now established an irrefutable, factual, and graphic argument. The *Brooks* was no longer merely an image; it had been transformed into documented empirical evidence which was beyond dispute. This one, apparently small, example from a maritime industry which dispatched thousands of ships to the African coast, and millions of Africans across the Atlantic, represented much more than a propaganda coup by abolitionists. It formed a remarkable and qualitative *shift* in the nature of the argument. Henceforth (and thanks largely to the research and investigations of Thomas Clarkson as he trekked up and down the country, visiting ports and poring over ships' logs and muster rolls) the arguments about the slave trade were grounded in statistical evidence. The slave ships yielded abundant information. How many Africans were carried, per ton, how many perished and how many survived? All this – obvious today (indeed it is the shank of modern slave trade scholarship) – formed a new direction both in analysis and in political debate. The abolitionists had, via the *Brooks*, steered the debate into an entirely new direction. It would be wrong, however, to ignore the simplest point: the *Brooks* also served a basic, more visceral function. It showed that a slave ship was "a place of violence, cruelty, inhuman conditions and horrific death."[14]

The initial Plymouth picture had a plain, almost clinical quality to it. It was issued as a leaflet, the top portion dominated by a view looking down on 294 Africans, lying in orderly fashion, naked except for loincloths, and all separated into four different compartments (for girls, boys, women, and men). As appalling as this image clearly was (and there is abundant evidence of contemporaries reeling in shock when they first saw it), it was a mere hint of the squalid reality of life on slave ship. It offers no suggestion of the turbulence, filth, and confused squalor (to say nothing of the noise and the stink) that characterized the slave deck. But how *could* it hope to convey the presence of the human waste, the agonized shrieks of the dead and the dying, the rats, and the movement – the lurching, sliding, colliding of manacled bodies as they pitched and rolled with the vessel at sea? Still, what people saw was bad enough.

The Plymouth broadside included an inset text to support the image, providing the specific measurements and space allotted to the slaves. Here was a seaborne experience which was an apprenticeship (for the survivors) to a life of unremitting toil. It was clearly a death trap for many Africans. But the debate which swirled around the *Brooks* also proved that the slave ships, far from providing a training ground for British sailors (as proponents of the trade regularly claimed), proved fatal, for black and white alike. With all this in mind, Plymouth's abolitionists urged everyone to step forward and protest against the slave trade, and add any information they had to the cause. As keen as they were to promote abolition, the Plymouth abolitionists must have been surprised by the instant success of the *Brooks* image. It was rapidly adopted by sympathizers across Britain and had, within the year, been revised and re-issued in New York and Philadelphia. But *the* critical changes, which both enhanced and expanded the original impression, came from the work of abolitionists in London. Despite the importance of the Plymouth initiative, London was the natural home – the center – for abolitionist activity, not least because the aim was both to rally national opinion *and* to win over parliament.

The new drawings which emerged from the London abolitionists, though shaped around the Plymouth broadside, were altogether more complex and detailed. Six new images were added to the original plan of the *Brooks*, all showing cross-sections of the vessel, and each one providing even more glaring evidence of the enslaved Africans' physical torments. Not only were the Africans packed cheek by jowl, but they were penned in, beneath low shelves and decks: pressing hard against each of their neighbors, and lying below other rows of Africans stacked on shelves above them. Every sailor on a slave ship knew that, before loading newly purchased Africans at the coast, the ships' carpenters were busy creating shelves in between decks. In effect they greatly increased the space available for packing Africans by adding new, temporary storage space, in the form of racks, between decks. The new and more sophisticated drawings from London, with more revealing illustrations, were also a reflection of the greater precision that was being invested in naval architecture of the period. It was a process evidenced in the mathematical details accumulated, and then reported, by Capt. Parrey.[15]

The drawings now available formed a broader idea of what a slave ship was like. They also reflected the findings of Thomas Clarkson in and around slave ships, notably in Liverpool. The new, more complex and more revealing images of the *Brooks*, now issued from London, confirmed the impression, already forcibly established by the Plymouth broadside. Once again, leaflets of the *Brooks* provoked a sense of horror. But it was a revulsion based not solely on offended humanity but one which had been given a sharper edge because of its factual evidence. It was, in graphic form, the very essence of Thomas Clarkson's analytical approach to the slave trade. What the London abolition committee produced in their newly expanded pamphlet (with accompanying detailed textual explanation) was a vessel (its human capacity now limited by the recent Dolben Act) loaded with 482 Africans.[16] All the same, all the obvious reservations still apply: where is the filth and traumatizing terror of the *Brooks* pitching and rolling in the heaving vastness of the Atlantic? And yet who could speak of that – except the Africans who had survived it?

Nonetheless, the *Brooks* picture achieved what its promoters wanted; it shocked and galvanized people. It helped, alongside a growing barrage of literary and political propaganda, to swing opinion against the slave trade. It worked alongside Thomas

Clarkson's invaluable data, gleaned from the papers of slave ships. Clarkson's new *methodology*, of trawling through written and printed evidence then weaving it into his testimony, helped to create a damning case against the slave trade, and undermined prevailing arguments in its favor. Whatever arguments were advanced in favor of the trade, Clarkson would cite chapter and verse to challenge and disprove them. He was confronted, notably in Bristol and especially Liverpool, by dogged (and sometimes threatening) opponents. More generally, the quaysides crowded with slave ships and their attendant clatter of business offered their own daunting evidence of the importance of those ships. But Clarkson persevered. Time and again he heard telling (and generally distressing) evidence from ordinary sailors: first-hand, undeniable evidence about the trade's destructive violence (both to black and white). In 1785 alone, of 5,000 sailors who left Britain on slave ships only 2,320 returned home.[17] This and similar evidence was accumulated, stored away, and eventually brought to light in his two major tracts published in 1788 and 1789 and, finally, in his monumental history of the campaign against the slave trade.[18] Evidence from men who knew the slave ships at first hand, sailors who had endured a working life on transatlantic crossings, provided irrefutable personal confirmation of what the simple geometry of the drawings of the *Brooks* suggested.

Through all this, Thomas Clarkson emerged as the single most important contributor in the public campaign against the slave trade. He braved personal dangers, was ostracized by merchants, yet he persevered, backed by the London Abolition Society and by local Quakers across the country. (By 1794 he had traveled more than 56,300 kilometers on his abolitionist journeys.) Throughout, a steady flow of tracts, pamphlets, and articles descended on British readers, many of them using the latest evidence from Clarkson's research, and many emblazoned with

images of the *Brooks*. In 1787–1788 the Abolition Society published tens of thousands of tracts, books, reports, and papers.[19]
These publications, like Clarkson's public lectures, struck an
unexpected chord, and it soon became clear that there existed a
broad body of opinion, across different sectors of society, which
was appalled by what they learned about the slave trade. Abolitionist lecture halls were so full that Clarkson sometimes had
trouble making his way to the front to speak. Tens of thousands
of people scribbled their names onto abolition petitions (destined for parliament in the hope of winning over legislators).
By 1788, the debate about the slave trade had entered parliament. And so too did the *Brooks*, in the form of an inch-perfect
wooden model. Two models were commissioned by Clarkson,
and given to Wilberforce to use as a visual aid in the parliamentary debates.

Clarkson had traveled to Paris (with uncanny timing) in
July 1789, on behalf of the London abolition committee. He
promptly introduced himself to the French abolition society,
the *Société des Amis des Noirs*, and mixed with members of
the National Assembly, and tried to use the turmoil of those
early months of the revolution to advocate abolition of the
French slave trade. London friends sent him a packet contain-
ing, among other things, translated copies of his own writings
and more than one thousand copies of the *Brooks* print – 'with
an explanation in French.'[20] It was now the turn of French abolitionists to be shocked by what they saw. The Archbishop of Aix
was stunned into silence. Mirabeau was so startled by what he
saw that he ordered his own wooden copy to be made. "It was a
ship in miniature about a yard long, and little wooden men and
women, which were painted black to represent the slaves, were
seen stowed in their proper place."[21] Mirabeau hoped to use the
model as the center-piece of a planned speech in the Assembly calling for immediate abolition of the French slave trade.

The French slave lobby, however, managed to have that debate cancelled. In London, Wilberforce was more successful, and his model of the *Brooks* was passed round the chamber, hand to hand, as the Commons discussed abolition.

The graphic illustrations, and the wooden models in London and Paris, reveal a great deal about contemporary Western society. The extremes of shock registered (on both sides of the Channel) when people *saw* the images and model of the *Brooks* suggest a real lack of awareness – simple ignorance perhaps – about the essential nature of the slave ships. And although it is true that the mass of publications which came flying off the abolitionist presses in the same years was instrumental in whipping up a deep outrage among the literate, the *Brooks* gave that growing outrage a sharper, and a more informed, edge. However brutal and vivid the printed texts about the slave trade, pictures of the *Brooks* managed to shift the viewer's attention to a different level. Although it has been argued that the *Brooks* was, at heart, a memorial to a disastrous historical experience,[22] its consequences were invaluable and far-reaching. How else can its enduring fame be explained? The *Brooks* continues to shock, not as a memorial but as a reminder of the realities of life, suffering, and death on the slave ships.

* * *

To this day, the *Brooks* sticks in the mind as a typical slave ship, a ship that not only carried thousands of Africans to an enslaved future but exemplified tens of thousands of other vessels engaged in the same commerce. Yet to view the *Brooks* as typical is to overlook the remarkable diversity and variety of slave ships. Moreover, every vessel was a slave ship for only *one* leg of what, for many, were complicated oceanic voyages. European and American ships *became* slave ships on the coast of

Africa. They were, essentially, flexible vessels, which could be easily adapted to loading and carrying a range of different cargoes, from humans to huge hogsheads of sugar and tobacco, from wooden cases of foodstuffs to large planks of timber. They had departed from their home ports bound for Africa with conventional cargoes, just like any other merchant ship. Likewise, they returned to their home base like other merchant ship, loaded with produce and goods from the Americas, or in ballast. What we remember, however, is not their mundane, everyday trading layout, but the voyage when they were packed with Africans. The *Brooks* is *not* remembered for what it looked like leaving Liverpool, or returning from the Caribbean, but as it appeared on the voyage between Africa and the Americas.

Just as the pictures of the *Brooks* (inevitably) fail to capture the full horror of the Africans' shipboard lives, so too do they obscure the complexity of the maritime trade in the era of Atlantic slave trading. Though the *Brooks*, at 297 tons and constructed in Liverpool at the height of that city's slave trading prowess, was comparable to its local contemporaries, slave ships came in all shapes and sizes. As early as 1586 Spanish slave ships had been restricted to carrying one slave per ton: the *Brooks* carried more than twice that ratio. Some late 18th-century slave ships were giants (we know of one from Liverpool of 566 tons), but at the other extreme, we know of one ship of a mere 11 tons. In the early days of the Atlantic trade, merchants used whatever vessel was available. The Dutch, for example, employed the *flute*, a bulk carrier, in their early slave trading, though by the late 18th century they were using barks, snows, yachts, but above all small frigates – all adapted by ships' carpenters to carry Africans on the American-bound leg. Most Dutch slave ships were, in fact, general-purpose merchant ships adapted for the occasion.[23]

From its early days, those involved in the slave trade realized that speed was of the essence. The longer a vessel remained at sea, loaded with Africans, the greater the risks to life and limb (and therefore to profits). Experience also brought about change. The pioneering slave trade gave way to an increasingly sophisticated business: merchants and sailors learned how best to navigate the waters of the African coast and the Atlantic and tried to keep to the best maritime routes and timings. New ship designs, and improved arrangement of sails, helped speed the Atlantic crossings. Bigger ships (Liverpool's ships grew from 70 to 200 tons over the course of the 18th century) enabled traders to carry large numbers of Africans. And much the same was true for vessels from the major French ports (Nantes and Bordeaux) and of Dutch and Danish ships. In and around the major ports, major shipbuilding industries flourished on the back of this trade. A total of 2,129 slave ships were constructed in Liverpool alone in the 18th century and 469 'Guineamen' were built in that city in the last twenty years of the century.[24] We know from the specific measurements of other ships that the crowding – the 'packing' – of Africans on the *Brooks* was not unusual. On Dutch vessels measuring only 37 meters long and weighing upward of 230 tons 300 Africans were carried.[25] The *Hall*, a Liverpool contemporary of the *Brooks*, was 375 tons, and measured 31 meters in length and 9 meters in width. She carried 245 Africans to Jamaica in 1791.[26]

Abolitionist investigations after 1787 into the exact details of British slave ships confirmed a simple point, though it was one which had been obvious to anyone who had worked or sailed on a slave ship. The space provided for Africans was tiny. Parliamentary scrutiny after 1788 revealed that the average space allowed on slave ships was 0.6 square meters per slave. Evidence suggests that French ships provided comparable space. Oddly, it became clear that smaller ships, not bigger ships, allowed greater space for the African. Yet as the century advanced, bigger slave ships came to dominate the trade. By the time

Liverpool was preeminent in the late 18th century North Atlantic trade, Africans were being forced into smaller spaces between decks than earlier victims. The restrictions on physical space seemed almost designed to cause maximum human suffering among people wedged together, on rough wooden boards, in frightful conditions of human filth, in stifling heat, and all on a pitching vessel in mid-ocean. Although Clarkson and his colleagues had initiated a scrutiny and discussion of these precise geometric issues, they also appreciated that simple facts and the figures, however vital in arguments, could never fully capture the trauma and claustrophobia of the Africans' shipboard experience.

Everyone involved – save for the Africans – knew that the most profitable form of Atlantic slave trading was a swift Atlantic crossing. As slave voyages got speedier, mortality rates on the ships decreased. Moreover, in the years *after* the Anglo-American abolition of 1807–1808, slave ships did indeed get faster. Now, however, with the preponderance of the trade in the South Atlantic, the ships (overwhelmingly Portuguese and Brazilian heading to Brazil) were being pursued and harried by the Royal Navy and the U.S. navy. Their journeys were shorter (and therefore faster) and many of them were in custom-built Baltimore Clippers, designed and constructed to outrun their naval pursuers. Such shorter voyages *ought* therefore to have been marked by lower slave mortality. But they were not. After 1831 (when Brazil abolished its own slave trade) the mortality rates on ships to Brazil actually *increased*. In what was a bizarre twist to Atlantic slave trading, the piratical traders of the 19th century were much more cavalier about the well-being of the Africans. Provisioning was slipshod, packing was worse – and casual brutality, even killing of Africans (jettisoning them overboard when being chased by naval patrols), was more common. In what proved to be the last phase of Atlantic slave trading,

850,000 Africans endured conditions that seem to have been *worse* than those suffered by Africans in the previous century.[27]

In the 19th century, officers on board American and British naval ships trying to stop slave ships compiled regular reports of atrocities at sea, in African rivers, and on the African coast, as slave traders hurried to load a crowded vessel and head to sea before being caught. Hundreds of Africans were rushed below deck in a matter of hours. Those same vessels reported levels of mortality which were horrific even by the standards of the Atlantic slave trade. In 1846, 373 of a total of 943 Africans died on one Brazilian ship – 74 of them in one night. The Royal Navy intercepted one ship (at 60 tons no bigger than the hoys playing from London to Margate) loaded with 400 Africans. Even smaller vessels were used to transfer Africans from the African coast to the close-by Atlantic islands. A vessel of only 7 tons shipped 30 Africans from Calabar to Principe: ten of them died. In 1819 the Royal Navy captured one slave ship, the *Nova Felicidad*, of only 11 tons carrying 71 Africans.[28]

Reports of such incidents regularly filtered back to the British and American press – telling of grossly overcrowded slave ships, with all the terrible consequences. But, in the chilling words of a sailor on one such vessel, "Nothing particular occurred during the voyage, excepting that a great many died."[29] The evidence from such vessels was sometime scarcely credible. One ship of 180 tons (which the Dolben Act would have restricted to 270 Africans) was found to be carrying 530. Another held 642 (where Dolben demanded 410). Inevitably, the losses were correspondingly high: 120 died out of 530, 140 from 642, and 200 from 600. The *Protector* was loaded with 807 Africans in 1818: 339 of them died.[30] Despite the uneven, faltering, and often ineffective efforts of the two major navies, and despite the punitive work of the *Courts of Mixed Commission* handling the cases of impounded slave ships, this was a trade which continued until the 1860s. It is an irony of inhuman proportions that the 19th-century Atlantic slave trade may have been the worst phase in the entire history of the trade, its sufferings heaped upon the heads of hundreds of thousands of Africans by the very efforts designed to put an end to the trade in the first place. In many respects, these were the darkest years of the Atlantic slave trade, and the details of a string of shipboard atrocities found their way back to London and Washington, in the outraged reports of naval officers – and inevitably found their way into the press.[31]

*   *   *

Today, few would challenge the view that the Atlantic slave ships were the crucible for a form of unrivalled human suffering: misery, sickness, and death on an epic scale. It is true that everyone who experienced long-distance maritime travel in the age of sail underwent seaborne terrors and privations. But even the most extreme of those experiences, among, for example, convicts transported to Australia, troops shipped to distant postings, and convicts sent to the 17th-century colonies, came nowhere near the suffering endured by millions of Africans crossing the Atlantic. All that, in the blink of an eye, is captured by the picture of the *Brooks*. The enduring importance of that image is that it *continues* to capture, instantaneously, the sufferings of millions. To scrutinize the image of the *Brooks* is to peer through a keyhole to see revealed the horrifying agonies of every African who suffered the Atlantic crossing. Which other piece of contemporary evidence achieves half as much?

Notes

1. James Walvin, 'The slave trade, abolition and public memory.' In *Transactions of the Royal Historical Society*, 2009, pp. 139–149.

2. 'Palace Green transformed into a slave Ship'. https://www.dur.ac.uk/durham .first/winter07/slaveship/ (retrieved 30/12/2015).
3. Michael White, 'Carrying the past into the present: Romauld Hazoumè, 'La Bouche du Roi.' http://www.history.ac.uk/1807commemorated/exhibitions/ art/ (retrieved 30/12/2015).
4. The *Brooks* has sometimes been known as the *Brookes*.
5. David Eltis and David Richardson, *Atlas of the Transatlantic Slave Trade*, New Haven, 2010, p. 203.
6. James Walvin, *Crossings: Africa, the Americas and the Atlantic Slave Trade*, London, 2013, Chapter 8.
7. Marcus Wood, *Blind Memory, Visual Representation of Slavery in England and America*, Manchester, 2000, pp. 33–34.
8. 50 pence stamp. A picture of Thomas Clarkson on a background of the *Brooks*. (Department of Culture Media and Sport), *Reflecting on the Past and Looking to the Future*, London, 2007.
9. Marcus Wood, *The Horrible Gift of Freedom*, Athens GA, 2010, Chapter 6.
10. Hugh Thomas, *The Slave Trade*, New York, 1997, pp. 520–521.
11. 'The Brooks', 'Summary Statistics', *Slavevoyages.org*.
12. John Oldfield, *Popular Politics and British Anti-Slavery*, Manchester, 1995, pp. 163–166.
13. Marcus Rediker, *The Slave Ship: A Human History*, London, 2007, p. 310.
14. Marcus Rediker, *The Slave Ship*, p. 309.
15. Marcus Rediker, *The Slave Ship*, pp. 310; 318.
16. Marcus Rediker, *The Slave Ship*, pp. 316–319.
17. James Walvin, *Crossings*, p. 173.
18. Marcus Rediker, *The Slave Ship*, pp. 319–326.
19. James Walvin, *Crossings*, p. 174
20. Marcus Wood, *Blind Memory*, p. 27.
21. Thomas Clarkson, *The History of the Abolition of the Slave Trade*, II, p. 153.
22. Marcus Wood, *Blind Memory*, p. 32.
23. James Walvin, *Crossings*, Chapter 3.
24. James Walvin, *Crossings*, pp. 65–67.
25. Johannes Postma, *The Dutch in the Atlantic Slave Trade, 1600–1815*, Cambridge, 1990, Chapter 6.
26. 'Hall', Voyage 81686 (1791), *Slavevoyages.org*.
27. James Walvin, *Crossings*, pp. 178–182.
28. James Walvin, *Crossings*, p. 182. See also Mary Wills, *The Royal Navy and the Suppression of the Atlantic Slave Trade, 1807–1867: Anti-slavery, Empire and Identity*, Ph.D. thesis, University of Hull, 2012.
29. James Walvin, *Crossings*, p. 179.
30. James Walvin, *Crossings*, p. 179.
31. James Walvin, *Crossings* pp. 179–180.

9

A Book
Slavery and the World of Print

Even today, it is hard to grasp the extraordinary impact of Harriet Beecher Stowe's book, *Uncle Tom's Cabin*. Within a week of its publication, in March 1852, 10,000 copies had been sold (it had initially appeared as articles in a Washington newspaper). A year later, 300,000 copies had been bought in the USA, and almost one million in Britain. Quickly translated into a host of languages (including Welsh), the book established its author as "the most famous writer in the world."[1] By the time of the Civil War, it had sold four and a half million copies, one million of them in the USA (in a population of 32 million). In addition, a string of serialized, children's, theatrical, and musical versions began to take the story to an even wider audience.

From the first, though *Uncle Tom's Cabin* was a best-seller it also divided opinion. However accurate or false, exaggerated, imaginary or realistic, *Uncle Tom's Cabin* outraged Americans, both north and south of the Mason–Dixon Line (though opinion about slavery was more complex and varied than merely two opposing sides: slave South versus anti-slavery North). *Uncle Tom's Cabin* had the effect of condemning slavery as a heartless, cruel, and irreligious outrage. Predictably, the South took a different view, loathing the book and its author in equal

Slavery in Small Things: Slavery and Modern Cultural Habits, First Edition. James Walvin.
© 2017 John Wiley & Sons, Inc. Published 2017 by John Wiley & Sons, Inc.

measure. Both were denounced, banned, and vilified throughout the Southern states. It was a book which seemed to aim a
poisonous literary blade at the very heart of the slave system.
For those wedded to Southern slavery, the book reinforced their
beleaguered mentality: the slave South was confronted by a hostile North.

Like any popular book, *Uncle Tom's Cabin* succeeded at a
number of levels. Above all, perhaps, it was a sermon, liberally sprinkled with biblical imagery and quotes, not surprisingly
since knowledge of the Bible coursed through the author's veins.
Mrs. Stowe was the daughter of one of the most important evangelical preachers of his age, sister to six clerical brothers, and the
wife of a theologian. Though the highly individual crisis which
brought Mrs. Stowe to pick up her pen against slavery was political (especially the recent pro-slavery Compromise and the Fugitive Slave Law of 1850[2]), her personal outrage was religious. Her
resolve to confront slavery was confirmed by a vision she had
experienced when taking Communion. Thereafter, she made it
her duty to rouse American Christians against what she took to
be the wickedness of the enslaved South. In effect, Mrs. Stowe
had launched a crusade, though no one (least of all the author)
could have imagined the enormous following that would rally
to her literary cause. Many people who, before 1852, had held
no views about slavery, were nudged towards abolition by an
emotional and religious disgust at what they read in *Uncle Tom's
Cabin*.

The book was an instant publishing and cultural phenomenon in the English-speaking world and, despite agree-
ing to a poor contract, the author became a rich woman.
In the first three months alone she earned $10,000 (some
$500,000 in today's money) but, personal gain aside, her book
helped to elevate American slavery to the center of international attention, generating an anti-slavery sentiment which was

remarkable for its global reach and influence. Here was a book which was purchased and borrowed by millions of people. Millions more had the book read to them, quite apart from untold legions who watched bowdlerized versions on the stage, in theatrical or vaudeville form. In the next century, many millions more watched the story on television and at the movies.

We have no way of knowing precisely how many people read the book, but it sold more copies than any other book in the USA with the exception of the Bible. Yet one critical element in this remarkable story is often overlooked. *Uncle Tom's Cabin* was an astonishing example of the cultural and political power of *popular literacy*. It was a book which, more than any other to date, illustrated the extent of mass literacy in the English-speaking world. Millions of people could now read, and what they read about slavery shocked and moved them. The power of the printed word – of what people read in black and white – was triumphantly proved by the impact of *Uncle Tom's Cabin* and mass literacy was confirmed as a critical weapon in the armory of the abolitionists.

Mass literacy was relatively new, though it had provoked arguments for centuries. From the early days of printing, men in clerical and secular authority recognized that access to cheap print might create a volatile, uncertain element among the newly literate. People able to read were likely to make up their own minds about religious or political issues. Disputes about printing the Bible in the vernacular (instead of Latin), for example, lay at the heart of the Reformation. Defenders of the *status quo*, in politics and religion, tended to distrust the rise of literacy and tried to contain the flow of cheap printed materials, whether it be a Bible or a radical tract. This was to prove a lost cause, and henceforth the world of print became what we now take for granted: a means of shaping opinion and a major forum for political and social debate. Indeed, *all* of the political battles which dominated the English-speaking world in the 17th and 18th centuries (from Britain's Civil War in the 1640s to the American Revolution after 1776) were waged not only in physical conflict, but also through the printed word.

Popular literacy was distrusted by those in power, and promoted by those seeking change. It was no accident that all the great reforming movements in the late 18th century (the beginnings of the 'Age of Revolution') turned to cheap print to advance their case and to win popular support. *Uncle Tom's Cabin* proved, perhaps more vividly than any other publication to date (more even than Tom Paine's seismic publications in the 1790s), the faith which reformers had long held in the power of the printed word. Teach people to read and write, and their literacy could change the world. So it proved in the USA in the wake of *Uncle Tom's Cabin*. Yet the pattern had already been set, in the previous seventy years, in the debates both in the USA and Britain about slavery.

The link between literacy and radical politics had been obvious from the mid-17th century. For all the difficulties of defining and tracing literacy, all the major indicators were there: the ability to sign marriage registers, the expanding number of books and of booksellers, and the widespread availability of tracts and cheap publications. London, for example, was dotted with printers, to the extent that competition drove many of them out of London into provincial towns. Philadelphia was to occupy a similar position in North America a century later. Cheap print became ubiquitous. Between 1620 and 1700, for instance, no fewer than 700 British newspapers and periodicals had appeared. In the next sixty years this grew to 900. Not even a succession of punitive government stamp duties on the press (designed to price knowledge and popular literacy out of the market) could check the rise. Newspapers found a natural home in alehouses and coffee shops where they were extensively read by customers: they were even stuck in the window of print shops to be read by passers-by. They reported, and at times even steered, political debate, and by the mid-18th century, an estimated one million people in Britain were reading a newspaper at some point each week. In North America, there were between 100 and 260 newspapers in the 1790s – and 400 by 1810.[3] In addition, many of 18th-century society's greatest contemporary writers practiced their art in the columns of newspapers and magazines. Through all this detail, it becomes possible to sense both the scale and the quality of cheap print, and of its widespread readership in the English-speaking world by the late 18th century.[4] Literacy itself was, however, a patchy affair and there were major regional variations in levels of literacy, as there were between different types of occupation. In England, literacy was at its highest in London (predictably perhaps) but Scotland was notable for its high levels of literacy among both men and women in the 18th century.

All this changed, and in unexpected ways, with the coming of industrialization. The new British factory towns, notably the textiles towns, actually set back popular literacy, especially among women, though in time the process was arrested by the rise of Sunday Schools, and day schools. Non-conformist chapels, with their emphasis on basic literacy to enable Bible study in the new industrial regions, also promoted literacy. Above all, however, it seems that ever more people *wanted* to read, both for the pleasure it afforded, and for the valuable and useful information it made available. Though much of this had a religious foundation (pamphlets and tracts issuing from a chapel or church), it established a new formula for the spread of learning and knowledge. Running through all this was a deeper, residual desire among large numbers of working people to improve themselves, to educate themselves – and this was most readily achieved via the Bible or scriptural publications. Gradually, too, British government took a hand. A string of Factory Acts (in 1802, 1833, and 1844) insisted on the provision of basic education for children trapped in the new work places, in the factories that now characterized the face of industrial Britain. Yet despite all this evidence about progress in literacy, swathes of the new industrial laboring class remained devoid of *any* form of education, and clearly lacked basic literacy. Hence the push from mid-century for the introduction of state education.[5]

Notwithstanding all the *lacunae*, and despite the patchy nature of the evidence, what is really remarkable is *how much* popular literacy took root: "how much could be achieved without the presence of the state or even of a widespread system of church education."[6] The foundations for popular learning were laid, not so much via formal institutions, but within the bosom of the working-class family. Illiteracy was defeated, as David Vincent has pointed out, by the efforts of illiterates themselves.[7] And this was the fertile soil in which new forms of popular politics and abolition thrived.

* * *

The question of slavery became an inescapable issue in the world of print in the last quarter of the 18th century. The use of slave labor throughout the Americas, and the transportation of millions of Africans across the Atlantic to feed the plantations, had long had its critics, but they were few and far between. For centuries, critical voices went largely unheard, or were drowned out by the cacophony of commercial success generated by slavery. How could moral or religious objections count against a system which yielded such enormous material bounty to all concerned (except to the slaves)? All that changed, quite suddenly and unexpectedly. In the last quarter of the 18th century a voice of critical dissent emerged, directing an ever more strident, popular (and politically influential) attack first against the Atlantic slave trade and later against slavery itself.[8] In the years immediately after American independence, criticism of the slave trade took off, and was swept along by an astonishing surge of cheap, printed literature.

The immediate origins of this development lay in the most unlikely of company – among American and British Quakers. Prominent Quakers had objected to slavery from the early days of the Society of Friends in the late 17th century. The real start of the campaign against the slave trade, however, was initiated by Quakers in the 1780s. This relatively small band of people, whose origins as a sect lay in the convulsions of the British Civil War a century before, had become famous for their severe piety, their distinctive dress code – and their commercial success. Quakers were also a notably literate group, dedicated to literacy, numeracy, and penmanship. Meticulous book-keeping, accountancy, and letter-writing were important factors in the way Quakers organized, worshipped, and secured their commercial success. They were also important advocates of the printed word, and were helped in large part by having major publishers and printers in their ranks in London and Philadelphia. In business, Quakers were to prove successful and influential out of all proportion to their numbers.[9] And so it proved with their political agitation, first against the slave trade and then against slavery.

American Quakers in Pennsylvania were among early voices raised against slavery. John Woolman and Antony Benezet in particular were following an earlier tradition which led back to George Fox himself, but which now urged Quakers and their organizations to speak out against bondage. It was no surprise that the American campaign against slavery took root in Philadelphia. The Pennsylvania Abolition Society led the way and their demands for an end to slavery – not merely the slave trade – was well in advance of British demands. Both Woolman and Benezet had proved greatly influential on their visits to England (Woolman died in York) and in the wake of those Americans' visits, Quakers in London picked up the challenge. British Quakers affirmed their collective revulsion for slavery in 1783, and the first British petition against the slave trade sent to parliament was drafted and delivered by Quakers. This was followed by a wave of cheap anti-slave trade literature, liberally scattered around Britain. Quakers were able to do this because they were among the few groups with anything remotely approaching a well-organized, national framework of associations and sympathizers. These early Quaker abolitionists believed that printing cheap material about the slave trade "might tend to the abolition of it."[10] As a result, much of the early literature against the slave trade came from Quaker pens, and was printed on Quaker presses on both sides of the Atlantic. The end result was the start of a propaganda campaign against the slave trade which was conceived, nurtured, and propagated by Quakers. Moreover, its strength and pervasive influence lay in its cheap printed format, and in its direct appeal to the literate. Quakers (and increasingly other non-Quaker sympathizers) also spoke out in sermons and lectures, and at religious and political gatherings across the face of Britain. Many of these verbal attacks on the slave trade often found their way into print. Indeed, between 1787 and the start of the American Civil War printed sermons against the slave trade and slavery came to form a truly enormous printed archive devoted to anti-slavery. To this day, one of the most substantial and voluminous forms of abolitionist literature lies in the collections of abolitionist sermons. Yale's Beinecke Library, for one, has hundreds of such printed sermons, bound and catalogued in its collection of tracts and American pamphlets.[11] From the 1780s onward, no preacher worth his salt, in Britain and the USA, seemed able to resist the urge to denounce (or support) slavery from his pulpit. Addresses from the pulpit then found their way into print, and hence were saved for posterity. It was the Quakers who had first grasped the power of the printed word as a weapon to be directed against slavery.[12]

In Britain in the late years of the 18th century, two powerful but relatively untested social forces converged: a tidal wave of free and cheap printed material, and a readership that was receptive (hungry even). No one could have predicted either. Thanks primarily to the Quakers, the British reading public was showered with abolitionist literature. Then, following another Quaker initiative, abolition petitions signed by many thousands of people began to pour into parliament in 1787. The extent of popular support for these petitions surpassed even Quaker expectations. In all this, the young Thomas Clarkson (though not a Quaker) was prompted and supported by Quakers, and emerged as the indefatigable foot soldier of the abolitionist movement. He traveled tens of thousands of miles on horseback to speak against the slave trade, and to undertake essential research into that trade. By the end of 1787, the newly formed London-based Abolition Society, working through Quaker contacts across the country, had scattered anti-slavery literature across Britain. Clarkson calculated that 51,432 books and articles, and 26,525 reports and papers, had been distributed, all in addition to regular articles on abolition activities in newspapers and magazines.[13] Some 15,000 copies of Clarkson's own tract (itself greatly influenced by Benezet) had been published, and a total of £1,000 had been invested in abolitionist publications.[14]

The West India slave lobby, surprised by the turn of events, rose to the challenge, publishing their own spate of pro-slave trade pamphlets, and by the end of 1787, the two sides (the Quaker-inspired abolitionists and the slave lobby) were locked into a political fight conducted not only in parliament but, crucially, in the public arena. Both sides were using print to secure the hearts and minds of the British people. To everyone's astonishment, within a year, the once-unchallenged slave lobby had lost the political and moral high ground. They were never to regain it. Commercial interests which had effectively gone unchallenged throughout much of the 18th century (Caribbean planters, merchants, agents, and shippers – indeed everyone who had thrived on slavery) found themselves outflanked and outgunned by the literary barrage unleashed by the Quakers and by the abolitionists. A mass British reading public had been exposed and it was bombarded with detailed information about the horrors of the slave ships. The more the British learned, the more they abhorred the trade – and demanded its termination.

Paralleling this literary campaign, a plethora of petitions demanding an end to the slave trade thumped onto the desk of the House of Commons. A total of 103 petitions, carrying tens of thousands of signatures, revealed not only the wide geography of British abolition sentiment but provided yet another important insight into the wide literate base of abolition. By the summer of 1788, members in both the Lords and the Commons were forced to concede that abolition was hugely popular. In public and in private, politicians based this assessment not on vague impressions but on hard evidence: the number of petitions, the number of signatures to those petitions, and the unprecedented volume of abolition publications devoured by British readers. All this was in addition to the large crowds gathering at abolitionist meetings. Time and again, the only limit on numbers attending abolitionist meetings was the capacity of the building.

From the first tracts, petitions, and speeches against the slave trade in 1787, through to the passing of the Abolition Act itself in 1806, this British campaign against the slave trade was waged at two levels. First, there was the public campaign, designed to whip up public outrage about the slave trade and to direct that anger at parliament in the hope of bringing a legislative end to the trade. Better known, of course, is the second battle *within* Parliament itself, and personified by Wilberforce, to win parliament over to ending the slave trade. The power and persuasiveness of the parliamentary campaign lay not merely in the moral and theological arguments against the slave trade which echoed through parliament and government offices, but in the *public* support which underpinned the entire campaign. That, in its turn, hinged on widespread popular literacy. As more and more people read about conditions on the slave ships, the wider and more vocal became the public outrage. The success of abolition was, then, forged in a society that was being fundamentally transformed by the emergence of widespread, popular literacy.

Sixteen years after the ending of the British slave trade, a new generation of British abolitionists roused themselves once more, this time to bring down colonial slavery itself. By then, the 1820s, Britain itself had begun to change. Urban growth and population growth in general, as well as the spread of new industries, were helping to shape a new kind of society. It was, moreover, a world characterized by changing literacy, a fact once again reflected in the print culture that formed the foundations of the revived abolition movement. This time, however, the evidence about slavery itself was even more striking and persuasive.

In the 1780s and 1790s the Abolition Society published tens of thousands of publications, but between 1821 and 1831, the Anti-Slavery Society issued *millions* of publications. In 1831 alone the abolitionists published almost half a million pamphlets, all in addition to an abundance of literature which issued from *local* anti-slavery societies across Britain. Printed anti-slavery messages and information smothered the reading public, choking off all efforts by the pro-slavery lobby to have their say.[15] A great deal of this anti-slavery literature was expressed in religious terms, not surprising, perhaps, because churches of all sorts and persuasions heeded the cry. British anti-slavery in the 1820s and 1830s was very much a religious crusade – whatever the fundamental economic issues at stake. When slavery was finally ended by parliament in 1833, it was universally denounced as a religious outrage. Yet a mere half century before, religious objections had been few and far between. Now, slavery was denounced, from a multitude of non-conformist chapels and Anglican churches in all corners of urban and rural Britain, and among large numbers of working-class men and women. Slavery was also condemned by those radical movements seeking to advance working-class political and laboring interests. From the Corresponding Societies of the 1790s through to the Chartists in the 1840s, the new plebeian politics denounced slavery as an outrage. It was as if slavery had been caught in a political pincer movement, trapped by the two major forces which spoke for large numbers of working people: their chapels, and their political organizations. In the words of Richard Oastler, the great Yorkshire factory reformer, anti-slavery and Chartism were "one and the same."[16] Like popular politics itself, abolition thrived on the dissemination, persuasiveness, and power of the printed word.

From the first, abolitionists had realized that their best hope for success was to shower the reading public with printed arguments. In the two generations which spanned the foundation of anti-slavery in 1787 and full emancipation in 1833, millions of Britons absorbed the printed word of the anti-slavery activists. The combination of those two factors – a public keen to read, and abolitionists anxious to persuade them of their cause – came

together, via the printed word, to create a powerful and ultimately irresistible political force. Abolition won because it was
popular.

Abolitionist literature after 1787 was not only popular, but
had a very different tone and content than any previous political literature. It was, in effect, a new genre of writing, characterized by much more than moral outrage. For the first time in
modern British politics, abolitionists based their case on careful analysis of empirical evidence. Thomas Clarkson led the way
with his research on board slave ships and in ships' papers (see
Chapter 8). He and later abolitionists began to make telling use
of *factual*, statistical data: using the figures derived from the
slave ships to expose the demographic realities about death and
sickness among Africans and sailors. It was an analysis which
exposed the hidden costs of the slave trade. What emerged was
not a simple, emotive case – nor even a religious dispute – but a
factually based argument which seriously challenged the long-
unquestioned benefits of the slave trade. The reading public was
presented with a wealth of facts and figures, tables, and itemized
data which was grounded in hard evidence and tight, empirical
analysis. Thereafter, and throughout the history of slavery, slavery's opponents sought to marshal *factual* evidence to attack the
institution.

Thomas Clarkson also opened up a major economic question, namely that of trade with Africa. Why did that trade have
to be predominantly in human cargoes? As he trekked round
the country, Clarkson carried with him his famous chest, each of
its many little drawers packed with commodities and products
from Africa (cotton, woods, dyes, seeds, spices, nuts, peppers,
gums, textiles, leather, shoes, and necklaces), all collected from
sailors and traders on the slave ships to West Africa. Each item
offered the prospect of a different kind of 'normal' trade with
Africa: an open, free trade in goods, instead of African slaves.[17]

It was an argument which was also promoted by Equiano in later editions of his autobiography.

More traditional objections to (and defenses of) slavery remained, of course, and many thousands of pages were given over to theological disputes about slavery: was it biblically ordained or not? Nonetheless, long before the British abolished their slave trade in 1807, arguments about slavery had shifted to arguments about the factual evidence. In addition, a new (and again unexpected) dimension developed to the arguments. What could be more persuasive, more forceful, than an African voice, speaking about the slave trade and slavery *from the inside*: telling that saga of human suffering from the point of view of lived experience? There were untold armies of Africans in the Americas, and small pockets in Europe, who could add their voice to the debate. An African spokesman, someone able to speak directly from slave experience, would offer a totally new kind of argument. In Britain the person who stepped forward to do that was an ex-slave and ex-sailor, known to his friends as Gustavus Vassa.

In the autumn of 1790, Vassa was lodging in London with a friend, the Scottish shoemaker Thomas Hardy, founder of the London Corresponding Society (LCS). At the time, Vassa was preparing a new edition of his autobiography, first published in 1789. From the first, Vassa, better known today as Olaudah Equiano, *assumed* that the radical working men attracted to the LCS would be abolitionists. More significantly perhaps, Equiano's own book – his autobiography – raced through a number of editions in the 1780s and 1790s. It was also noticed in the USA in 1790, and published there in 1791. Today, Equiano's *Interesting Narrative* has become astonishingly famous. His name and image (taken from the frontispiece of his book) adorn dozens of popular and scholarly books, articles, exhibits, and organizations. Equiano now lends his name to a society, and he has come to personify a host of modern causes: the history of black people in Britain, the story of African writers, and the fate and experience of millions of Africans who had been consigned to anonymity. Equiano's autobiography has been extensively edited, anthologized, and reprinted. His face even appeared on British postage stamps in 2007, and was displayed on huge posters draped across civic buildings in Birmingham, and in the foyer of the city's main railway station. Today, more so than in his own lifetime, Equiano's voice not only speaks for millions but he has become a revered figure whose international status is virtually unimpeachable. Equiano was not, however, the first African whose writing offered an insight into the life of an enslaved African. A number of other Africans left earlier written accounts (sometimes mere fragments, sometimes letters) of their life as an enslaved person in the 18th century.[18] But none of them, at the time or since, had the impact of Equiano. He remains the most celebrated black writer of the period.

Equiano's book sold well and had an important impact on the abolition debate in Britain between 1789 and 1793. Thereafter, however, the shadow of the French revolution and the turmoil in Haiti obstructed both abolition and the broader cause of radical reform. Despite that, the strength of Equiano's book was its African heart: it was a first-hand expression of African life in the era of the slave ships, and was quite unlike any previous publication. It had a powerful political and cultural resonance.

Today, Equiano's writing is lauded and valued as the preeminent African voice of freedom and attainment in the 18th century. The author was also an astonishing self-made man who published and promoted his own book, and achieved a healthy financial success which can be measured in his assets at his death.[19] His financial and material success – no mean thing for an ex-slave in 18th-century Britain – barely registers, however, when we compare it what happened, fifty years later, in the world of abolitionist writings in the USA. The comparison is unfair, of course, for Equiano, though speaking for millions, was working from within a small London-based African community. The African-American writers of the early 19th century in the USA, on the other hand, formed an integral part of a massive, enslaved population which was central to the North American economy. To a remarkable degree, the US economy was driven by the cotton-based South and its millions of enslaved people. The 700,000 American slaves of 1790 had almost doubled by 1810, had reached two and half million in 1840, and four million by the time of the Civil War. The USA boomed, with its legendary expansive frontier, its flourishing cities, and its vast geography gradually succumbing to man's management and control via the proliferation of canals and, increasingly, railway tracks. It attracted Europe's poor in ever growing numbers, and the country's population more than quadrupled in the half century before 1850, to 23 million people. Throughout, however, the USA continued to depend on slave-grown cotton as a major stimulus to rising well-being (both in the North and in the South).

American slave-grown cotton was king, and was shipped down the Mississippi to be exported through New Orleans and Mobile to all the world's major manufacturing countries, but especially to industrial Lancashire, as we saw in Chapter 6. By 1860, the value of exported cotton formed 50% of the entire export trade of the USA, and income from cotton exports substantially financed the nation's imports. Moreover the economic benefits of slave-grown cotton were not restricted to the South. Merchants, manufacturers and bankers in the North all profited from their business dealings with the South. Profits from the plantations found their way into the expansion of railroads and other industries, into improved river and oceanic shipping. Everyone recognized that slavery – and cotton – was vital to

the well-being of the nation as a whole, as well as to the South.
The prime obstacle to American arguments against slavery was,
then, not just the entrenched power of the South itself, but the
pivotal and mighty power of slave cotton within the broader
economy of the USA.[20]

US slavery lay at the very heart of North American life
and well-being, but throughout, it posed a myriad of problems. The principal conundrum was political. The USA was a
society founded on democratic principles (the Declaration of
Independence and the Constitution) but it was also home to
millions of slaves. Indeed, the USA was *born* arguing about
slavery, and those arguments swept back and forth, in the North
and the South, from pulpits, state legislatures, and public meetings. The published disputes about slavery, already prefigured in
Britain a half century earlier, reached new levels of intensity as
the 19th century advanced, as the economics of slavery became
more vital, and the moral issues more troublesome. Much of this
was, again, made possible by the convergence of two critical factors: the existence of widespread literacy and modern technolo-
gies of print and distribution.

As we have seen, the first two generations of North American democracy were paralleled by an astonishing growth in
print culture. Printed materials and letters (private and business) moved ever more freely via the new postal system. As in
Britain, the widespread debate about democracy in the 1790s
was sustained and promoted by cheap publications, none more
spectacularly successful, on both sides of the Atlantic, than
those of Tom Paine. (When Paine – *the* great radical and abolitionist scribe of his generation – died in New York in 1809, his
coffin was followed by 'two negroes.')[21]

Canals and railroads transformed communications in the
USA. So, too, did the telegraph. Tens of thousands of miles
of telegraph lines criss-crossed the USA (greatly helping the

conduct of the cotton industry among others).[22] Now, the printed word flashed almost instantly, from one corner of the US to another. (After 1866, it could even travel by cable underneath the Atlantic.) Printed materials in bulk – bundles of newspapers and magazines, parcels of books – could be shipped and delivered promptly from printers to shops and street corner vendors. All this helped to open up a massive market for the printed word, and not surprisingly the enslaved were also able to find their voice in this new mass market.

This outpouring of all kinds of North American printed material was remarkable. Most notable among the authors were freed slaves: men and women who had escaped from bondage and who henceforth devoted themselves to denouncing slavery in print and in public, and campaigning for the freedom of their brothers and sisters across the USA. They took to the road and railways, even crossed the Atlantic, taking their demands for freedom to large audiences throughout the USA and Europe. They also wielded their pens for the same cause. Some, unable to write, dictated their stories to others. In speaking and writing about the lives of enslaved people, freed men and women were making much more than a political argument: they were also breaking free from their own slave past. These slave narratives have spawned an enormous (and disputed) recent historical scholarship. Nonetheless, as a *genre* they confirm the point already made about Britain: the literature of slavery struck so powerful a chord because of widespread, popular literacy. Most famous of all, perhaps, was Frederick Douglass who had escaped slavery at the age of 20 and who in 1845 published his *Narrative of the Life of Frederick Douglass, An American Slave*. He confessed that it had been literacy that had opened his eyes: being able to read and write was "the light [that] broke in upon me by degrees." Literacy freed him to say what he wanted and without restraint. He could write, speak, and publish, and he did so with astonishing success. His work laid waste to contemporary support for bondage, and Douglass devoted his life to the cause of black freedom. Inevitably, his book was denounced by supporters of slavery: some flatly refused to accept that so complex and sophisticated an argument could have been written by a black man.[23]

Douglass was the very personification of a fear long nurtured by slave owners everywhere: that literacy was a dangerous force in the hands of the enslaved. Throughout the Americas, slave owners worried about literate slaves (their resistance was of course one of the reasons why illiteracy remained so high in the slave communities). But preachers, led by the Moravians, nonconformist chapels with their Bibles, hymnals, and opportunities to preach and to study the Scriptures, proved corrosive of the slave owners' resistance. What one had called 'The magic of the written word' gave slaves a power they had long been denied. As one slave had said about the Bible "The book will make me wise."[24] Planters in the South, like those in the Caribbean and Brazil, disliked and resisted the approaches of missionaries, and worried that their slaves would be "incited by emissaries, books and pictures to servile insurrection."[25] Though literate slaves were few in the era of slavery itself, their literacy became a corrosive force of the structure of slavery. Literacy among plantation slaves remained stubbornly low, but the *fear* of literacy, and its association with Christianity, was equally persistent among planters.

Frederick Douglass was a unique figure, but he was not alone. A number of freed slaves, like Equiano before them, published their own narratives in the USA in the early 19th century. In the century before the Civil War, upward of seventy such narratives were published in Britain and the USA. Today, some of them are revered as iconic classics: one recently became the subject of a major movie. Moses Roper (1845), William Wells

Brown (1847), Solomon Northrup, *Twelve Years a Slave* (1853), Sojourner Truth (1847), and Harriet Jacobs, *Incidents in the Life of a Slave Girl* (1861) stand out in popular and historical memory. Some used an amanuensis, others strengthened their case by appending letters of support from prominent backers. But all proved themselves to be much more than simple storytellers. Each, in their own distinctive way, made available a set of unique introductions to the world of slavery. Many of them were 'runaways': some remained as fugitives, always fearful of recapture and being returned to slavery (as had happened to Equiano). But all who put pen to paper did more than narrate their own story, real or imaginary; they spoke out for freedom and independence, though their work was successful because of the literacy of the wider American society they addressed. The parallel with Britain in the late 18th century was close. The voice of the enslaved found a sympathetic audience among the literate at large.

The American slave narratives were oddly ignored by historians until the 1950s, but in their own day they enjoyed a massive and enthusiastic readership. Frederick Douglass, for example sold 5,000 copies of his *Narrative* within four months, and 30,000 by 1860. There were clearly huge numbers of people, in the North (and in Europe), keen to read about slave lives. The narratives were after all also remarkable adventure stories which recounted daring and dangerous escapes *en route* from slavery to freedom. They were tales which described triumph in the face of great adversity, and were testimony to the human desire for freedom. Slave narratives were overwhelmingly true accounts which worked at all kinds of levels. And their readership wanted more.

For many readers, slave narratives were a revelation about the brute reality of slavery in the South. Just as Equiano and Thomas Clarkson had presented the reading public with hard evidence of the horrors of the slave ships (evidence which no amount of writing by the slave lobby could effectively deny or rebut), so, too, did the American slave narratives inform their readers of the personal and communal horrors of Southern slavery. Time and again, freed slaves spelled out the pains and inhumanities of slavery; of brutal treatment and work, family separation, of sexual violence and personal and family grief on a scale which outsiders could hardly comprehend. Despite all this, the narratives also informed readers of the achievements and virtues of slave life, of the strength of the slave family and community, forged in adversity, of shared pleasures and of Christian devotion, all wrested from the bleakest of oppressive environments. The narratives described people and their customs which strangers (outsiders living thousands of miles away from the slave plantations) could recognize, sympathize with, and admire.

For all the undoubted impact of the slave narratives, and for all the political gains achieved by those publications among American and European readers, they formed but a preface to the seismic impact of a single novel about slavery, written by a white woman, and which, to this day, dominates perceptions of American slavery. But *Uncle Tom's Cabin* also emerged from the politics of American abolition. The revitalized abolition movement after 1831 (led by William Lloyd Garrison) had 250,000 members, 1,300 local organizations and, naturally, tens of thousands of publications: tracts, articles, petitions. The movement was troubled by splits, factionalism, and personality clashes – but its essence was rooted in a religious objection to slavery. American abolitionists, faced with the indisputable benefits of cotton, found it hard to master an economic critique of slavery. It was as if abolition was a branch of the evangelical movement itself. And this was the setting – the social context – in which *Uncle Tom's Cabin* made its tremendous impact.[26]

Among the large numbers of American readers deeply moved by the stories in the slave narratives, few were to be more influential than Harriet Beecher Stowe. Indeed, the possible links between her book and the slave narratives became an instant source of controversy, and the debate continues to the present day.[27] Some black abolitionists immediately saw a direct connection: a number of black authors even claimed that their work – and their lives – had been the direct inspiration for various characters in *Uncle Tom's Cabin*. Stowe, however, simply denied the connection. "None of the characters in *Uncle Tom's Cabin* are portraits."[28] The truth, unsurprisingly, was more complex because she drew her inspiration and evidence, and shaped her characters and incidents, from a variety of printed sources and personal experiences. There was, after all, no shortage of printed material available to her when she was working on the book. We know that she was familiar with the slave narratives by Frederick Douglass (1845), Lewis Garrard Clarke (1846), William Wells Brown (1847), Henry Bibb (1849), and Josiah Henson (1849). She also personally met a number of freed slaves whose stories doubtless provided detail for her writing. Without relying on any particular person or narrative, Stowe was obviously influenced by the writing of freed slaves. The life of Frederick Douglass was too rich, too striking in detail and accomplishment – and too persuasive in its argument – *not* to have left a deep impression on Mrs. Stowe. In particular, Douglass's account of his pleasure at reading offered persuasive evidence for her conviction that slaves could improve themselves through self-education. Of all the slave narratives, Douglass's was the most compelling argument for slave self-improvement.

There was also a darker side to the narratives, namely the violent world of slave masters and overseers. The accounts are strewn with horrifying details of systematic and random acts of violence against slaves. One after another told similar

stories, and their accounts were too alike, too similar, to be coin-
cidental or contrived. They had a ring of authenticity. It was
the ubiquity and the extremes of that violence which supplied
the most shockingly persuasive evidence in wooing readers over
to the side of abolition. Torture, whippings, sexual attacks – all
hung over slave communities everywhere, and the authors of the
slave narratives did not hesitate to spell out the grim details for
their readers. Douglass and other freed slaves had no reason to
pull their literary punches, regaling their readers, in their early
pages, with the gory inhumanity that was often the lot of Southern slaves. Stowe, however, fought shy of repeating such graphic
details. The cries and the sounds of whippings and sufferings
were hinted at rather than spelled out. Here, she parted company
with the slave narratives, and has left a historical legacy which
has been used to diminish the book's credibility. The impression
in *Uncle Tom's Cabin* is of a more benign Southern system, with
the author hoping that there was still time for the slave owners to
see the folly of their ways. Douglass and his colleagues had no
truck with any such appeasement. Slavery was rotten and had
to go.

Stowe and the narratives converged on a number of issues.
The sheer incongruity of US slavery was astonishing: extremes
of physical and sexual violence were features of a system which
claimed to be defending Christian values against the dangers of
African savagery. Nor was the problem restricted to the South.
Many of the most violent men to be found on the plantations
hailed from the North: men born and raised in the North but
now living and working among the Southern slaves. The cumu-
lative impact of all this on the image of mid-century America
was damning. Stowe blended her personal observations of life
in the North with her reading of life in the South, to portray
an American society thoroughly corroded by racial antipathy
towards the slaves (and freed slaves). Nor was she was alone

in claiming that the USA was shamed by deep-seated racial prejudice. Visitors, American observers and of course African-Americans, all claimed that racial prejudice was not restricted to the slave South, though such prejudices seemed to find their origins in Southern slavery.

Uncle Tom's Cabin was, then, written by a devout Christian mother who was appalled by what she learned of Southern slavery: its violence, its corruption of Christian values, and, above all perhaps, its violations of family life. And yet, however emotive Stowe's account of the enforced break-up of the slave family, it was as nothing compared to what we know of the extent and damage of the reality. Between 1790 and 1860 one slave marriage in five was wrecked by enforced separation: one child in three was separated from parents.[29] The devout Mrs. Stowe looked at slavery and its role in the USA and decided that slavery could only be discarded "if the nation faced up to its sins." She thus took up her pen to draft a novel that would help to confront the nation with its manifold sins. What even she could never have imagined was the degree to which her book "moulded public opinion."[30] Who could have guessed that the power of print could be wielded to such effect – and by the humble wife of a cleric? Among its many achievements, *Uncle Tom's Cabin* illustrated that the USA was a remarkably literate society. Print culture had become basic to the way Americans lived and thought about themselves.

Today, even in the midst of a digital revolution, we are so accustomed to the world of print that we scarcely notice it. Yet it shapes and defines the way we live. There are few greater disadvantages in life than being illiterate. Being unable to share in the vital and informative world of print is to be underprivileged at a basic and disabling level. Yet this world of print and of mass literacy is relatively new. In the English-speaking world it flourished as never before in the great 'Age of Revolution' which transformed the Western world after 1776. At the heart of that all-pervading revolution was the rise of popular literacy, and the huge volumes of printed materials which fed it. Among the dominant issues which characterized political and social debate in those years, slavery proved to be the one of the most striking. The slave trade and slavery caught the public eye like no other contemporary matter – not even women's rights, or the popular franchise. Slavery angered critics of all sorts and conditions, from humble working people to an elite of contemporary writers, poets, painters, and thinkers. It also it made heroes of ordinary people. A preacher's wife (Harriet Beecher Stowe) and ex-slaves (Frederick Douglass and Equiano) secured a place for themselves among the major iconic figures of the era, via their use of the printed word to attack and undermine slavery.

Today, it is perhaps tempting to pick up their writings and simply slip them back onto the bookshelf: they may seem but simple examples from an abundance of literary objections to slavery. In the 18th and 19th centuries, however, theirs were books which did much more than fuel the readers' imagination. They ignited a passion which became the most destructive force undermining support for slavery. Slavery ended its days as the most detested of human conditions. And it was detested because millions of people had learned about it through the printed word.

Notes

1. *Uncle Tom's Cabin*, London, 1995 edn., Keith Carabine, Introduction, p. v.
2. The Missouri Compromise (1820) was designed to regulate slavery on the western regions of the USA. The Fugitive Slave Law (1850) required captured runaway slaves to be returned to their former owners.
3. Eric Foner, *Give me Liberty! An American History*, New York, 2005, p. 280.
4. Frank O'Gorman, *The Long Eighteenth Century: British Political and Social History, 1688–1832*, London, 1997, pp. 127–129.
5. E. Royle, *Modern Britain: A Social History, 1750–1985*, London, 1987, pp. 343–354.

6. David Vincent, *Literacy and Popular Culture. England, 1750–1914*, Cambridge, 1989, pp. 53–54.

7. David Vincent, *Literacy and Popular Culture*, pp. 53–54.

8. At first the point of attack was the slave trade. Later, with the slave trade abolished in 1807, the attack was directed at colonial slavery.

9. James Walvin, *The Quakers: Money and Morals*, London, 1997.

10. Thomas Clarkson, *History of the Abolition of the Slave Trade*, vol. I, pp. 276–277.

11. *American Tracts*, Beinecke Library, Yale University.

12. Christopher Leslie Brown, *Moral Capital: Foundations of British Abolition*, Chapel Hill, 2006, Chapter 7.

13. Ellen Gibson Wilson, *Thomas Clarkson: A Biography*, London, 1989, p. 42.

14. Abolition Committee Minutes, 12th August 1788, *Add Mss* 21,255, (British Library).

15. James Walvin, 'The propaganda of anti-slavery.' In James Walvin, ed., *Slavery and British Society, 1776–1848*, London, 1982, pp. 60–61.

16. Betty Fladeland, '"Our cause being One and the Same": Abolitionists and Chartism.' In James Walvin, ed., *Slavery and British Society*, p. 99.

17. 'Thomas Clarkson's African Box. Exhibition Catalogue Item 22, in Stephen Farrell, Melanie Unwin, and James Walvin, eds., *The British Slave Trade: Abolition, Parliament and People*, Edinburgh, 2007, pp. 305–313.

18. Vincent Carretta, ed., *Unchained Voices: An Anthology of Black Authors in the English-Speaking World of the Eighteenth Century*, Lexington, 1996.

19. Vincent Carretta, *Equiano, the African: Biography of a Self-Made Man*, Athens GA, 2005, p. 366.

20. For a compelling discussion about the centrality of cotton, see Sven Beckert, *Empire of Cotton: A New History of Global Capitalism*, London, 2014.

21. Moncure Daniel Conway, *The Life of Thomas Paine*, New York, 1892, 2 vols., II, p. 417.

22. Robert William Fogel, *Without Consent or Contract: The Rise and Fall of American Slavery*, New York, 1989, p. 67.

23. David Blight 'The Slave Narratives: A Genre and a Source.' At http://www.gilderlehrman.org/history-by-era/literature-and-language-arts/essays/slave-narratives-genre-and-source (retrieved 30/12/2015).

24. Sylvia Frey and Betty Wood, *Come Shouting to Zion: African American Protestantism in the American South and British Caribbean to 1830*, Chapel Hill, 1998, p. 85.

25. Edward Ball, *Slaves in the Family*, London, 1998, p. 324.

26. Robert William Fogel, *Without Consent or Contract*, Chapter 8.

27. David S. Reynolds, *Mightier than the Sword: Uncle Tom's Cabin and the Battle for America*, New York, 2011, Chapter 3.

28. Quoted in David S. Reynolds, *Mightier than the Sword*, p. 103.

29. James Walvin, *Crossings: Africa, the Americas and the Atlantic Slave Trade*, London, 2013, pp. 137–138.

30. David S. Reynolds, *Mightier than the Sword*, p. 116

10

Chains
The Ironware of Slavery

Among the many celebrations of August 1st, 1834, the day slavery was formally abolished in British colonies, a mezzotint was published in London, suitably entitled 'The First of August 1834.' Painted by David Lucas, it showed a delighted slave family – all beaming with joy, one digging a hole in which they were busy burying chains and manacles. The father raises his arms to the heavens in thanks, his hand pointing to a notice of emancipation pinned to a tree. His wife holds a baby aloft – a child destined to live the life of a free person. It was a picture that was to be widely used, adapted, and copied, in Britain and the USA, to illustrate black freedom. Two things leap out from the picture: the delight of the former slaves – and the burying of the chains.[1]

Few objects provoke more immediate thoughts of slavery than a link of chains. Ask people what they imagine slavery to involve and as likely as not, they will describe an African in chains. Modern publications frequently use pictures of chains to convey the impression that the book is about slavery. In 2007 a British church campaign used a picture of chains, and sugar cubes, to adorn its publicity.[2] In 1954, when the sculptor Jacob Epstein was pondering how best to sculpt African slaves, he created a bronze piece, of an African man and woman, the

Slavery in Small Things: Slavery and Modern Cultural Habits, First Edition. James Walvin.
© 2017 John Wiley & Sons, Inc. Published 2017 by John Wiley & Sons, Inc.

man raising his hands clad in chains.[3] In fact the iconography of slavery teems with images of chains and manacles. Among the many hundreds of images of slavery, large numbers involve chains: pictures of Africans heading to the Atlantic coast, of Africans chained below deck on a slave ship, of Africans being punished in the Americas, secured in metal restraints. Even the imagery of freedom – the ending of slavery and the end of the slave trade – often come ready packaged with metal manacles. Commemorative statues of emancipation show Africans proffering broken chains which once bound them. Freedom gained can be simply represented by shattered chains. Even the literature of slavery, and of freedom from slavery, clanks along to the sound of metal ware: 'breaking the chains' is a phrase, a motif, which seems to capture the complex nature of emancipation from bondage. At its worst, this association between chains and slavery has become a grotesque caricature: a lazy and partly misleading visual and literary shortcut to coping with a hugely complex issue. Not surprisingly, this imagery of the manacled African, and the broader reliance on images of chains to depict slavery, has prompted a cultural backlash. Today, chains provoke a hostile response, especially among black people, not least because they suggest African defeat and submission; Africans on their knees, secured by the brutal metal ware of slavery, speak to a debatable and contested historical narrative. Yet, for all that, the chains of slavery also tell another, very different story. They suggest resistance, not defeat. Without the chains, African slavery could not have survived. There is, however, much more to this story than chains. There is a complex but revealing story to be told about the connections between slavery and ironware. The ironware of the slave system evokes the wider story of slavery itself, and of its significance in the way the economies of the Western world thrived and boomed on the back of African slaves.

Chains were only the most obvious of metal goods which formed an integral feature of the Atlantic slave system. This was a system built around metal production, and which needed huge volumes of metal for shipbuilding, fortifications, for the guns, pans, and metal bars, all used in enormous volumes for exchange on the slave coast. Similarly, plantations across the Americas needed an array of metal implements for planting, cultivation, harvesting, and processing crops. American slavery stimulated an astonishing industrial output. This, in its turn, raises the thorny question of the impact of slavery on the emergence of industrial society.

But above all else, chains were ubiquitous. From the loading of the slave ships at the European and American dockside, to the African coast, in mid-Atlantic, and finally on the plantations of the Americas, chains were inescapable in the world of Atlantic slavery. Yard upon jangling yard of chains were loaded onto every slave ship bound for the African coast, alongside a vicious array of other metal items; handcuffs, leg irons, speculums for forced feeding – right down to the simple, excruciating thumb-screws, used to force confession from potentially rebellious Africans. These items were not merely a reflection of a fearful and punitive mentality among the slave traders but also provide important evidence about the collective mentality of the Africans themselves. Without physical restraints, enslaved Africans would simply have disappeared: escaped, fought back, rebelled – and melted away.

On their protracted journeys to the Atlantic coast, when Africans were herded into the baracoons, forts, and holding pens on the coast, in the pestilential holds of the slave ships, even at the moments of exercise on the deck, they threatened to escape: into the bush, down the nearest river, over the ship's side into the ocean. If they could, they would rise up collectively, in an instant, and be at the throat of their captors and tormentors. Slave ships required chains to restrain and contain their human cargoes. Chains were equally vital in the Americas, when slaves were detained for sale, for punishment, or when they were being moved onward to a new destination. Clearly, not all were manacled, and not all posed the risk of escape or resistance. But enough of them did to warrant the slave owners' heavy investment in metal restraints.

The difficulty of restraining Africans was at its most acute, and most dangerous, on the slave ships. On the thousands of ships, which ranged from tiny sloops to some of the biggest of contemporary trading ships, small handfuls of sailors (their numbers invariably depleted by tropical disease and death on the African coast) confronted swelling numbers of Africans as the human cargoes gradually increased in the long periods at anchor off Africa. What had previously been a normal trading vessel was gradually converted into a floating prison, its crew members themselves transformed into guardians of swelling ranks of disaffected, resentful, and potentially turbulent Africans. The Africans were dangerous. Any slave captain – any ordinary deck hand – who did not appreciate that essential fact placed themselves in great personal danger. How could the small crew – a band of apprehensive men – physically control huge numbers of aggrieved Africans? They needed physical restraints (as well as weaponry placed at appropriate commanding positions). And they needed to use harsh, highly visible, and extreme corporal and capital punishments against Africans who rebelled. Survivors of ship-board rebellions, and by-standers, needed to be shown what happened to Africans who threatened their captors: they had to be exposed to the power of their captors in its most savage and unforgiving form. All this required hardware disgorged by iron industries on both sides of the Atlantic.

Shipboard rebellions were frequent. One in ten voyages – perhaps even more – experienced some form of slave resistance (most of it erupting on the African coast itself, rather than in mid-Atlantic). It seems indisputable that without the brutal hardware of incarceration, most notably the chains and fetters, open rebellion would have been even more widespread and more successful. The point is simple. Without chains and manacles, no slave ship could have survived very long. Chains were, at one and the same time, an indication of the slave traders' prudence, of the sailors' deep fears – and of the Africans' rebelliousness. No chains – no slave trade.

Chains are, then, not so much a reflection of African defeat, but of the Africans' pervasive and unquenchable resistance to enslavement. Every slave ship we know of carried chains and other metal restraints. They were loaded in the vessel's home port, and manufactured by local or regional metal industries. The slave trade – indeed the entire Atlantic slave system – generated an enormous volume of commercial and economic activity, at all points of the compass: in Europe, Africa, and the Americas. Less obvious, at first sight, is the industrial hardware spawned by this system, of which chains are only the most visible and most debated.

Every slave ship needed a range of items produced by metal industries. Although slave ships were timber vessels, they all required massive volumes of metal in their construction. Between 1701 and 1810, 8,087 British ships were engaged in the slave trade (one quarter of them constructed in Liverpool shipyards).[4] All of them were held together, and sailed, thanks to metal work: nails, anchors, screws, bolts, iron fittings. Towards the end of the 18th century, they were also fitted with large volumes of copper. By the 1780s, ships' hulls were sheathed in copper, protection against the rotting of the ships' timbers caused by shipworm, so dangerous and common in tropical waters. This was, of course, the story of all kinds of sailing ships. The famous 'wooden walls' were dependent for their construction and for their very movement on a myriad of metal items. Metal craftsmen worked alongside the joiners, shipwrights, and other tradesmen in the construction and maintenance of sailing ships. In British shipyards, for the Royal Navy and for commercial vessels, skilled metalworkers were as critical as the shipwrights. From the mid-17th century, the massive expansion of the Royal Navy, and the parallel transformation of commercial shipbuilding, saw a proliferation of dockyards around the British coastline. There, the complex business of shipbuilding evolved with its reliance on a host of traditional skills harnessed to technical innovations and improvements. The most eminent historian of the Royal Navy has described that process quite simply: the dockyards saw the development of "the industrial age a hundred years before the rest of the country."[5]

The British had traditionally imported substantial volumes of foreign iron, mainly from Sweden. But the story of the British iron industry in the 17th and 18th centuries was closely related to the development of Britain's overseas trade and expansion. Traditional sources of iron ore, in the Forest of Dean and the Weald, were augmented by discoveries and expansion elsewhere: in South Wales, the West Midlands, Shropshire, Staffordshire, Birmingham and the Black Country, Derbyshire, Lancashire, Cumberland, and Sheffield. Ores differed of course, and the nature and quality of the resulting metals varied greatly. But the end result was a network of local (sometimes very small) metal industries able to dispatch their crude or manufactured products to neighboring ports (by sea, river, and canals) thence to the outbound ships to all corners of Britain global trading system. The value of Britain's iron exports increased at a remarkable rate, especially in the course of the 18th century. The £85,000 value of iron exports in 1700 had grown to £400,000 by 1748 and to £1 million before the end of the century.[6] Huge volumes were shipped to Africa, the Caribbean, and North America. The Atlantic slave empire was a key element in driving forward particular areas of domestic British growth – in this case the iron industry.

The increased volume of shipping in the 18th century was remarkable.[7] So, too, naturally, was the explosion in the import and export of goods in British ships. The tonnage of British shipping increased threefold in the course of the 18th century, and what had once been primarily a coastal trade was now, increasingly, global. (20,000 people were employed in coastal waters in 1810–1811 compared to 200,000 in foreign trade at the same time.) All this had a massive impact, via wages, on domestic consumption. The tonnage, and the value, of new ships constructed to cope with this expansion were huge. By the last twenty years of the century between £2.6 and £3 million worth of shipbuilding and repairs took place, much of it at the five major shipbuilding yards scattered around Britain. The shipping industry was, then, an enormous manufacturing industry and the expansion in shipping was closely related to the iron and copper industries, themselves at the very heart of industrial change in Britain.

Building ships for this trade was costly, and much of the cost was for metal. The construction costs of the *Guineamen* in Liverpool, for example, provide a clear indication of the importance of metal in the construction of those ships. The Liverpool ship *Blayds*, built in 1782, cost £1,665. Of that sum £633 went into iron work, £232 in copper sheathing, £91 in nails and braces, and £368 in gun and shots. *The Earl of Liverpool*, built in 1797, cost £1,688.14s, of which iron work accounted for £283, guns £119, and copper £423.[8] What is clear from the few examples we have is that, timber aside, the largest amounts of money invested in slave ships were devoted to metal. Dockyards were, then, an important stimulus to a number of British heavy industries, which in their turn lay the foundations of industrial change from the late 18th century onward.[9]

Slavery lay at the heart of Britain's Atlantic economy, the whole business safeguarded by the Royal Navy, and sustained and secured by Navigation Laws (which kept foreign ships and merchants outside the British imperial and trading zones). By the end of the 18th century, almost half of Britain's foreign trade was to West Africa and the Americas, and central to that commerce was the slave trade and the slave ships which headed out from British ports (often stopping *en route* to collect other commodities) to their chosen trading locations on the Atlantic coast of Africa. They left their home ports stocked with the variety of manufactured goods which they knew were wanted by African middlemen.

The slave trade was more costly than other forms of maritime trade, for example, the coastal or European trades. The value of slave trading to the broader British economy was therefore much greater, and the impact of the slave trade on the wider economy, and its consequences for industrial change, much greater than might initially be expected. In addition to the industrial development of shipping and its ancillary industries, many of the cargoes bound for Africa were manufactured items. Ships trading to West Africa and to the slave colonies carried a host of items which were themselves produced by British industries. The slave colonies, and the trading posts in West Africa, absorbed huge volumes of metal goods from Britain. By the end of the 18th century, 60% of *all* iron exports from Britain went to West Africa and the Americas.[10] Much earlier, in the late 17th century, the Royal African Company exported large volumes of metal goods to West Africa, and those goods were among the most highly valued of all exported commodities.[11] It was, however, the slave *plantations* which absorbed the largest volumes of metal goods. Plantations could only function – survive even – by massive importations (including, above all of course, enslaved African labor). The nails that held the buildings together, the metal implements needed to plant, harvest, and process the tropical produce, the equipment for haulage and transport, all these items and more needed metal goods from British industries. In addition to the most obvious metal goods – nails by the ton, for example – tropical plantations required copper and lead for the boilers, pipes, and cisterns in the factories built to process sugar. The huge demand from the sugar plantations was made possible by the major 'take-off' of British copper mining in the 1680s. Wrought brass and copper, iron, lead, and tin all emerged from expanding British industries, to be shipped in ever increasing volumes to the Caribbean, North America, and West Africa.[12] By the late 17th century, there were legions of small factories dotted throughout the Caribbean islands, all of them employing simple industrial equipment manufactured in Britain. Cog wheels and rollers, cauldrons, pipes and cisterns, boilers and stoves – all these found their way from craftsmen in the British metal industries to the slave plantations. (Travel around the Caribbean to this day and you can still find mounds of rusty cog and fly wheels, large metal vats, pans and boilers, all heaped together, overgrown and hidden in the local bush.)

This growth in demand from the slave economy was substantially responsible for the rapid improvements in methods, and in financing, of Britain's various metal industries. At the same time, the plantations (and the basic human settlement of the American colonies) also demanded a great variety of tools; hand tools for agricultural and industrial work. Every working slave in the tropics was, at some stage of their working life, equipped with tools: bills, hoes, axes, machetes, spades, and rakes. The plantations of the Americas, but especially the dominant sugar plantations, could not have evolved and become the major force they were without huge imports from British metal industries.

There is an abundance of graphic images to illustrate the metal ware of slavery, at all points of the Atlantic – at sea, on the African coast, and in the slave colonies. Perhaps the most obvious, and dramatic, of metal objects are the guns, of all sorts and sizes. Swivel guns on the decks of the slave ships, heavy gun emplacements on the major European settlements in West Africa and the Caribbean, hand guns and firearms of various kinds carried by white people (when surrounded by large numbers of Africans). The European dependence on guns is seen at its most striking in the major West African forts and castles. A string of forts (many modelled on medieval European castles) were constructed along the coast from Arguin in the north to Whydah to the south-east, though the great majority are clustered along the Gold Coast. They were chosen for their strategic location, and designed to afford protection against external threats from the sea, and from the land. European nations feared both their European rivals (who also wanted the location and trade in Africans) and Africans themselves. To the rear of the forts lurked that immense and largely unknown danger that was Africa. Large canons were placed along the fort walls, at strategic gun ports which commanded a view over maritime and land routes to the fort itself. Original plans, and sketches by transient sailors and traders, clearly show the firepower the forts could muster. The bigger forts were defended by dozens of cannons, organized in intimidating ranks, their muzzles poking through apertures in the fort. The major forts had their own armorers, their magazines and powder stores, but the most obvious sign of their firepower were the muzzles of their guns pointing out to sea or covering the paths to the fort.[13]

Today, the major forts are significant tourist sites and many of the guns are still there, useless now, but imposing reminders of the warlike nature of this slave trading presence, and of the

astonishing impact those distant outposts had on European
metal and armament industries. Moreover there were similar
(and generally less noticed) forts which Europeans constructed
throughout their major settlements in the Americas. Again, to
this day, the visitor is struck not only by the astonishing physical impression left by these (often massive) buildings, but by
their reliance on European armament industries for their effec-
tiveness. European settlements, especially those commanding
approaches by land, sea, or river, or which looked over capital cities and towns, often grew around forts or military bases
and dockyards. The Caribbean is littered with such military
structures – Brimstone Hill, St. Kitts; *Citadelle Laferrière*, Haiti;
Fort George, Grenada; Forts Charles and Henderson, Jamaica;
Morro Castle, Havana; San Cristobal fort, at San Juan, Puerto
Rico – and many more.

Less obvious, but much more significant in terms of industrial output, were the huge volumes of firearms consumed by
the slave trade. From an early date, slave traders supplied guns
to African middlemen, as part of the mixed cargoes of textiles,
alcohol, and manufactured goods which formed the basis of that
trade. By the mid-18th century, everyone interested in the slave
trade simply assumed that guns were a vital part of the trade
to Africa and guns were shipped to West Africa in remarkable
volumes.[14] In addition to the guns needed by slave traders and
Europeans living and trading on the coast, huge numbers of
guns were exchanged for African slaves. In the early days, Dutch
gun-makers provided both gunpowder and the most sought-
after weapons (they were better and cheaper than the British
versions).[15] British ships sometimes sailed first to Holland to
acquire a cargo of Dutch firearms for Africa.[16] This African
demand for guns proved an important stimulus in the rise of
British gun manufacture, and British copies of successful Dutch

guns (along with knives and swords) became a major item in the cargo, alongside textiles, of early 18th-century slave ships to West Africa. In the years 1701–1704, for example, the Royal African Company exported enough firearms, in the words of their historian, "to equip a fair-sized army."[17]

These weapons clearly had a major impact *within* Africa. Some African societies came to depend for their political and regional strength on imported guns (and powder) to enhance and strengthen their power over neighboring states. From about 1700, for example, Ashanti traders from the north began to trade at the coastal forts, and the guns they acquired greatly bolstered their emerging power against rival states far from the coast.[18] In 1730, a Dutch memorandum noted that "The great quantity of guns and powder that the Europeans have brought here from time to time has caused terrible wars among the kings, princes and caboceers [local elite] of those lands, who made slaves of their prisoners of war...."[19]

During its relatively brief history, the Royal African Company had enjoyed a flourishing trade in firearms (and gunpowder and knives) to the African coast. Between 1673 and 1704, the Company exported almost 60,000 firearms to West Africa.[20] But the massive expansion of the slave trade in the following century, after the ending of the Company's monopoly, made these numbers look small. In the second half of the 18th century, the English alone exported between 150,000 and 200,000 guns *annually* to West Africa as part of the slave trading system.[21] It was, however, an uneven trade which varied greatly between African regions and in different periods. Nonetheless, it was a massive operation which channeled every conceivable type of firearm into a great number of African societies. From a total of 64,828 guns traded into West Africa between 1757 and 1806, one scholar has found more than thirty different *types* of gun.[22] Moreover, the value of each firearm traded to Africa was much higher than that of other individual items. Slave traders could exchange more for a gun than, say, a pan, kettle, or piece of textile.

So great was the demand for guns that traditional gun manufacturers (notably in Birmingham) had trouble keeping up with the demand from the slave traders, and new gun industries sprang up. Liverpool, for example, had its own gun-makers who supplied the slave ships.[23] Gunsmiths in that city were just one of many skilled groups whose products were destined for the African coast.[24] Slave ships around Britain departed for Africa with guns in their cargoes; when the *Hope* left Lancaster for Africa in 1792 her cargo included almost £500 worth of metal goods, £414 of textiles, and £337 worth of guns.[25]

The story of gun exports to Africa provides some of the best evidence of the impact of the enslaved Atlantic on British industry. In the mid-17th century the armaments industry (primarily in the West Midlands) had been a small affair, but by the end of the 18th century, it had grown to become one of the region's major industries. Birmingham alone employed upward of 5,000 people in arms manufacture by 1788. When the nation was at war (as it was so frequently in that century), government contracts kept them busy. In peacetime they were, according to a major manufacturer, "almost entirely supported by the African trade, a business so very different to any other, that their whole existence may be said to depend on it."[26] Manufacturers recognized that wartime orders for guns, though more specific and demanding than peacetime orders, were largely viewed as a windfall compared to the regular trade in guns to Africa. Moreover, the guns rejected by the government for the military generally found their way to African markets. The order books of gun manufacturers accurately reflected the demand from slave traders: one order from Liverpool in 1772 was for 6,410 guns.

Not surprisingly, the gun manufacturers were strongly opposed to the abolition of the slave trade:

> By such abolition the greatest, and perhaps only,
> efficient nursery for artificers in the art of manufacturing
> guns, would be destroyed.[27]

At times, the demand for guns to Africa was so high that British manufacturers simply could not find enough skilled men to complete the orders from slave traders. Liverpool merchants were especially needy. In 1754 one order was for 1,400 guns for two Liverpool slave ships. In 1772, one manufacturer had orders on his books for 15,900 weapons destined for West Africa. Another Liverpool order was for 6,410 guns. A Liverpool agent, working for a gun manufacturer, had to construct three warehouses and workshops next to his home in the city to cope with the gun trade. In 1771 one Liverpool slave trading firm bought 4,991 guns and 1,250 cutlasses from a Liverpool gun manufacturer.[28]

Africans acquiring guns – and powder – also acquired the power that went with gun ownership. Even if they were not used, the possession of armaments bestowed a power, a terror, which alarmed and intimated opponents. The consequences on African societies were incalculable. But so, too, was the impact on British manufacturing industries. (When the slave trade ended in 1807, and the traditional flow of arms dried up, African states which had come to depend on those armaments found their power correspondingly reduced.[29])

Another major export of metal goods to Africa was in the form of iron bars. Initially trans-shipped from Sweden, but increasingly shipped direct from British iron industries, iron bars formed a regular trade in the barter and exchange for slaves in West Africa. In parts of West Africa such bars became a major means of exchange (though other regions rarely took iron). In places, the ledger accounts of transaction with African traders were kept in terms of iron bars, as well as in pounds and pence.[30] Iron bars passed into African societies where they were melted down and refashioned into a host of implements, tools, and weapons. In the 41 years to 1704 (i.e. before the British trade became the dominant force in the North Atlantic), the Royal African Company alone exported almost 6,000 tons of iron bars to their merchants on the African slave coast.[31]

This trade in iron and iron goods to West Africa was just one aspect of a wider export trade in ironware within the Atlantic slave system. The development and the successful functioning of the Caribbean and, initially, early North American colonies, was also made possible by a host of exports from European industries. Among the most popular (and most reprinted) images of a sugar plantation in the age of slavery were the ten aquatints of Antigua by William Clark in 1823.[32] Although painted in the last decade of British Caribbean slavery, they reveal in great detail the nature of slave work in the fields, in the sugar factory, and in the cumbersome business of transporting barrels of sugar to the coast and onto the waiting ships. At every turn, the African slaves, toiling at their various tasks, depended on metal implements, tools, and machines – all produced and exported by British iron industries.

Slaves first prepared the sugar fields, digging, weeding, and clearing the land for the later planting of sugar. One picture shows a line of 18 slaves, a good number of them women, advancing across the field wielding hoes, clearing the field (which is divided into square grids), and creating holes into which other slaves plant the sugar cane. Another gang of slaves is shown planting the cane ratoons, using spades, hoes, and sticks – and all working under the beady eye of a supervisor who is armed with a whip to ensure that there is no back-sliding

or truculence among the laborers. But perhaps the most revealing image of slaves using metal tools is Clark's picture of the
cane cutters. A line of slaves (the 'First Gang') again, both men
and women, advance on the high wall of fully grown sugar cane,
hacking away at its base with the machete (which remains the
basic tool of all cane cutters to this day). Here, perhaps, was the
most strenuous of tasks, undertaken by slaves chosen for their
strength and endurance. Behind them, younger and older slaves
(the Second and Third Gangs) are tying up the cane and loading it on the wagons for transport to the factory. Surplus 'trash'
is also bundled up for use as fuel in the factory. In all this, metal
agricultural tools were essential.

This dependence on imported metal tools is confirmed
by an examination of the cargoes of ships destined for the
Caribbean, and the account books of individual plantations.
One of Jamaica's oldest continuous plantations, Worthy Park
(founded in 1670 and producing sugar to this day), required a
huge range of imported items to function as a working sugar
plantation. In 1789 three vessels delivered a variety of metal
goods for Worthy Park. The *Betsey* from London regularly
brought barrels and boxes of goods from England and Ireland:
food, hats, and clothing for the slaves, coal, oil, paint, lead,
gunpowder, flour, stationery, leather goods, seeds for the fields,
medicines, rope – and a host of metal items. A 300-gallon boiler,
brass strainers, copper ladles, metal clamps, lead sheets, casks
of cooper's nails, nails for shingles (for roofing), hoes and bills,
tools for the carpenter and for the smith, an anvil for the farrier,
iron axles and metal hoops for barrels – and chains for the cattle. That same year, the *Edward* from Bristol delivered 120 sets
of hoops for the puncheons (the large barrels or hogsheads used
to export the sugar) and the *Henniker* from London shipped in
machine parts for the factory; mill cases, gudgeons, and various
materials to use with the machinery.[33] All this was in addition

to the great variety of metal goods Worthy Park bought or borrowed from local merchants and neighbors, in order to keep the slaves fully employed at sugar and rum production.[34]

The number of slaves employed in factories on sugar plantations was relatively small – but they were of course vital in converting the raw sugar cane into the puncheons of sugar and rum destined for the Atlantic ships and the markets of North America and Britain. William Clark's picture from Antigua again captures that steamy, and sometimes dangerous, work. Large metal rollers in the windmill crushed the juice from the cane: the juice was then filtered and run through piping into the boiling house. There, the juice was slowly transformed into crude sugar – passing through large coppers, clarifiers, and thence to large copper boilers, and finally emerging as crystallized sugar, to be cooled and packed into large barrels (hogsheads), which were kept firmly in place by imported metal hoops. Stored for some weeks, the hogsheads allowed the sugar to drain, the residue collected and converted to rum. The sugar, loaded onto carts pulled by cattle and horses, was transported to the nearest port or jetty, sometimes held in warehouses before finally being loaded onto small boats, thence on board the awaiting vessels. At every level of production, from planting to packing and storing the finished product, metal goods were important; from the hoes used in the field, to the hoops round the puncheons, and the chains used for harnessing oxen to the carts and wains.

By the late 18th century, there was an even greater reliance on imported metal goods because of the revolution wrought by the new steam engines, machines that were being imported from Birmingham to power sugar factories. In the 1780s, Matthew Boulton was keenly aware of the potential for his new engine on Caribbean sugar plantations, and personally knew planters "who wish to see steam answer in the lieu of horses." In fact, James Watt received financial support from men with a commercial interest in the sugar plantations. Not surprisingly, then, between 1788 and 1825 more than one hundred steam engines were ordered for the Caribbean from the Birmingham factories of Boulton and Watt.[35]

By the time the British emancipated their 750,000 slaves in 1838, Britain itself was being transformed by population and urban growth, and by creeping industrialization. Those changes are often characterized by the rise of steam power: it is often referred to as the age of steam. But steam engines had *already* made an impact on the old sugar plantations of the Caribbean, and were to have an even greater impact on the modernized sugar industries of Cuba and Brazil in the 19th century. In all those cases, on the sugar plantations of Jamaica, Cuba, and Brazil, the labor involved was slave labor. This slave labor, introduced into the Americas three centuries earlier, was now part and parcel of the modernizing industrial world.

Yet in many critical respects, slavery in the Americas had *long* been linked to Europe's early industries, nowhere more obviously than in its dependence on the myriad metal goods. Long before Britain became the prototype industrial society (driven forward by cotton) modern industry, in the form of factories, was scattered across the face of the slave colonies.

We do not have precise figures, but most large and medium-sized sugar plantations had their own factories: a series of (often large) buildings, on the plantation, where sugar cane was transformed into sugar by an industrial process. These crude sugars were then dispatched to the sugar refineries which dotted the skyline of European port cities. (In 1753, there were about 120 sugar refineries in England and Scotland, 80 of them in London and 20 in Bristol. A string of such 'sugar-houses,' many owned by Liverpool slave traders, lined the streets of Liverpool close to the docks.[36])

Curiously, the sugar factories have been overlooked by historians of British industrial change, perhaps because they represented an industrial process that was deceptively camouflaged by its rural and agricultural setting. Yet those clouds of smoke and steam traditionally associated with the north of England and the Midlands could be seen belching from sugar factory chimneys in the Caribbean. Clark's pictures of a sugar factory in Antigua in 1838 are only the best known of a host of similar images. Landscapes, sketches, and book illustrations from the earliest days of slave settlement provide clear visual evidence of sugar factories at work; crushing, boiling, filtering, and potting sugar in a process that was clearly industrial. Time and again, contemporary pictures show smoke billowing from the factory chimneys into the Caribbean sky.[37]

Factories, and even steam engines, were commonplace on sugar plantations by the time of emancipation in 1833. Above all, however, the one metal object that epitomized slavery was, of course, the chain. David Lucas's mezzotint of 1834, showing Africans burying their chains was a vivid reminder of the pre-eminent symbol of slavery: the chains that shackled slaves to their owners and to the land. Vital on the slave ships, chains had become a visual symbol of slavery, even though the millions of enslaved Africans across the Americas did *not* work (indeed *could not* work) when shackled. It was not possible to work in the tobacco, sugar, and cotton fields burdened by chains – though many found themselves clapped back into chains for punishment and restraint, or when being moved from place to place. It is now, surely, time to think of those chains in a different light. We need to see the chains of slavery as a sign of slave resistance, not of defeat.

Notes

1. Tim Barringer, Gillian Forrester, and Barbara Martinez-Ruiz, *Art and Emancipation in Jamaica: Isaac Mendes Belisario and His Worlds*, New Haven, 2007, p. 369.
2. *Set All Free*, 2007, Published by Churches Together in England.
3. Jacob Epstein, 'Study for Slave Hold,' 1954, Bolton Museum.
4. James Walvin, *The Zong: A Massacre, the Law and the End of Slavery*, London, 2011, p. 23.
5. N.A.M. Rodger, *Command of the Ocean: A Naval History of Britain*, London, 2006, p. 189.
6. J.R. Harris, *The British Iron Industry 1700–1850*, London, 1988.
7. Joseph E. Inikori, *Africans and the Industrial Revolution in England*, Cambridge, 2002, p. 268.
8. Joseph E. Inikori, *Africans and the Industrial Revolution in England*, pp. 307–308.
9. Joseph E. Inikori, *Africans and the Industrial Revolution in England*, p. 312.
10. Joseph E. Inikori, *Africans and the Industrial Revolution in England*, p. 460.
11. Nuala Zahediah, *The Capital and the Colonies: London and the Atlantic Economy, 1660–1700*, Cambridge, Table 6.2, p. 249.
12. Nuala Zahediah, *The Capital and the Colonies*, Table 6.9. p. 272.
13. The most detailed study of the forts is still A.W. Lawrence, *Fortified Trade Posts: The English in West Africa, 1645–1822*, London, 1963.
14. Joseph E. Inikori, 'The import of firearms into West Africa, 1750 to 1807.' In Joseph E. Inikori, ed., *Forced Migration: The Impact of the Export of the Slave Trade on African Societies*, London, 1982, pp. 129–131.
15. Joannes Menne Postma, *The Dutch in the Atlantic Slave Trade: 1600–1815*, Cambridge, 1990, pp. 103–104.
16. K.G. Davies, *The Royal African Company*, New York, 1970, p. 173.
17. K.G. Davies, *The Royal African Company*, p. 177.
18. K.G. Davies, *The Royal African Company*, p. 288. For a study of warfare in the region see John K. Thornton, *Warfare in Atlantic Africa, 1500–1800*, London, 1999.
19. Robert Harms, *The Diligent: A Voyage Through the Worlds of the Slave Trade*, New York, 2002, p. 135.
20. K.G. Davies, *The Royal African Company*, p. 356.
21. James Walvin, *Black Ivory: A History of British Slavery*, London, 1992, p. 30.
22. Joseph E. Inikori, *Africans and the Industrial Revolution in England*, 'Imports,' Table II, pp. 142–143.
23. Jane Longmore, 'Cemented by the blood of a Negro? The impact of the slave trade on eighteenth-century Liverpool.' In David Richardson *et al.*, eds., *Liverpool and Transatlantic Slavery*, pp. 243–244.
24. Jane Longmore, 'Cemented by the blood of a Negro?', p. 240.
25. Melanie Elder, *The Slave Trade and the Economic Development of 18th century Lancaster*, Halifax, 1992, pp. 211–212.

26. Quoted in Joseph E. Inikori, *Africans and the Industrial Revolution in England*, p. 458.

27. Joseph E. Inikori, 'Import of firearms.' In Joseph E. Inikori, ed., *Forced Migration*, pp. 129–130.

28. Joseph E. Inikori, *Africans and the Industrial Revolution in England*, pp. 464–466.

29. Gareth Austin, 'Between abolition and jihad.' In Robin Law, ed., *From Slave Trade to Legitimate Commerce*, Cambridge, 1995, p. 93.

30. K.G. Davies, *The Royal African Company*, p. 238.

31. K.G. Davies, *The Royal African Company*, p. 351.

32. William Clark's ten aquatints are most easily seen in Tim Barringer *et al.*, *Art and Emancipation in Jamaica*, pp. 319–320.

33. Michael Craton and James Walvin, *A Jamaican Plantation: Worthy Park, 1670-1970*, London, 1970, pp. 320–322.

34. Michael Craton and James Walvin, *A Jamaican Plantation*, pp. 324–327.

35. Ian Grosvenor, Rita McLean, and Sian Roberts, eds., *Making Connections, Birmingham Black International History*, Birmingham, 2002.

36. Richard B. Sheridan, *Sugar and Slavery: An Economic History of the British West Indies, 1623-1675*, Jamaica, 1994 edn., pp. 29–30; Jane Longmore, 'Cemented by the blood of a Negro?', p. 245.

37. See, e.g., J. Hinton, 'A Representation of the Sugar Cane and the Art of Sugar Making,' (1749); James Hakewill, 'Water Colours, 1820–21.' In Tim Barringer *et al.*, eds., *Art and Emancipation in Jamaica*, pp. 315; 322.

11

Cotton

Slavery and Industrial Change

In 1842 the recently incorporated city of Manchester acquired a Coat of Arms, providing its own colorful version of a heraldic tradition that went back centuries. It is a vivid compilation of heraldic symbols and significant images. The eye is immediately attracted by two prominent themes: bees and a sailing ship. The bees – always busy – seem clear enough and represent the city's industriousness. But the sailing ship seems oddly out of place. Manchester, after all, is an inland city, a full thirty miles from the sea, and not readily associated with seafaring. Yet in 1842 the city chose to portray itself via an image of a sailing ship in full sail. The explanation lies in Manchester's claim to be a city founded on global trade – above all a global trade in textiles.

At the time, Manchester had become infamous as the 'shock city' of the industrial revolution, a 'land of long chimneys,' home to a rapidly expanding but largely ill-housed population which consisted overwhelmingly of grimly exploited immigrant work-ers, drawn from its immediate hinterland– and Ireland, most working in the factory-based manufacture of a range of textiles. It was also a city which had a steady stream of curious visi-tors, attracted not by its natural beauty but by the raw industrial and human curiosity that was Manchester. Like generations that

Slavery in Small Things: Slavery and Modern Cultural Habits, First Edition. James Walvin.
© 2017 John Wiley & Sons, Inc. Published 2017 by John Wiley & Sons, Inc.

followed, such visitors were struck by a landscape dominated by factory chimneys, and by the terrible living conditions of the people working in those factories.

In the mid-18th century, some maps of England did not even include Manchester on their list of English towns,[1] but a century later, it was unmissable. Its population stood at 223,000 in 1831 and had quadrupled in the space of fifty years. It had become a new kind of urban, industrial phenomenon (but one that was to become increasingly familiar around the world in later years). Manchester was also the center of a new 'cotton empire': a city at the heart of a regional network of towns and villages scattered across the north-west of England which absorbed vast amounts of raw cotton and then refined, spun, weaved, bleached, dyed, and transformed it into millions of yards of cheap textiles, dispatching the finished products all over the world. And the world at large quickly took to, and dressed itself in, Britain's cheap cotton exports.[2] This global market evolved partly because of Lancashire's flying start, partly through its competitive edge, but also as a result of Britain's astonishing political and colonial reach – a reach which obliged millions of people to trade with and buy from Britain on terms that were favorable to British industry. The bees and the sailing ship on Manchester's Coat of Arms were, then, the perfect symbols for an industrious city which prospered by exporting its products around the world.

There had been nothing quite like Manchester before, and visitors traveled to that damp, murky place to see for themselves what was happening.[3] Indeed, some of the most vivid of historical memories of Manchester in its early industrial phase are to be found in the accounts from the steady trickle of curious British and foreign visitors, whose wide-eyed descriptions of the town quickly entered the literary and political folklore of industrial history. Manchester established itself not merely as an industrial city, but (odd as it may seem today) as a tourist destination for the socially curious. They were the early Victorian equivalent of today's 'dark tourists,' people whose (generally horrified) accounts of what they saw provided rich pickings for later historians.

Time and again, visitors reacted with astonishment to the filth and degradation that underpinned, seemed even to characterize, life and work in Manchester. The list of commentators and writers influenced by their time in Manchester is long and distinguished, but however different their political views, they were united in the shock they felt at the condition of the place. The eminent French critic Alexis de Tocqueville passed through in 1835, and penned some of the most memorable and caustic of remarks about Manchester's filthy, money-making environment. More famous still, of course, was the literary and political reaction of Frederick Engels, the intellectual son of a German textile manufacturer, sent to Manchester by his father in 1842 to work in the Victoria Mill, in the hope that his radical political views might be changed by life in the city. Engels found his spiritual home in Manchester's Chetham's Library where he continued his studies and writings, and where he met and talked with Karl Marx. The essays and articles he sent to Karl Marx in 1844 to 1845 about Manchester became the basis for his classic publication, *The Condition of the Working Class in England*, published first in German in 1845, but not published in English until 1887.

In a different but nonetheless powerful vein at mid-century, the novels of Elizabeth Gaskell had made their own literary impact on the debate about the nature and condition of Manchester. The city also provided Charles Dickens (who serialized Mrs. Gaskell's *North and South* in the journal *Household Words* and visited Manchester 19 times) with evidence for a number of his works. The city's fame spread among armies of readers who knew little about the place except via the printed word. But millions more learned about Manchester through the cheap textile goods they bought in ever greater volumes. By the time Manchester acquired its Coat of Arms, it had secured a distinctive place for itself in the contemporary literary and political imagination.

Visitors were astonished by the distant sight of the place long before they entered the city itself. It looked like no city had before it, its panorama shaped and defined by factory chimneys, by the numerous large factories themselves, and by the shroud of industrial smoke that seemed to hover permanently overhead. Cities the world over had traditionally been dirty and smelly – but there had been nothing like Manchester: nothing to approach the concentration and intensity of large buildings, towering chimneys, and belching smoke. And though it seemed to function under a permanent gloom of industrial smoke, it was brightened by artificial gas lights spilling from thousands of factory windows: the very lights that kept the workers at their tasks long after the sun had disappeared.

The rise of the East India Company had seen large volumes of Indian textiles shipped into Britain (though large amounts were also re-exported). But Britain had its own long tradition of textile manufacturing, too. An early textile industry, for instance, had emerged in East Anglia among refugees from the Low Countries, but cotton spinning seemed better suited to the damper climate in Lancashire, and that early industry also had the advantage of being located close to Liverpool for the import of cotton from Smyrna in Turkey and the Caribbean. The real transformation in textiles, however, was wrought by the technological changes in the 18th century – mechanical improvements in weaving and spinning, the application of water power, and, finally and most dramatic of all, the application of steam power to both spinning and weaving. The simple data from these changes is staggering. In India it took 50,000 hours of hand operative work to produce 100 pounds of cotton, but by 1795 the same amount of cotton could be produced in Lancashire by

300 hours of industrial labor. By 1825, it took only 135 hours.[4] The incubation of this technological revolution – the origins of the Industrial Revolution – took place in villages and valleys close to Manchester, and it drew its finance and raw materials from *existing* commercial systems. The industry also used cotton grown by slaves in the Caribbean, and drew on finance which was available from men already established in trade to and from Africa, India, and the Americas. In addition, Britain's remarkable commercial and colonial reach and global dominance provided ready-made markets for the end products: the textiles which spilled out from Lancashire's factories. There were other enterprising and pioneering industrialists in Germany, Brazil, and the USA: Lowell Massachusetts paralleled the story of Manchester, with its massive mills and armies of exploited laborers, large numbers of them young women and girls. But none of these countries had access to the global markets that Britain had created (and jealously guarded) in the course of the 18th century.[5] To cap it all, Britain's textile pioneers also had access to very cheap labor in the form of child and female labor. Cotton manufacture boomed.

At the end of the 18th century Britain boasted 900 cotton factories, but the subsequent revolution in cotton production can perhaps best be gauged through the number of cotton spindles at work. In 1788 there were 50,000 spindles, but by 1821 it stood at 7 million.[6] Most were humming away in cotton mills, the very factories that created the new skyline of Manchester, and in a string of smaller industrial towns in the region. Writing of Oldham in 1824, a local historian commented that "Sixty years ago there was not a cotton mill in the chapelry [parish]; at the present there are no fewer than sixty-five, of which all, except two, have been built during the present century."[7] Such mills were powered first by water, then by steam, and these large buildings, some of them six storeys high, quickly established themselves as the quintessential image of industrial society, first of all in Britain, but soon in other parts of Europe and North America. The age of the modern factory had been born. Curiously, however, the concept of the factory was already well established, not in industrial Europe, but on the slave plantations of the Americas. Sugar plantations throughout the Caribbean and Brazil not only cultivated sugar cane but also processed the cane into refined sugar and rum in a factory close to the cane fields. Late 18th-century pictures of sugar plantations invariably showed the factory chimney, its smoke trailing skyward above the plantation. Long before the rise of the cotton factory, slave plantations had used recognizably modern industrial systems to produce commodities for export to the wider world. These same places – plantations and their factories – also developed a discipline of labor which was tightly regulated and marshalled, and all this *long* before the rise of the clock-based discipline of industrial life in Europe and North America. Yet today, when we speak of early 'factories' we tend to think of the large buildings pioneered by the cotton industry. In fact, sugar came first.

Lancashire's new cotton manufacturers required a raw material that was cultivated thousands of miles distant from their factories. Again, the British had an advantage. Cotton had been cultivated on Caribbean islands (as it had in South America) from the 1630s, and had been among the exports from the slave empire throughout its existence. As demand in Britain increased in the late 18th century, Caribbean planters turned to marginal lands, or land in newly acquired colonies, to plant cotton, and as demand grew, planters in frontier regions of South America, notably Surinam and Demerara, turned to cotton too. Brazilian cotton (indigenous and a long-standing if relatively minor industry) also boomed. Cotton exported from British Caribbean colonies quadrupled in the decade after 1781, and planters in Tobago and the Bahamas similarly turned to cotton (having grown little or none earlier). By 1787, the Bahamas was dispatching almost half a million pounds of cotton to Britain.[8] It was, however, in Barbados that the most dramatic change took pace. After the devastating hurricane of 1780, which all but destroyed the sugar industry, cotton was planted, and that island quickly established itself as the most important source of cotton in the British Caribbean. The French, too, doubled their Caribbean production. (The French islands produced 56% of all Caribbean cotton, much of it finding its way, via France, back to British manufacturers.) By the end of the 18th century 8 million pounds of cotton were imported into Britain.

In all these locations, from the Bahamas south through the Caribbean islands and into Brazil, cotton was cultivated by slaves. It was this slave-grown cotton which arrived at European ports, most notably at Liverpool, in staggering volumes. These sources of cotton, however, very rapidly went into decline in the 1790s. War between Britain and France, the devastating slave rebellion in St. Domingue (Haiti) after 1791, and competition for land from expansive sugar industries all served to undermine the slave-based cotton production which had served the initial rise of industrial Britain. There was, however, a new region available for the development of cotton cultivation – the rich frontier lands of the new American Republic.

The USA had land beyond imagination (if we ignore, for a moment, the rights of native Americans to that land) and though American demand for labor would inspire waves of immigrants from Europe, the USA already had a large and growing labor force at home: the enslaved population which had transformed the face and economy of the Old South. It was clear enough to a number of observers and politicians that the collapse of Caribbean cotton, and the demand of Britain's

booming cotton industry, offered the USA a major opportunity. There had been, moreover, a variety of older efforts to
grow cotton in colonial America. But it was the success of Sea
Island cotton, well-suited to Manchester's requirements, which
made the difference. The real leap – the transformation – came
about, as it had in the British textile industry, by technological
change, and the impact of Eli Whitney's cotton gin after 1793.
Whitney's device (for removing seeds from the cotton) was an
instant success and swiftly and massively enhanced cotton production. Cotton cultivation quickly spread from coastal South
Carolina into the hinterland of that state and on to Georgia.
Settlers poured in, converting land to cotton production, using
slaves they took with them, and shipping their produce to Liverpool. The pattern was established for the transformation of great
swathes of the USA, and cotton cultivation seeped across the
face of the South, taking slavery along with it. Settlers and their
enslaved laborers moved like an invading army, across Alabama
and Louisiana, Mississippi and Arkansas and as far as Texas.
The rich, untapped soils, especially of the Mississippi Delta, provided a luxuriant environment for cotton cultivation, and as the
acreage of cotton cultivation increased, so too did the enslaved
population. The US production of cotton grew at an astonishing rate. The 1.5 million pounds produced in 1790 had grown
to 36.5 million in 1800, and to 167.5 million by 1820. By 1850,
the US South was producing 2.5 million bales of cotton – each
one weighing 181 kg. Yet a decade later, that figure had doubled
again.[9] On the eve of the Civil War cotton had become not only
the principal export from the USA but its value was greater than
all other American exports combined.[10]

British cotton imports increased at a scarcely believable rate.
They grew sevenfold between 1800 and 1820.[11] In 1772 (before,
that is, the rise of Southern cotton), Britain imported 4.4 million
pounds of cotton; by 1800 that had grown to 41.8 million. The

figures for the following decades reveal the astonishing impact of American cotton:

65 million in 1811
141 million in 1821
249 million in 1831
452 million in 1851.[12]

Behind these figures lay not only the transformation of the US South (and indeed of the wider US economy) but also of Lancashire, most notably the rapid expansion of the city of Manchester. But textile factories, often of a specialized kind, sprouted across south-east Lancashire, with the associated growth of small towns in their shadow. Where cotton spinning thrived, there we find advances in steam power. As late as 1870, 30% of all the steam power used in British industries was to be found in the cotton spinning industry.[13]

The rise and rise of the Lancashire textile industry was also reflected in the story of Liverpool. It had become a major port in the 18th century via the Irish and the Atlantic trades, and was, by the end of that century, recognized as Britain's major slave trading port. Fears that the ending of the slave trade (in 1807) would bring the port to its knees proved groundless, though what subsequently happened was ironic. The port which had boomed on the back of the slave trade had in place all the necessary elements for the later development of the import and export of cotton and textiles. One slave economy (the slave trade) helped to lay the foundations for another slave economy in cotton. After abolition, Liverpool continued to expand and thrive, and much of this was down to the trade in cotton from the USA. Within a decade of the ending of the slave trade, cotton had become the Liverpool's major import. By 1850, 80% of the nation's imported cotton landed at Liverpool. The pattern of Liverpool's exports was similar. By the 1820s, exports from Liverpool even surpassed exports from London. In 1857, 42% of the value of Liverpool's entire export trade consisted of cotton goods.[14] Liverpool brought "the world's resources and markets almost to the doorstep of south-east Lancashire..." – all greatly helped by major improvements in transportation in the region.[15]

As Britain devoured ever more raw cotton, its cotton mills spat out correspondingly vast volumes of textiles. But the markets buying Lancashire textiles changed in the course of the 19th century, largely because new textile industries in other parts of the world ate into Lancashire's initial dominance. Before 1820, Europe and the USA bought about 70% of British textile exports. By 1850, that had dropped to 26%, though by then Lancashire was pouring its textiles into Latin America, the Middle East, and, above all, India. (There, the British exercised decisive political and commercial power, and could wield critical commercial control over a captive market.)[16]

Time and again, Britain's booming textile industry was lauded as an astonishing commercial success. Its size, its unprecedented growth, the number of people it employed, the material and social benefits it yielded in the form of cheap and healthy clothing for millions of people around the world – all were part of an extraordinary story. But at the heart of this commercial success lay the human tragedy of slavery. Lancashire's success was carried along on the back of American slaves. A new breed of planters had tapped the wealth of the rich lands of the US South using the labor of armies of slaves. This time, however, planters had no need to turn to Africa for their labor force, as their forebears had done. There was an expanding slave population closer to hand, in the Old South, and from there a new kind of slave trade emerged: the internal North American slave trade, which saw huge numbers of slaves bought and sold, forcibly moved on from their original homes. This enormous demand for slaves in the South also stimulated the economies of other states. The value of slaves increased, and slave owners in the old slave-holding states capitalized on the demand by shipping their human possessions onward towards the Cotton Belt. The end result was that twice as many slaves traveled along these *internal* American slave routes as had crossed the Atlantic from Africa to North America.[17] They often passed through a variety of hands, down the rivers, by coastal craft (from Norfolk to New Orleans, for example), by steamboat and on foot, until they reached the auction blocks of the South, thence into the cotton fields. It was a merciless process which destroyed slave families, broke slave hearts, and left a deep scar on American life which has remained unhealed to this day. Almost one million people endured the enforced movement to the cotton fields of the South, leaving in their wake a trail of emotional dismay and misery. One in five slave marriages were destroyed by these migrations, one child in three was parted from parents. Once sold, and prodded onward, the departing slave effectively disappeared, just as their ancestors had disappeared from their African homelands when they were removed to the Atlantic coast and to the awaiting slave ships.

Today, the image of the western migration of the American people is proclaimed in popular culture as one of the heroic features of the shaping of the USA and its peoples. It is an image, however, which hides a much darker story, or rather two related stories. It is the story of the brutal removal of native peoples from their traditional lands, and the enforced migration of hundreds of thousands of enslaved peoples. Time and again, the US government and its army forced native peoples to move, to sign treaties which surrendered their lands and saw them transported to distant, alien locations. When they resisted, the US army used its military power to move them. The essence of what took place is a bleak, depressing story: the exercise of raw power against native peoples, and the enforced movements of slaves to re-occupy and transform that land. That land was then brought into profitable cultivation by the use of slave labor – and all for the benefit of the new landowners and their financial backers in the North (and in Europe). It is, to repeat, a story which runs counter to popular myth: the heroic saga of the American frontier and the West, familiar to millions mainly via movies. The truth of this American surge westward was altogether more rapacious.

Cotton transformed the US South, the land quickly refashioned into a patchwork of plantations and farms, with slavery the dominant form of labor. In a matter of decades, major urban areas sprouted, much as they did in the Lancashire textile regions. Southern states swelled with migrant populations. Louisiana contained only 77,000 people in 1810: forty years later this stood at half a million. Alabama increased its population, in the same period, from 9,000 to 772,000. A majority of those inhabitants were slaves. Cotton had created a new human phenomenon in the USA: regions where a majority of the population was black. This had long been true in the Caribbean and Brazil. (Indeed, until 1840, the Americas as a whole formed an extension, not of Europe, but of Africa.[18]) In the South, slavery shaped and determined local life. Slave ownership was widespread but most slaves were owned in relatively small groups, with most slave owners owning fewer than ten slaves. Only 2.7 % of Southern slaveholders owned more than 50 slaves in 1860 but one quarter of Southern slaves lived on properties that were home to 50 slaves or more.[19] Most Southern slaves lived on small, modest properties, often working alongside their owners. But to this day it is the large cotton plantation that catches the popular imagination. It is, once again, the image of *Tara*, established by *Gone with the Wind* (see Chapter 5). Most of the cotton grown in the South in 1860 was picked by slaves working on larger plantations.[20] At mid-century, more than one third of a million Americans owned slaves: of the 4 million slaves in the USA in 1860, the great majority worked in cotton.[21] It was not the small farmer, but the planter – the man in the fashionable Great House – who commanded an army of slave laborers and who dominated Southern life. They were the men who shaped the ideals, values, and culture of the South.[22] Before the meteoric rise of the railroad and steel barons, America's wealthiest men were the planters of the South, and their surviving homes confirm their wealth, their social aspirations, and their power. Slavery defined Southern life far beyond the boundaries of the cotton plantations. And, of course, it is their lavishly restored homes that continue to attract tourists, and thus reinforce the popular image of what the slave plantation was really like.

Like slaves throughout the Americas, slaves in the South undertook whatever task they were ordered to do. On bigger Southern properties, there were retinues of servants catering for every domestic need of the planter's family, from child-rearing to cleaning and cooking. Often, too, they satisfied the sexual demands of the men of the house. Visitors to the US South (and to Brazil in the same period) were astonished by the numbers, and the inescapability, of slaves in the planters' homes (as they had been in the Caribbean in the 18th century). Slaves also forged the physical transformation of Southern society at large: building the towns, the railroads, the riverboats, and manning local industries, from logging to mining. But they were most visible and most obvious in the laboring gangs in the fields across the Cotton Belt, which stretched from South Carolina to Texas. And it was here that the slave drivers and overseers exercised that harsh and often brutal discipline which characterized slave labor. In the words of Solomon Northrup (now famous for penning the memoir that inspired the movie *12 Years a Slave*), the overseer needed "utter heartlessness, brutality and cruelty."[23] Overseers emerged as a distinct 'professional' class, famed for (and boastful of) their ability to handle truculent slave gangs. The larger the plantation, the more complex the organization of slave labor, and the more brutal the methods needed to handle them. Everywhere, however (and this was true throughout the Americas), slaves were always exposed to the capricious whim, personal quirks, and idiosyncrasies of the owner and overseers. In general, slaves had few effective defenses, though they devised their own strategies of resistance. Yet the overseers themselves rarely satisfied their employers' expectations, and found themselves caught between the dangerous hostility of the slaves and the often unrealistic plans of their bosses. Whatever their working and personal frustrations, overseers found relief by taking out their anger on the slaves.

Cotton was a labor-intensive commodity, and slavery – in gangs – was ideally suited to its cultivation. The plantation, the key to the success of cotton, had already proved its value in other parts of the Americas, in the cultivation of tobacco, rice, sugar, and coffee (and a host of other crops which are generally overlooked). Plantation labor had been organized in a variety of ways, in gangs, at task work, via hired gangs of jobbing slaves. But whatever the system, few doubted that the key to successful development was the use of slave labor anchored to plantations. Unlike cotton manufacturers in Europe, cotton planters had total control over their labor force (and they faced little opposition, until late in the day, about how they operated that control). The labor discipline available to planters must have been the envy of industrialists who were restrained by a host of moderating forces: local and political scrutiny, radical critics, and legal restraints. Planters were more or less free to do what they wanted with their enslaved labor force.

Not surprising, then, the plantation became the crucible for social and economic life across the US South. It was both workplace and home, the center of soaring profitability for some, and a life of inescapable misery for most. More than that, the men who controlled the South, the planters and the cotton merchants (with all their ancillary backers), had the ear of Washington and of state and regional government. They needed, and secured, the political backing and authorization to expand their businesses using slave labor on land which initially belonged to others. Political support for the Southern planters was especially important, for instance, in the decisions to route the new railway lines to facilitate the movement of cotton and people within the Cotton Belt. At first sight, it might seem that the US South was physically distant from the center of US power, but it was integrated in the key decision-making in the nation's capital, at a time when the planters held political sway in the South itself.

The main artery of what became a massive and geographically dispersed slave system was the Mississippi. Millions of tons of cotton were shipped down that massive waterway, by steamboat and barge, to New Orleans, which quickly became the key cotton port for the USA. In 1817 there were only 17 steamboats working there. By mid-century, there were 700. Ten years later, more than 1,500 steamboats were transporting two millions tons of cotton.[24] On the eve of the Civil War more than 4 million bales of cotton were being produced in the Cotton Belt.[25]

Such statistics, astonishing as they are, can nevertheless serve to mask the stark reality of slavery, and the brutality and violence which underpinned it. The hidden cost of the cheap textiles which poured from Lancashire's factories was not merely the exploitation of local working people (notably female and child labor) but the gross violence done to millions of American slaves. Transporting, selling, corralling, and ordering slave labor could not be done without the threat – and the reality – of physical force. Scratch any slave narrative – listen to the voice of any slave remembrance – and violence quickly surfaces as a commonplace feature of slave life. Yet it is also true that managing and working a plantation involved a more complex structure of command than simple force. There was also a degree of give-and-take, the promise of bonuses and of benefits, the making of concessions – all to persuade and cajole slaves to work. Even so, slaves were under no illusions about the ultimate sanction: no one doubted who held the whip-hand (the phrase itself redolent of slave life). Moreover, those who knew the US Southern cotton industry at first hand, for example the British merchants and traders who paid regular business trips to the South, fully recognized the brute reality: cotton needed slavery (and where would Lancashire be without it?) and the organization of slavery was lubricated by violence.

As early as 1802, US cotton dominated the British market. Thirty years later it dominated the entire European market. It was also the largest US export, constituting 32% of all US exports in 1820. Indeed, cotton drove forward the astonishing emergence of the US economy in the first half of the 19th century – courtesy of slavery.[26] This transatlantic flow of cotton had its most astonishing impact on industrial Lancashire. An estimated 3.5 million people in Britain worked in the cotton industry at mid-century, but such a dependency came with obvious risks. What would happen to the British industry if US cotton faltered, or was diverted elsewhere (to factories in the north-east of the USA, for instance)? And what would happen if US slavery was abolished? This question was no mere theoretical speculation. The rising tide of abolition sentiment, in the US North and in Britain itself, was committed to bringing slavery to an end. The British, flushed with their own success at emancipation in 1833, directed an increasingly critical voice at US slavery. Twenty years later, after *Uncle Tom's Cabin*, North American slavery was firmly in the sights of a powerful and expanding transatlantic abolitionist lobby. Worried Lancastrian manufacturers began to look elsewhere, notably to India, then (with more success) to Egypt, for alternative supplies of cotton, just in case the unthinkable happened – and US slavery was abolished.

Here was an apparent paradox. The first industrial society was steered towards a more broadly based industrial growth by a textile industry that was reliant on slave labor on the far side of the Atlantic. Cotton c. 1850 had come to occupy a similar position to sugar c.1750; a commodity grown thousands of miles from its main consumers, which was an integral feature of a massive and complex global commerce. And both were dependent on enslaved labor from Africa. The British after 1807 (abolition) and then 1833 (emancipation), repeatedly congratulated themselves on their abolitionist triumph in ending their slave trade and colonial slavery. They had apparently washed their hands of the pollution of slavery. Yet Britain's drive towards industrialization was inextricably and causally linked to slavery in the American South. For a century and a half, sugar had been the main and dominant import into Britain. After 1820, it was replaced by cotton, both of them the fruits of slave labor.[27]

Cotton had become a golden crop, and industrializing societies – not just Britain – simply could not get enough of it. Speculators invested in new cotton lands wherever soil and climate seemed suitable. Cotton mills sprouted in the most unlikely of places: across Europe and the north-east of the USA, Mexico, India, and Brazil. Often they imitated the British pioneers, sometimes even encouraged by British exports of equipment, skilled manpower, and investment. European and American businessmen and investors flocked to Lancashire to see the process at work, returning home with ideas, plans, drawings, machines, and a zest to transform their home industries on the Lancastrian model.[28] Everywhere, the old ways of spinning cotton and of manufacturing textiles were simply washed away by a proliferation of cotton mills able to produce unprecedented volumes of cheap textiles.[29]

For the time being the British dominated. British cotton production increased at an annual rate of 5% to 1850; its exports by 6.3%. In 1835 there were 1,500 British cotton manufacturers. By 1860, 4,000 people owned cotton mills in Britain. It was in those mills, and other factories like them, that industrial labor, mainly child and female, was instilled with a new kind of discipline (one we accept and take for granted today): the discipline imposed by the clock, by the machine, and by the mechanical dictates of the place of employment.[30] At both ends of the cotton cycle – in the cotton fields of the US South and the factories of Lancashire – a harsh work discipline was essential. It was no accident that the pioneer of factory reform in Britain, Richard Oastler, denounced 'factory slavery' in Britain's mills. Of course the analogy was flawed, and the links were not as simple or direct as Oastler suggested: however harsh, factory owners could not treat their workers as planters treated their slaves. Yet the parallel was close enough to have the required political effect. Forging the link, in the public's mind, between slavery and factory labor was a clever political ploy. Nor was it a simple political trick, because it possessed a historical reality (one which perhaps even Oastler himself did not fully grasp). Factory labor and American slavery were indeed linked. Both were integral features of a massive industry which had slaves working the rich soils of the US South to cultivate a commodity which was then transformed by exploited factory workers into cheap textiles.

* * *

Liverpool was the vital conduit between the slaves in the Cotton Belt and Lancashire's factory workers. That port's well-established systems of maritime and global commerce had been developed in the 18th century by its expanding trade to Ireland, Africa, and the Americas. Liverpool men – the ship owners, merchants, brokers, and traders – had long been accustomed to looking to the far side of the Atlantic for profitable business, and US cotton was just the latest branch of their enterprising activities. The homes and civic buildings which had, in the 18th century, proclaimed the local importance of Africa and of Africans (street names, African heads on buildings) were now joined by massive docks, warehousing, and commercial premises devoted to the trade in cotton and textiles. Cotton flowed in, and textiles flowed out, with the grey skyline dominated by a forest of masts, and, after 1830, of smoke stacks of the new steam ships, all plying their trade between Liverpool, Boston, New York, and the Gulf ports. On the dockside, a multitude of laborers, many of them Irish, toiled at loading and unloading the cargoes (forming yet another badly exploited group of working people in the cotton system). They shifted bales of cotton from ships' holds to warehouses, thence to the barges on the canals which had come to form a spider's web of commercial links to Liverpool's hinterland. From the mid-18th century, a string of vital waterways had linked the Mersey to a large inland interior. Canals, and improved rivers, snaked their way into Cheshire, to the Potteries, and onto the Midlands, across the Lancashire coalfield and onto Yorkshire and Leeds. The critical artery was the Bridgewater canal to Manchester (designed initially to carry coal). From the 1830s onwards, of course, the new railway companies offered their own commercial ties between Liverpool and inland urban and industrial centers.

This massive movement of cotton passed through the hands of Liverpool's cotton brokers, who congregated on the flags outside the Exchange (reputed, at the end of the working day, to be white with cotton fluff). From 1808 they had offices to occupy inside the new Exchange Building. From there, Liverpool's brokers exploited the old trading links to North America to manage the massive expansion of cotton imports pouring into the city. The 246,759 bales shipped into Liverpool in 1810 formed 44% of the nation's imports. By 1825, the 646,776 bales constituted 72% of national imports.[31] As trade flourished, Liverpool brokers began to publish weekly newsletters (these later formed a 'General Circular' from all brokers) to their customers, keeping them abreast of the latest news about cotton, prices, sales, stocks. They displayed samples of freshly arrived cotton to potential customers, who then chose the most suitable, with the bales then passing onto the packhorses, mules, barges, and, most crucially, after 1830, onto trains destined for the clusters of textile towns in the Lancashire interior. The new railway companies greatly reduced the cost of transport, provided their own secure warehousing *en route*, and were able to transport cotton bales safe from the weather (especially the rain, which damaged cotton in transit). Just as the age of steam speeded the transport of cotton to the mills, the arrival of steam ships, from 1840, substantially cut the time of a transatlantic crossing.

By then, Liverpool was the main port for this extraordinary flow of slave-grown cotton to the Lancashire textile mills. In its turn, Manchester become the center not merely of a dispersed manufacturing system across Lancashire, but of the distribution of finished textiles, its massive warehouses and stores (many of them still there, ornate Italianate in design) filled with finished textiles. The Manchester Exchange (Royal after 1851) was another Italianate design, dominated by three glass domes (now housing a theater), which became a meeting place for upward of 8,000 traders – spinners, manufacturers, merchants, and agents – where deals were struck silently (unlike in the rowdy shouting matches of other exchanges). The key player was the 'Manchester merchant', "the link between the Lancashire cotton industry and the foreign consumer of cloth." These men bought unfinished cloth from manufacturers, then bleached, colored, or printed it as required, before packing and shipping it.[32]

And so it was that men crowded into a lavish commercial headquarters in the center of that land-locked city, completing deals which dispatched finished textiles onto the outbound ships waiting at Liverpool's docks, and destined for the far reaches of trade and commerce. Lancashire cotton goods, cheap to buy, easy to wash, now clothed people the world over. Above all, it was the massive sales of textiles to the British empire, especially to India, which sustained the Lancashire textile industry throughout the second half of the 19th century,[33] allowing the industry to expand further into new, distant markets (in Japan, China, and Brazil). By then, of course, the nature of the business had changed substantially because of the US Civil War and the ending of slavery in North America. But until 1860, the entire industry had been grounded in slave labor. From its origins in the technological revolution of the late 18th century, Lancashire textiles had used cotton cultivated by slaves, first in the Caribbean, then – in unimaginable volumes – in the Cotton Belt of the US South. The two major industries marched in step: Southern slavery and Lancashire textiles. It was not surprising, then, that Manchester chose that sailing ship as a prominent image in its new Coat of Arms. Ships were essential to the rise of modern Manchester, and of the wider Lancashire region. They delivered slave cotton and exported finished Lancastrian textiles. These two great cities, Liverpool and Manchester, also marched in step. The one had emerged as the major North Atlantic slave port in the 18th century, the other as the world's first industrial city, via slave-grown cotton shipped across the Atlantic in spectacular volumes. In 1858, the president of a Southern railway company, Mr. Richard B. Kimball, said this of his visit to Manchester:

> ...I said to myself, what connection shall
> there be between Power in Manchester and
> Nature in America? What connection shall there
> be between the cotton fields of Texas, and the Factory, and
> loom, and spindles of Manchester?...[34]

The link was there, lurking in the Coat of Arms: busy bees and a sailing ship: two continents linked by the labor of slaves.

Notes

1. 'A Current Map of Europe.' In Malachy Postlethwayt, *Universal Dictionary*, vol. I.
2. Ronald Findlay and Kevin O'Rourke, *Power and Plenty, Trade, War, and the World Economy in the Second Millennium*, Princeton, 2007, Table 6.2., p. 314.
3. The essay by Asa Briggs on Manchester in *Victorian Cities* (London, 1971 edn.) remains perhaps the best single essay on Manchester.
4. Ronald Findlay and Kevin H. O'Rourke, *Power and Plenty*, p. 320.
5. Sven Beckert, *Empire of Cotton: A New History of Global Capitalism*, London, 2014, Chapter 3.
6. Sven Beckert, *Empire of Cotton*, p. 67.
7. Edward Baines, *Baines' Lancashire*, 2 vols, 1824 (1968 edn.), Newton Abbot, II, p. 440.
8. Sven Beckert, *Empire of Cotton*, pp. 89–90.
9. James Walvin, *Crossings: Africa, the Americas and the Atlantic Slave Trade*, London, 2013, p. 198.
10. Peter Kolchin, *American Slavery, 1619-1877*, London, 1995, p. 95.
11. Sven Beckert, *Empire of Cotton*, pp. 103–104.
12. John Walton, *Lancashire: A Social History*, Manchester, 1987, p. 104.
13. John Walton, *Lancashire*, pp. 106–107.
14. John Walton, *Lancashire*, pp. 112–113.
15. John Walton, *Lancashire*, pp. 114–115.
16. John Walton, *Lancashire*, pp. 200–201.
17. Peter Kolchin, *American Slavery*, p. 96.
18. I owe this point to David Eltis, Lecture given in University of Pittsburgh, April 17th, 2015.
19. Peter Kolchin, *American Slavery*, pp. 101: Tables 4 and 5; pp. 243–244.
20. Sven Beckert, *Empire of Cotton*, pp. 109–110.

21. Robert William Fogel, *Without Consent or Contract: The Rise and Fall of American Slavery*, New York, 1989, pp. 29–34; Giorgio Riello, *Cotton: The Fabric that Made the Modern World*, Cambridge, 2013, pp. 205–207.

22. Peter Kolchin, *American Slavery*, Chapter 6.

23. Solomon Northrup, *Twelve Years a Slave*, London, 1853, p. 127.

24. Walter Johnson, *River of Dark Dreams: Slavery and Empire in the Cotton Kingdom*. Cambridge MA, 2013.

25. Peter Kolchin, *American Slavery*, p. 95.

26. Sven Beckert, *Empire of Cotton*, p. 118.

27. Ronald Findlay and Kevin O'Rourke, *Power and Plenty*, pp. 328–329.

28. Sven Beckert, *Empire of Cotton*, pp. 152–154.

29. Sven Beckert, *Empire of Cotton*, pp. 139–140.

30. E.P. Thompson, 'Time, Work-Discipline and Industrial Capitalism,' *Past and Present*, No. 38, December 1967.

31. See the website of the *International Cotton Association*: www.ica-ltd.org (retrieved 30/12/2015).

32. John J. Parkinson-Bailey, *Manchester: An Architectural History*, Manchester, 2000, pp. 93–94.

33. Sven Beckert, *Empire of Cotton*, pp. 164–165.

34. Quoted in Sven Beckert, *Empire of Cotton*, pp. 81–82.

Conclusion

For centuries, slavery in the Americas was an integral feature of the Western world, and the West greatly enjoyed the
material benefits derived from that slave labor. Not surprisingly, slavery was highly valued. Today, that outlook seems
bizarre, offensive even, but for the three centuries during which
slavery cast its shadow across the Atlantic, it went largely
unchallenged. Who could denounce slavery in the face of the
prosperity it yielded? It seemed to enhance the well-being (and
the pleasures) of all sorts and conditions of consumers throughout the Western world – and beyond. Who was to deny the poor
the comfort they found in a sweet cup of tea? Or the masculine
conviviality of a smoke-filled alehouse or coffee shop? And who
could dispute that poorer sorts were better off for being able to
buy cheap cotton clothing spilling from Lancashire's textile factories? Yet all of the commodities involved – sugar, tobacco, cotton – were produced by slaves.

Behind all this lay one of slavery's great paradoxes. Slavery –
the brutish exploitation of millions – also created refinement,
fashion, and luxury. It made possible pleasurable and refined
habits for wealthy people on both sides of the Atlantic. Prosperous people flaunted the wealth and status acquired on the

Slavery in Small Things: Slavery and Modern Cultural Habits, First Edition. James Walvin.
© 2017 John Wiley & Sons, Inc. Published 2017 by John Wiley & Sons, Inc.

back of slavery. This was at its most extreme and most glaring in the fashionable homes of those who profited from the plantations, the slave ships, and the trading houses. Their wealth was reflected in the buildings, the grounds, the furnishings and fittings, the porcelain and portraits that characterized such lavish dwellings. Clearly, slavery was not the sole force behind the rise of Western material luxury and refinement in the 17th and 18th centuries, though in many specific cases it was. Today, it is popular to point to stately homes as an example of the profits of slavery, but the fruits of slave labor were remarkably invasive, working their way into the most inaccessible and wretched crevices of Western life. While the rich provided the most striking examples of the benefits of slavery, even the poor were able to pick up crumbs under slavery's lavishly heaped table. The benefits of slavery could, then, be found in all corners of Western life – among rich and poor alike. Though not, of course, in the slave quarters of the Americas.

All this makes all the more puzzling the point I made at the start of this book: that the history of slavery passed largely unnoticed by British historians until the last fifty years. And despite the fact that evidence about slavery and its consequences is all around us. It is at its most obvious in the presence of people of African descent scattered to the four winds by the slave trade. That diasporic surge of African peoples was first started by Europe's voracious demand for ever more cheap African labor to tap the wealth of the Americas. All this, now, is so obvious, so familiar, that it seems hardly worth stressing. Yet it was not so obvious to earlier generations of scholars and historians. Today, by contrast, scholars have come to accept the historical significance of slavery, and we can appreciate the intellectual change involved when we look at the prodigious volumes of research by modern scholars on the subject. The 2013 'Annual Bibliography' of slavery, for example, ran to one hundred pages of closely printed entries.[1] In addition, the *popular* fascination with slavery (which is itself largely derivative of scholarly work) continues to attract huge audiences, both to movies and TV series. In recent years, four major movies (*Lincoln*, 2012; *Twelve Years a Slave*, 2013; *Django Unchained*, 2014; and *Belle*, 2014) have all focused on slavery. Even as I wrote these pages, a major two-part BBC television series (*Britain's Forgotten Slave Owners*, 2015) was attracting great praise as well as an audience of two million viewers. It is as if the Western world has finally woken up, after a very long intellectual and cultural slumber, to the enormity that was slavery.

However, this abundant and expanding scholarship on slavery can easily confuse. For a start, it is difficult to keep pace with scholarship which ranges far and wide across the chronology and geography of slavery. Faced with this plethora of information, slavery might seem so varied and diverse that generalities fall apart in the teeth of a multitude of exceptions and differences. We should not, however, let this complexity intimidate us, or prevent us from offering a judgment. The nub of the problem is simple. In essence, the individual elements of this vast sprawling system of far-flung empires coalesced into a simple unity. They were variants of a grossly exploitative and brutal labor system that ensnared millions of Africans for the benefit of Europe, their settler colonies, and for the nation-states which emerged from those colonies. We can also sense the pervasive influence of slavery by simply looking around: the evidence is there for all to see. Even in small things.

Note

1. Thomas Thurston, 'Slavery: Annual Bibliographical Supplement (2013),' *Slavery and Abolition*, vol. 35, No. 4. December 2014, pp. 681–781.

Index

Slavery in Small Things: Slavery and Modern Cultural Habits, First Edition. James Walvin.
© 2017 John Wiley & Sons, Inc. Published 2017 by John Wiley & Sons, Inc.

Index